PEARSON
Prentice
Hall

"Think for yourself."
prentice hall

Prentice Hall's *Basic Ethics in Action* series in normative and applied ethics is a major new undertaking edited by Michael Boylan, Professor of Philosophy at Marymount University. The series includes both wide-ranging anthologies as well as brief texts that focus on a particular theme or topic within one of four areas of applied ethics. These areas include: Business Ethics, Environmental Ethics, Medical Ethics, and Social and Political Philosophy.

Anchor volume
Michael Boylan, *Basic Ethics*, 2000

Business Ethics

Michael Boylan, ed., *Business Ethics*, 2001

James Donahue, *Ethics for the Professionals*, forthcoming

Dale Jacquette, *Journalistic Ethics*, forthcoming

Murphy, Laczniak, Bowie and Klein, *Ethical Marketing*, 2005

Edward Spence, *Advertising Ethics*, 2005

Joseph DesJardins, *Environmental Business*, forthcoming

Environmental Ethics

Michael Boylan, ed., *Environmental Ethics*, 2001

J. Baird Callicott and Michael Nelson, *American Indian Environmental Ethics: An Ojibwa Case Study*, 2004

Lisa H. Newton, *Ethics and Sustainability*, 2003

Mary Anne Warren, *Ethics and Animals*, forthcoming

Medical Ethics

Michael Boylan, ed., *Medical Ethics*, 2000

Michael Boylan and Kevin Brown, *Genetic Engineering*, 2002

Rosemarie Tong, *New Perspectives in Healthcare Ethics*, 2003

David Cummiskey, *Global Healthcare*, forthcoming

Social and Political Philosophy

R. Paul Churchill, *Human Rights and Global Diversity*, forthcoming

Seumas Miller, Peter Roberts, and Edward Spence, *Corruption and Anti-Corruption: An Applied Philosophical Approach*, 2005

Deryck Beyleveld, *Informed Consent*, forthcoming

Kai Nelson, *Social Justice*, forthcoming

D0023968

Please contact Michael Boylan (michael.boylan@marymount.edu) or Prentice Hall's Philosophy & Religion Editor to propose authoring a title for this series!

Ethical Marketing

PATRICK E. MURPHY
University of Notre Dame

GENE R. LACZNIAK
Marquette University

NORMAN E. BOWIE
University of Minnesota

THOMAS A. KLEIN
University of Toledo

PEARSON
Prentice
Hall

Upper Saddle River, New Jersey 07458

Library of Congress Cataloging-in-Publication Data

Ethical marketing / Patrick E. Murphy . . . [et al.].
    p. cm. — (Basic ethics in action series)
    Includes bibliographical references and index.
    ISBN 0-13-184814-3
    1. Marketing—Moral and ethical aspects.   I. Murphy, Patrick E.   II. Basic ethics in action.

HF5415.E796 2005
174'.96588—dc22   2004006840

VP, Editorial Director: Charlyce Jones-Owen
Senior Acquisitions Editor: Ross Miller
Assistant Editor: Wendy B. Yurash
Editorial Assistant: Carla Worner
Director of Marketing: Beth Mejia
Marketing Manager: Kara Kindstrom
Marketing Assistant: Jennifer Lang
Production Liaison: Joanne Hakim
Manufacturing Buyer: Christina Helder
Cover Art Director: Jayne Conte
Cover Design: Bruce Kenselaar
Project Management: Jessica Balch/Pine Tree Composition, Inc.
Composition: Interactive Composition Corporation

Pearson Education LTD., London   Pearson Education North Asia Ltd
Pearson Education Singapore, Pte. Ltd   Pearson Educación de Mexico, S.A. de C.V.
Pearson Education Canada, Ltd   Pearson Education Malaysia, Pte. Ltd
Pearson Education–Japan   Pearson Education, Upper Saddle River, NJ
Pearson Education Australia PTY, Limited

10 9 8 7 6 5 4 3 2

ISBN 0-13-184814-3

To our wives:
Kate, Monica, Maureen, and Karen
for your love, support and understanding

Contents

Acknowledgments

A book-length manuscript is never the product of only the authors. Thus, we would like to acknowledge the efforts of several individuals who have assisted us in the various stages during the preparation of *Ethical Marketing*.

At our institutions, several people should be singled out for their efforts. At Notre Dame, our biggest debt is to Deb Coch, who worked through the many revisions of our chapters, turning our sometimes untidy manuscript into final form. In the early stages, Sandy Palmer was helpful in numerous ways. Several student assistants deserve mention: Diana Laquinta, Jami Kirk, Erin Powell, and Monica Smith. We want to thank colleagues at Notre Dame who critiqued various aspects of the book: Georges Enderle, Mike Etzel, and Betsy Moore. A number of MBA classes in marketing ethics at Notre Dame, especially the one in Fall 2003, commented on or contributed to earlier versions of the chapters. From Marquette, we thank Wayne R. Sanders, former CEO of Kimberly-Clark, for his specific support of the Wayne and Kathleen Sanders professorship in business at Marquette University and his general dedication to the advancement of higher education. At other schools, we thank Andrew Abela of Catholic University for his contribution to Chapter 3 and Lauren Strach of Andrews University, who classroom tested several chapters.

At Prentice Hall, Ross Miller, Senior Acquisitions Editor, signed the book and was patient with our slow start. Wendy Yurash, Assistant Editor for

Philosophy and Religion, was helpful in providing editorial guidance throughout the project and was very supportive. At Pine Tree Composition, we appreciate the assistance of Jessica Balch. Michael Boylan, the series editor for *Basic Ethics*, read the entire manuscript and gave us helpful direction at several stages. We are also thankful to the two anonymous reviewers that Prentice Hall commissioned to comment on an earlier version of the manuscript.

Despite the assistance of these individuals, undoubtedly some omissions and errors remain. We take full responsibility for them.

PEM
GRL
NEB
TAK

Introduction

The dawning of the 21st century saw a general optimism in the world, with the hope that the new millennium would be a prosperous time for the world economy in general and business in particular. It did not take long for the dot com bubble to burst in April 2000. Along with the financial collapse, we heard a host of ethical questions being asked of the "new technology" companies. These included small boards of directors made up mostly of insiders, cronyism, nepotism, inflated CEO pay, and a general "me first," egoism that reflected the booming economic times.

More broadly, the early years of this new century have witnessed business ethics scandals of unprecedented proportions. In late 2001, the sixth largest firm in the United States—Enron—collapsed under the weight of a host of ethical transgressions including conflicts of interest, unethical (if not illegal) offshore accounts and a pervasive hypercompetitive "see no evil," "take no prisoners" culture, both within the firm and in its dealings with many of its stakeholders. Enron's demise also brought down Arthur Andersen, perhaps the most revered public accounting firm of the 20th century. These meltdowns were quickly followed by major ethical and legal problems at Adelphia, Merrill Lynch, Tyco and WorldCom. 2003 was labeled as a "bad rerun" of the previous scandal-ridden year of 2002: ". . . the resignation of American Airlines' chief executive [for concealing a preferential executive bonus during difficult union negotiations that produced a significant reduction in wages and benefits], the restatement of revenues at food marketing giant Ahold, and the charges against HealthSouth and Richard Scrushy—happened . . . just one year after the biggest wave of corporate scandals in decades and after the passage of new legislation to combat corporate malfeasance."[1] In early 2004, Italian dairy-food giant Parmalat had "prosecutors scrambling to find out what happened to $8.5 billion to $12 billion in vanished assets. That sum makes Parmalat one of the largest financial frauds in history."[2] Unfortunately, current corporate misconduct has the appearance of an epidemic yet to run its course.

While these scandals have been most directly linked to accounting irregularities and financial misdeeds, some advocate that marketing ethics is not far removed from these problems. Marketing executives were obviously compliant in some of the situations where sales and revenue were grossly overstated. And, as big accounting firms became more marketing oriented and moved away from simply auditing services and into consulting, critics believe a lack of marketing ethics directly contributed to their decay. Similarly, marketing misconduct clearly had a role in the scandals involving financial services firms, as supposedly objective analysts inflated profit projections and hid bad news in order to sell tarnished securities to unknowing clients.

Business schools, where professors and students come together to study business theory and practice, are also not immune from criticism. *Business Week, Financial Times,* and *The Wall Street Journal* have all leveled charges at business education for teaching short-term financial performance as the main "gospel" of business success. We understand these charges and agree with them to a certain extent. However, one of our purposes in writing this book is to take on the challenge from one business writer who said: "Can business schools teach students to be virtuous? . . . In the wake of all the corporate scandals, they have no choice but to try."[3]

One consideration in this attempt is a recognition that the news coverage accorded these scandals has left a residue of extreme cynicism in public attitudes toward business, unmitigated by the thousands of companies where ethical conduct is the rule, unremarked upon by a press corps seeking the latest "aha!" And business students are not immune from this cynicism. Ed Schultz, retired CEO of Dana Credit Corporation (the leasing arm of automotive supplier Dana Corporation and a Malcolm Baldrige Quality awardee), recently told one of the authors, "Our biggest single challenge with new employees is to overcome their belief that business is mostly about "dog eat dog" and "survival of the fittest" and to convince them that unethical behavior will get them fired, not promoted." As will be shown in pages of this book, many successful companies and executives are distinguished by their ethical underpinnings and most firms certainly recognize and follow ethical principles.

TITLE OF THE BOOK

The title of this book, *Ethical Marketing,* is purposeful for several reasons. First, despite the spate of scandals mentioned above, we remain optimistic about the future of the economic and marketing system. Furthermore, we believe too much attention has been devoted to *unethical* business and marketing. When someone talks about ethics, it usually is in terms of something we shouldn't do, rather than something we should. Our focus, therefore, is to accentuate the positive practices that business firms can employ to bring about more ethical marketing. These are highlighted at the end of each chapter and throughout the text.

A second reason for the title is that we see ethical marketing as being proactive and the logical implementation of the marketing concept. The cherished "marketing concept" is usually thought to have three pillars: customer orientation, integrated marketing, and organizational gain (interpreted in business as profit). To be customer oriented requires a level of *trust* to exist between marketer and consumer that is based on an ethical foundation. For the integration of marketing to occur, marketing personnel must work honestly across areas of responsibility and with their counterparts in production, engineering and finance. Finally, the organization, whether it be for profit or nonprofit, can only be successful if it truly satisfies its customers and other key stakeholders and does so in an integrated fashion. Much has been made in recent years of customer relationship management and relationship marketing. Both of these concepts seem to us to require ethical marketing perspectives and practices.

Third, we see ethical marketing as taking primarily a long-term view. Firms that are highly ethical are not willing to bribe or give favors to gain market share or new business. This means they may actually lose out in the short term. However, good ethics is good business in the long run. These companies must sometimes make a stand and literally "walk away from business." Several global firms that we admire for taking this long-term marketing orientation are bp (British Petroleum), IBM, Medtronic (a medical devices company), SUEZ (a French firm), and Toyota.

ETHICAL MARKETING DEFINED

In an earlier book on this topic, we indicated that *ethics* deals with the morality of human conduct. We went on to say that:

> Marketing ethics is the systematic study of how moral standards are applied to marketing decisions, behaviors, and institutions.[4]

The fact that marketing ethics, like legal and medical ethics, is an applied field is an important aspect of the definition. Marketing decisions pertain to a host of specific issues like selling cigarettes to teenagers, violence-oriented products, pricing at a level that gouges unsuspecting consumers, and so on. The behavior governed by ethical principles involves all personnel involved in marketing—top management, sales, distribution, customer service, advertising and public relations. Finally, marketing ethics issues arise in SMEs (small and medium size enterprises), MNCs (multinational corporations) and NFPs (nonprofit organizations).

Our approach here is similar, but subtly different because we take a normative, prescriptive approach. Therefore, we define ethical marketing as:

> practices that emphasize transparent, trustworthy, and responsible personal and/or organizational marketing policies and actions that exhibit integrity as well as fairness to consumers and other stakeholders.

Because ethics sometimes deals with subjective moral choices, the question becomes *what* moral standards ought to be applied to *which* ethical questions in marketing. For example, is it proper for an advertising copywriter to use a blatant (but legal) sexual appeal, which some see as exploitive and demeaning of women, when the agency has demonstrated that such appeals sell more of a client's cosmetics products? Cynics claim issues like these tend to generate much disagreement and, thus, illustrate the futility of dealing with the "always subjective" ethics area. However, as we shall show repeatedly in the following pages, in many industries and in many situations, there is more consensus about what is accepted by the majority as "proper" than many casual observers suspect.

THE TWO ASPECTS OF ETHICS

We see ethics, or the study of moral choice, as having two dimensions. First, ethics, via its foundation in moral philosophy, provides models and frameworks for handling ethical situations, i.e., various approaches to ethical reasoning. For instance, ethics leads us to consider whether we should judge the moral appropriateness of marketing decisions based on the *consequences* for various stakeholders or on the basis of the *intentions* held by the decision-maker when a particular action is selected. Often, differing approaches lead us to similar conclusions about the "ethicalness" of a particular action. Unfortunately, different approaches sometimes lead to divergent conclusions. We set out to discuss the fundamental approaches to analyzing marketing ethics in Chapter 1, and we explain what rationale lies behind the way people deal with ethical problems.

The second dimension of ethics addresses the question: "What is the 'right' thing to do?" This is the *normative* aspect of marketing ethics. When people say that someone is acting ethically, they usually mean the person is doing what is *morally correct*. The underpinnings for understanding what one ought to do come mostly from our individual values. These are shaped by our family, religious training, experience, and personal feelings about how we should treat other people. A prominent manager once remarked that some of the elusiveness about what constitutes an ethical person could be overcome if the word *trust* were substituted for ethics; that is, ethical marketing managers are *trustworthy* in that they can always be counted on to try to do the right thing.

It is also true that ethics is a subject where people cannot say anything of substance without revealing quite a bit about their own values. Throughout this book, we will make normative judgments about various marketing practices. While some of our evaluations may cause debate and disagreement, our major purpose is to increase students' and managers' sensitivity to the ethical questions which regularly occur in marketing and to assist them in making more consistently ethical decisions.

A NORMATIVE WORLDVIEW

This text is part of a series of books, *Basic Ethics in Action*, published by Prentice Hall, that emphasizes a consistent worldview toward ethics. As noted above in the definitions, ethics in marketing is applied ethics. In the first chapter especially, but also throughout the book, we subscribe to the notion that normative theories of ethics can be applied to moral issues facing marketers.

There are two aspects of this worldview: the personal and shared community moral imperatives. The first aspect says that "all people must develop a single comprehensive and internally coherent worldview that is good and that we strive to act out in our daily lives."[5] In this manner the individual is able to imagine just what it would be like to live in a world informed by ethical theory. It is our hope that this volume will assist each reader in attaining his or her personal worldview.

The shared community worldview imperative argues for a broader context in which ethical decisions are made.

> Each agent must strive to create a common body of knowledge that supports the creation of a shared community worldview (that is complete, coherent, and good) through which social institutions and their resulting policies might flourish within the constraints of the essential commonly held core values (ethics, aesthetics, and religion).[6]

As this definition indicates, the community worldview draws from several areas—ethics, religion, and family. We would add the corporation to this list because individuals' views are often shaped by the corporate community in which they work. Therefore, it is important that one realizes that ethical attitudes and behavior can be influenced by organizational affiliations. One of the common refrains about Enron was that its culture changed the moral compass of many of its workers to one in which ethical principles always were secondary in importance to financial success.

MANAGERIAL APPROACH TO THE SUBJECT

Our approach also has a distinct managerial flavor. We believe that if ethical decisions are to occur within marketing organizations, managers must shape a corporate culture hospitable to such outcomes. Therefore, we use ethical theories and reasoning as a foundation for managerial decision-making. In each chapter, we identify some key issues and then move to providing guidance for resolving them. Every chapter concludes with an "Ideas for Ethical Marketing" section outlining several options available for overcoming ethical obstacles. Managers can use these ideas as guideposts for moving their companies toward more consistently ethical decisions and actions, in terms of both corporate policies and individual conduct. We believe that the professional practice of marketing is *self-actualized* only when marketing strategy and tactics are tempered with an underlying and abiding concern for high ethical principles.

A FINAL NOTE

We are frequently reminded by colleagues, students, and working executives that good ethics, whether in marketing or other domains of business and life, is a journey that cannot be mapped out by a few simple decision rules. We are also troubled by the prospect that business schools have come to forget that this same truth applies to those areas where we mostly teach from a decision rule perspective—finance, accounting, operations, and even some aspects of marketing. Our concern is twofold. First, there is necessarily an ethical dimension to most problems that we face, whether in business or elsewhere in our personal, family, and community life. Teaching marketing and other business subjects as if revenues minus expenses, no matter how complex the formula, is all that matters misses that dimension. Second, and more importantly, we have learned through studying hundreds of organizations that business judgments containing ethical dimensions are best made when they follow open communication. Such dialogue takes healthy advantage of the experiences and perspectives available and tends to bring in a broader range of viewpoints than any one individual is likely to command.

We began this introduction with a catalogue of recent business scandals that have captured worldwide attention. In studying these stories and others like them, we find that discussions about the ethical aspects of, for example, trading energy futures, financial reporting, and executive compensation not only did not take place but were suppressed. The lives of both managers and aggrieved parties, such as other employees and shareholders, have been seriously disrupted. The fact that those companies with fine reputations are now in shame and/or bankruptcy should not be lost in the debate about how ethical business conduct is to be taught and learned.

ENDNOTES

1. J. Kurlantzick, "Liar, Liar," *Entrepreneur* 31 (10) (2003), 68.
2. G. Edmondson and L. Cohen, "How Parmalat Went Sour," *Business Week* (January 12, 2004), 46.
3. R. Alsop, "Right and Wrong," *The Wall Street Journal* (September 17, 2003), R9.
4. G. Laczniak and P. Murphy, *Ethical Marketing Decisions: The Higher Road* (Boston: Allyn and Bacon, 1993).
5. M. Boylan, *Basic Ethics in Action* (Upper Saddle River, NJ: Prentice Hall, 2000).
6. M. Boylan and K. Brown, *Genetic Engineering: Science and Ethics on the New Frontier* (Upper Saddle River, NJ: Prentice Hall, 2002).

Chapter One

Ethical Reasoning and Marketing Decisions

Scenario 1

Buzz marketing is a relatively new marketing technique. Its objective is to seek out trendsetters in each community and subtly push them into talking up the brand to their friends and admirers. These people are hired to generate favorable word of mouth. This approach builds on the well-known "opinion leader" concept and the influential nature that some individuals hold over their reference group. With teenagers, companies strive to seek out kids who are "cool." Buzz marketing is catching on with many marketers, particularly those selling sneakers, jeans, cars, and certain packaged goods. This technique is a special favorite of cigarette and liquor manufacturers for which advertising is restricted.[1]

- Buzz marketing is different from other forms of marketing in that the consumer usually does not know that the product endorser is being paid (either in money, free goods, or some other item) by the company to promote its product.
- The marketers "plant" the product in areas of high traffic and use these salespersons to create a "buzz" about the product.
- While some consumers think these are spontaneous encounters, most situations are carefully orchestrated by the marketers.

An example is Ford's introduction of the Focus. Rather than spend a lot of money on 30-second commercials, Ford recruited several opinion leaders in a few markets and gave them each a Focus to drive for six months. The responsibility of these individuals was to hand out Focus trinkets and talk up the car to anyone who expressed interest in it, but not to tell them that Ford had given them the car to drive. **Is this an ethical technique? Why or why not?**

Scenario 2

Recent commercials in the United States for Swiss-based Roche Group's weight-loss drug Xenical appear to break new ground. Xenical is an oral prescription designed to help considerably overweight people shed pounds by blocking about one-third of the fat in food from being digested.

Under Food and Drug Administration rules, a full-length commercial touting a product by name for specific medical conditions must include a sometimes lengthy list of unpleasant side effects. Roche, however, got around that requirement by advertising Xenical not with one full-length commercial but two shorter ones separated by unrelated commercial time.

The first Xenical ad describes the condition—unhealthy weight gain—the drug is designed to treat, and shows an image of a cuddly baby morphing into a heavyset woman. But it doesn't name the drug. The second ad uses the same images and music and mentions the drug by name, but says nothing about losing weight. This ad states, "Your doctor cared about your health then: He cares about it now. Ask about Xenical." When taken together, the two commercials are 45 seconds long, or longer than many full-length spots. But side effects never are mentioned.[2] **Is this advertising ethical?**

VIEWS OF MARKETING ETHICS

The opening section of this book examines several different views toward marketing ethics. We begin with the personal or individual view. Then we turn our attentions to the organizational view. Since most ethical issues arise in a business setting, this view is particularly important to understand. The third view is an industry one. A number of concerns such as *fairness* in the marketing system and protection of the physical environment fall under the societal view. The final view is a "stakeholder" one. This concept is utilized throughout our book. So it is essential to introduce, define, and illustrate the stakeholder view at the outset.

A Personal View of Marketing Ethics

Some marketing managers contend that they are relatively exempt from ethical dilemmas or that moral pressures do not generally affect them. In reality, most studies confirm that between 65 and 75 percent of all managers do indeed face major ethical dilemmas at some point in their careers. An *ethical dilemma* is defined, for our purposes, as a situation where it is not clear what choice morality requires. The situation may involve the trade-off between one's personal moral values and the quest for increased organizational or personal profit. However, it may not involve trade-offs such as a decision to cut the labor force to increase shareholder wealth. Marketing managers sometimes feel compelled to do things that they feel ought not be done. Based upon the reports of practicing managers, most marketing executives are *not* exempt from dealing with ethical concerns. Our view is that most marketers do face ethical dilemmas, but that they may not recognize them. Judging from the questions being raised about the propriety of marketing practices, many marketing decisions clearly have significant consequences.

An Organizational View: Corporate Versus Individual Ethics—Is There a Difference?

The ethics of the organization and the values held by the individual manager may not be the same. The issue is, When does a person follow individual values and when do they follow corporate values? When these values are not compatible, a conflict may arise between organizational pressure that impels a particular action and what the individual believes ought or ought not to be done. The typical conflict in such cases involves a manager or employee who holds a higher standard of behavior than that expected by the organization. In such situations, the manager may be pushed toward an action that reflects ignoring or lowering personal standards in order to achieve some organizational goal. These dilemmas produce "moral stress" in the manager, because the core values of the organization, as embodied in the corporate culture, seem to imply a choice different from that which would be selected by the manager based upon personal values. Another real issue occurs when the boss orders you to do something that violates organizational values, as well as your own values. One way organizations have addressed this issue is to explicitly develop a "values statement" for the firm. For example, Hanna Andersson (the maker of high quality children's clothes) lists three major values: respect, integrity, and responsibility.[3] They guide this firm when it is faced with the quandaries discussed earlier.

Corporations with an organizational climate that causes managers to act contrary to their individual values need to understand the *costs of* unethical behavior articulated in this chapter. Sometimes managers who choose to follow organizational pressures rather than their own conscience rationalize their decisions by maintaining that they are simply *agents* of the corporation. In other words, as company agent, the manager assumes the duty to do exactly what the organization most desires—often translated to mean maximizing return on investment, sales, or some other managerial objective.

The weaknesses of assuming that managers are merely organizational agents who need to override their personal values are several, including:

1. Managers can never totally abdicate their personal responsibility in making certain business decisions. The defense of being an agent of the corporation sounds suspiciously like the defense given by certain war criminals that they were only following orders. (Companies frequently prosecute rule breakers to make an example of them, even if the manager's intention was to help the firm.)
2. It is quite possible that the manager does not *fully* understand what is in the best interest of the organization. Short-term profits, even if advocated by the manager's immediate supervisor, may not be the most important consideration for the organization.
3. The manager has an irrevocable responsibility to parties other than his organization. This understanding moves us to the *stakeholder concept* (explained below) that explicitly identifies various publics to which organizations have duties and obligations.

While the trade-off involving appropriate personal values and questionable organizational values, suggested earlier, is most typical, other situations are also found. We can envision instances where organizational values should trump personal ones, such as when the employee has a character flaw or does not subscribe to legitimate corporate expectations. One other circumstance involves organizational values that are more rigorous than personal values. Here the manager may not appreciate the reasoning behind certain policies (along the lines described in number 2) and, for personal or organizational gain, is inclined to violate them. To avoid values misalignment, senior management must bring clarifying ethical standards into employee selection, orientation and training, and advancement or dismissal decisions. (These issues are treated in more depth in the final chapter.)

Still another situation generating ethical anxiety is when an employee's ethical standards are overly *scrupulous*, leading to actions—or omissions—that unnecessarily disadvantage the employer. For example, concerns about lavish customer entertainment may prompt an inexperienced sales representative to avoid even modest lunch or dinner expenditures and, thus, neglect the kind of social interaction upon which sound customer relationships may be built or reinforced. If the goal is to establish a workable set of ethical norms for an organization and its marketing personnel, management policies and programs must strive for agreement between what individuals and companies view as acceptable and unacceptable. Openness in communications is necessary for this goal to be attainable.

An Industry View

Industries vary greatly in the approach they take to ethical issues. Some industry sectors have out of necessity developed detailed strategies to address ethical problems peculiar to their sector, such as the promotion of responsible drinking by the brewing industry. Other industries, such as the chemical industry, are highly regulated by government. And still others, such as private waste haulers and construction trades, have a reputation for being somewhat tough minded in the way they operate. The point is that the amount of ethical guidance an individual manager receives from "industry norms" is highly idiosyncratic. Nevertheless, whatever norms are operant should be learned and integrated into the manager's ethical decision-making calculus. Companies and their marketing managers can take some *cues* from the industry, but as we advocate in this chapter and throughout the book, each firm must make a conscious attempt to set and maintain high ethical standards.

A Societal View

From the vantage point of society in which our economic system is nested and provisioned through marketing activities, the role of marketing ethics can be seen as critical to both social order and justice.[4] *Trust* is an essential ingredient of a fair and efficient marketing system.[5] Market participants—buyers and sellers of goods and services—should have faith that transactions in which they take part are characterized by openness or transparency, that is, that they are not being deceived by untruthful claims or unknowingly exposed to risks associated with unsafe products. They also need to have faith that they are being treated fairly, not being discriminated against because of circumstances that are regarded as inappropriate bases for differential pricing, quality, or service levels. Absent these characteristics, market transactions lead to distortions in the level of welfare generated by the market. When such faith is not present, buyers or sellers are subject to exploitation, extra costs of inspection are incurred, and, when damages are experienced, injured parties undertake efforts to resolve disputes adding additional costs. In other words, lack of disclosure, unfair treatment, and unexpected risks lead to inefficiencies in the form of injuries and dispute settlement that would be avoided if transactions occurred in a more open and ethical manner. For example, the emerging economies of eastern and central Europe are struggling with how to attain a political-economic system that fosters these characteristics.[6]

Societies also have an interest in marketing systems in the more profound sense that their sustainability and prosperity depend on the conservation of resources that are not directly involved in buying and selling. Economic activity depends on the availability of natural resources—air, water, and land. The depletion or pollution of these resources places the long-term survival of communities and nations at risk. When people recognize the prospect of such risks, they seek ways to ensure survival through means that replace or intervene in markets—laws and administrative procedures that prohibit or limit pollution or depletion or that tax or penalize marketers to compensate for the *social costs* associated with these events. Economists refer to these effects of marketing as *externalities,* unpriced outcomes that are not accounted for among the costs and benefits that constitute the conditions of market transactions. A societal view on marketing ethics requires that marketers: (1) avoid, wherever possible, actions that expose societies to disorder and to the prospect of inadequate resources, and (2) respect those laws and regulations formulated to ensure order and sustainability for all citizens and future generations.[7]

A Stakeholder View

A perspective that now must be considered, because marketing is usually undertaken in the context of an organization, is the *stakeholder concept.*

> *A stakeholder in an organization is . . . any group or individual who can affect or is affected by the achievement of the organization's objectives.*[8]

For example, typical corporate stakeholders include customers, stockholders, suppliers, employees, host communities or countries (where the company has operations), and various other parties. To this list might be added other individuals and groups that may affect the company's success, even though they may not be usually affected by the company's activities, for example, regulatory agencies and the media. The stakeholder concept is useful in ethical analysis because it provides a framework for weighing obligations and gauging the impact of decisions on all relevant groups, not just the firm and its managers.

At times it is useful to distinguish among the *primary, indirect,* and *secondary stakeholders.* Primary stakeholders have a formal, official, or contractual relationship with the firm; indirect stakeholders have an ongoing or abiding interest in the firm but no direct transactional contact; and all others are classified as secondary stakeholders. Primary stakeholders are the owners, suppliers, employees, and customers of the organization. Citizens who may be affected by pollution are a good example of an indirect stakeholder. Secondary stakeholders encompass public-interest groups, the media, consumer advocates, and local community organizations that have occasional interest in the various corporate activities. For example, the amount of paper and plastic packaging generated by fast-food chains is a concern of local environmental groups, whereas the media may be more interested in the

EXHIBIT 1-1   Stakeholder Analysis for Amazon.com

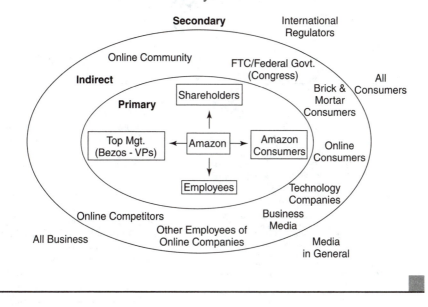

firm's treatment of its minority employees. Exhibit 1-1 illustrates the three types of stakeholders for Amazon.com.

Although primary stakeholders have a direct relationship with the firm, they should not always receive the greatest weight because a manager determines which particular strategic option to choose. For instance, an action that may be in the best interest of stockholders and customers, for example, building a distribution center on recreational parkland, may be villainized by the media (a stakeholder group) to the local community (another stakeholder group), generating overall public opinion (a third stakeholder) against the project. Organizations that subscribe to the stakeholder concept largely try to see that its primary stakeholders attain their objectives, while at the same time keeping other stakeholders satisfied. One management expert characterizes the goal of stakeholder analysis as creating the classic "win-win" situation for all stakeholders.[9] In other words, the task of marketing management is to seek solutions that ideally will achieve the goals of *all* stakeholders. Failing that, management must at least select options that generally optimize net stakeholder benefits.

One example of an organization that has apparently internalized this approach is Johnson & Johnson (J&J). Its corporate "Credo," an embodiment of the stakeholder concept, is shown in Exhibit 1-2 in both English and Arabic. This document recognizes responsibilities to consumers,

EXHIBIT 1-2

J&J

Our Credo

We believe our first responsibility is to the doctors, nurses and patients, to mothers and fathers and all others who use our products and services. In meeting their needs everything we do must be of high quality. We must constantly strive to reduce our costs in order to maintain reasonable prices. Customers' orders must be serviced promptly and accurately. Our suppliers and distributors must have an opportunity to make a fair profit.

We are responsible to our employees, the men and women who work with us throughout the world. Everyone must be considered as an individual. We must respect their dignity and recognize their merit. They must have a sense of security in their jobs. Compensation must be fair and adequate, and working conditions clean, orderly and safe. We must be mindful of ways to help our employees fulfill their family responsibilities. Employees must feel free to make suggestions and complaints. There must be equal opportunity for employment, development and advancement for those qualified. We must provide competent management, and their actions must be just and ethical.

We are responsible to the communities in which we live and work and to the world community as well. We must be good citizens - support good works and charities and bear our fair share of taxes. We must encourage civic improvements and better health and education. We must maintain in good order the property we are privileged to use, protecting the environment and natural resources.

Our final responsibility is to our stockholders. Business must make a sound profit. We must experiment with new ideas. Research must be carried on, innovative programs developed and mistakes paid for. New equipment must be purchased, new facilities provided and new products launched. Reserves must be created to provide for adverse times. When we operate according to these principles, the stockholders should realize a fair return.

مبادئنا

إننا نؤمن بأن مسؤوليتنا الأولى هي أمام الأطباء والممرضات والمرضى، وأمام الأمهات والآباء وغيرهم من أولئك الذين يستعملون منتجاتنا ويستفيدون من خدماتنا. فمن أجل تلبية احتياجاتهم يجب أن يكون كل ما نقوم به في مستوى عالٍ رفيع. علينا أن نعمل دائماً على تخفيض تكاليفنا للمحافظة على أسعار معقولة وكذلك يجب أن تلبى طلبات الزبائن بسرعة ودقة، وأن يكون لموزعينا ومورّدينا فرصة للربح.

نحن مسؤولون تجاه موظفينا، أولئك الرجال والنساء الذين يعملون معنا في جميع أنحاء العالم. يجب النظر لكل منهم على أنه إنسان علينا احترام كرامته وتقدير فضائله. يجب أن يشعر موظفونا بالأمان في أعمالهم. كذلك يجب أن تكون الأجور عادلة وكافية، وظروف العمل نظيفة، مرتبة وآمنة. كذلك يجب أن يشعر الموظفون بأن لهم الحرية في تقديم الإقتراحات والشكاوى، ويجب أن تكون أمامهم فرص متساوية للتوظف والتطور والتقدم للمؤهلين منهم. علينا أن نوفر إدارة تتمتع بالكفاءة وتتّسم تصرفاتها بالعدالة والخلق.

نحن مسؤولون أما المجتمعات التي نعيش ونعمل فيها وأمام المجتمع الدولي. كذلك علينا أن نكون مواطنون صالحين - علينا أن نؤيد الأعمال الصالحة والخيّرة وأن نتحمل نصيباً عادلاً من الضرائب. يجب أن نشجع أيضاً تحسين الظروف المدنية الصحية والتعليمية. ويتوجب علينا أيضاً المحافظة على البناء الذي كُرّمنا باستعماله، وحماية البيئة والمصادر الطبيعية.

أما مسؤوليتنا الأخيرة فهي لحاملي أسهمنا. يجب أن نحقق رباحاً مناسبة، وعلينا القيام بتجربة الأفكار الجديدة. يجب مواصلة الأبحاث، وتطوير البرامج المبتكرة والمحاسبة على الأخطاء. يجب شراء معدات جديدة، وتوفير التسهيلات الحديثة، وتقديم منتجات جديدة وعلينا إيجاد احتياطيات تحسباً لأوقات الشدة. عندما نعمل وفقاً لهذه المبادئ فلابد لحاملي أسهمنا من تحقيق مردود جيد.

جونسون و جونسون (مصر) ش.م.م.

Johnson & Johnson (Egypt) S.A.E.

Source: Johnson & Johnson, New Brunswick, New Jersey. Reprinted with permission.

employees, communities, and stockholders (top line of each paragraph). The Credo was first introduced in 1943. In the 1970s, former J&J Chairman James Burke held a series of meetings with the firm's 1,200 top managers; they were encouraged to challenge the Credo. What emerged from those meetings was agreement that the document functioned as originally intended; it was slightly reworded but substantially unchanged from when the Credo was originally published. The company has now reprinted the Credo into 36 languages for non-English-speaking employees.[10]

Most important, the Credo still influences how J&J conducts its operations. In recent years, the company has surveyed all 100,000 employees in its 200 companies about how well the company meets its responsibilities to its four principal stakeholders. The survey questions employees from all 54 countries where J&J operates about every line in the Credo. The tabulation and reporting of results are confidential. (Department and division managers receive only information pertaining to their units and composite numbers for the entire firm.) A J&J employee recently told one of the authors that a low score for a unit causes substantial discussion about how it might improve.

Does J&J's Credo work? Top management feels strongly that it does. The Credo is often mentioned as an important contributing factor in the company's exemplary handling of the Tylenol product recall twenty years ago when that product was subject to tampering. It appears that the firm's commitment to its Credo makes ethical business practice a high priority.

Increasingly, more and more organizations are accepting the stakeholder concept. They are beginning to develop procedures for linking stakeholder concerns to the strategies they conceive. In order to implement a stakeholder management approach, organizations need to do several things including:

- Identify the company's stakeholders.
- Determine which ones are primary, indirect, and secondary, as well as exactly what stakes each group holds in the organization.
- Establish what responsibilities (economic, ethical, legal, or philanthropic) the organization has to each stakeholder group.
- Identify any conflicts between stakeholder criteria.
- Decide how the organization can best respond strategically to the opportunities and threats inherent in stakeholder claims, especially where conflicts are likely to require creative compromises.

Again, the rights and interests of various stakeholders are important, as they are the objects (some may say moral subjects) to which the different ethical theories or frameworks are applied. Since a large part of ethics is *deciding what is properly owed to whom*, identifying stakeholders and their claims is analogous to establishing the interests in a legal case. Consider the example of a public-relations firm asked to represent a foreign country seeking economic development as a client. Suppose the country has acceptable diplomatic relations with the United States, but is also accused of violating human rights. The stakeholders include the employees of the public-relations agency, the U.S. government, the client country's government, the stockholders of the public relations firm, other customers, the media, and the citizenry of both the United States and the nation being considered as a client. Each group might very well view the ethical stakes involved in this controversy from a different perspective. Agency employees are concerned with their right to earn a living; the U.S. government may be preoccupied with maintaining cordial relations with the developing country; stockholders are motivated by the prospect of a client signing a lucrative, long-term contract; and the media may be energized by the news value associated with the apparent hypocrisy of helping a government most U.S. citizens find abhorrent—which may also complicate the agency's ability to service its less controversial clients. Meanwhile, the prospective client nation's citizens may be torn between the value of anticipated improvements in their economy and dismay that such improvements may imply foreign approval of their country's human rights record. The complexity of stakeholder analysis is apparent from this example.

PRINCIPLES FOR ETHICAL DECISION MAKING

What standards do marketers use to grapple with questions that have ethical implications? Several shorthand decision rules are often used by business people. We offer two types of simple *Rules of Thumb* for marketers. The first is the ABCs of Marketing Ethics, and the second is a list of maxims.

ABCs of Marketing Ethics

One easy way to examine the major thrust of marketing ethics is to think of a series of words/phrases that begin with A, B, and C. This is a short and relatively straightforward approach to simplifying marketing ethics. However, we must caution you that behind each of these relatively basic ideas is a complex set of issues. The three As are applied, above the law, and aspirational. The three Bs are beneficial, beyond the bottom line, and breaking new ground. The Cs are compliance, consequences, and contributions.[11]

Applied

Marketing ethics is an applied discipline, like legal, engineering, and medical ethics. Each of these professional fields draws rules from moral philosophy or religious traditions, and applies them to the problems specific to the relevant area. For example, we apply these standards to dilemmas faced by marketing managers, salespeople, advertising executives, and retail managers throughout the book.

Above the Law

Ethical questions are those that exist somewhere above the legal minimum. Unfortunately, some companies view ethics as synonymous with legal requirements. We view the law as the floor. As a response to the scandals discussed in the Introduction, the floor was raised by the passage of the Sarbanes Oxley Act in the United States during 2002. As an illustration, one might think of a famous dance of the baby-boom generation, the limbo. The purpose of this dance was to continue to dance under a stick progressively closer to the floor. The challenge was, How low can you go? This, unfortunately, also describes marketers who try to do the moral minimum.

Aspirational

Marketing ethics at its best should be aspirational. Both junior and senior marketing executives should aspire to do better from an ethical standpoint. This approach is covered within the virtue ethics and moral development models examined later in the chapter. For a number of years, one of Levi Strauss & Company's ethics publications was called its "Aspiration Statement," which signaled to the world that Levi aspired to a high level of ethics, even though they did not always attain it.

Beneficial

This point means that good ethics is beneficial to the firm. The one caveat is that it is beneficial in the "long run." There are good theoretical reasons for believing that practicing good ethical behavior is beneficial. We admit, however, that the empirical evidence is mixed with respect to whether good behavior usually results in increased profitability. We do know that a systematic lack of transparency with customers, stockholders, and the public is financially disastrous. Immoral behavior can ruin a company (e.g., Arthur Andersen and Enron).

Beyond the Bottom Line

Marketing managers must think beyond just the financial impact of their decisions. They should understand the environmental and safety implications of their products, whether toys or automobiles. In fact, Royal Dutch Shell now regularly provides information on what they call a "triple bottom line," including economic, environmental, and social performance. The latest report can be found online.[12]

Breaking New Ground

The most ethical firms think "outside the box" and employ moral imagination in dealing with intractable ethical problems.[13] In particular, problems for which the most obvious alternative solutions all involve harm to multiple stakeholders call for creative thinking to devise a solution that either minimizes such harm or, ideally, produces results that permit the parties in conflict to gain. For example, pollution control efforts sometimes generate cost reductions (e.g., less waste) with economic value.

Compliance

At minimum, marketing managers must comply with the policies and rules of their companies, as well as those of their nation's legal system. In fact, most corporate codes of ethics are written as compliance documents by spelling out prohibitions and approved responses to ethical situations known from company experience. In research we have done with large companies, about half report taking a compliance approach to ethical issues facing their firm.[14]

Consequences

Virtually all marketing managers worry about the consequences of their actions. In fact, one set of ethical theories uses the yardstick of whether good or bad consequences will result in deciding whether a decision is ethical or unethical. For instance, a decision to move a manufacturing plant to a lower cost of labor country will likely mean good consequences for the company in terms of lower costs of production. **What negative consequences for the company can you think of arising from this decision?**

Contributions

Most marketing managers and other top managers of companies do *not* look at their position or corporation as just being in the business of making money. They often speak in much more enlightened terms such as improving convenience for our consumers or offering more product choice. Thus, marketing contributes to a more productive economy and happier society. Whether this vision is always fulfilled is debatable, but business men and women often see themselves as contributing to society and not just in a narrow microeconomic sense.

Maxims for Ethical Marketing

Several maxims that might aid a marketer facing an ethical dilemma are the following:

The Golden Rule.   Act in a way that you would hope others would act toward you.

The Professional Ethic.   Take only actions that would be viewed as proper by an objective panel of your professional colleagues. (The new American Marketing Association Ethical Norms and Values for Professional Marketers presented in Exhibit 1-3 is an example of a professional code.)

The TV/Newspaper Test.   A manager should always ask, "Would I feel comfortable explaining this action on TV or in the front page of the local newspaper to the general public?" (This is sometimes referred to as *The Wall Street Journal* or *Financial Times* Test.)

When in Doubt, Don't.   If a manager feels uneasy about a decision, there is probably reason to question it. We advise our students that if the decision does not seem right in the head, heart, or gut, then the decision should be postponed. The individual should probably seek guidance from a trusted person before proceeding with the decision.

Slippery Slope.   This maxim suggests that companies must be careful not to engage in debatable practices that may serve as a precedent for undertaking other even more questionable strategies later. For example, there could be good reason for a sales manager to push sales "up the channel" toward the end of a fiscal quarter so that a hardworking group of sales reps achieve their bonuses. However, such tactics may lead to an increasing acceptance by management that it is okay to be "fast and loose" with inventory figures (i.e., the slippery slope). (Although this maxim does occur in marketing, we see the recent scandals that plagued several firms and the accounting profession as classic illustrations of the slippery slope.)

Kid/Mother/Founder on Your Shoulder.   Would a naive child, your mother, or the company founder be comfortable with the ethical decision being made? Could you explain it to them in commonsense terms they would understand?

Never Knowingly Do Harm.   This implies a manager would not consciously make or sell a product deemed to be unsafe. Certain observers call this the "silver rule" because it does not hold marketers to as high a standard as the Golden Rule does. **(What marketers might be guilty of not following this guideline?)**

Some thumbnail rules are difficult to apply in specific situations. The application of different rules of thumb to the same situation may sometimes lead to quite different solutions. For example, if salespeople pad their meal expense accounts 15 percent because customary gratuities (i.e., tips) are not technically reimbursable in the absence of a receipt, the *professional ethic* might indicate the practice is okay despite its variance from the letter of

Exhibit 1-3   **American Marketing Association**
Ethical Norms and Values for Marketers

Preamble

The American Marketing Association commits itself to promoting the highest standard of professional ethical norms and values for its members. Norms are established standards of conduct expected and maintained by society and/or professional organizations. Values represent the collective conception of what people find desirable, important and morally proper. Values serve as the criteria for evaluating the actions of others. Marketing practitioners must recognize that they serve not only their enterprises but also act as stewards of society in creating, facilitating and executing the efficient and effective transactions that are part of the greater economy. In this role, marketers should embrace the highest ethical *norms* of practicing professionals as well as the ethical *values* implied by their responsibility toward stakeholders (e.g., customers, employees, investors, channel members, regulators and the host community).

General Norms

1. Marketers must first do no harm. This means doing work for which they are appropriately trained or experienced so they can actively add value to their organizations and customers. It also means adhering to all applicable laws and regulations, as well as embodying high ethical standards in the choices they make.
2. Marketers must foster trust in the marketing system. This means that the products are appropriate for their intended and promoted use. It requires that marketing communications about goods and services are not intentionally deceptive or misleading. It suggests building relationships that provide for the equitable adjustment and/or redress of customer grievances. It implies striving for good faith and fair dealing so as to contribute toward the efficacy of the exchange process.
3. Marketers should embrace, communicate and practice the fundamental ethical values that will improve consumer confidence in the integrity of the marketing exchange system. These basic Values are intentionally aspirational and include: Honesty, Responsibility, Fairness, Respect, Openness and Citizenship.

Ethical Values

Honesty—this means being truthful and forthright in our dealings with customers and stakeholders.
- We will tell the truth in all situations and at all times.
- We will offer products of value that do what we claim in our communications.

- We will stand behind our brands if they fail to deliver their claimed benefits.
- We will honor our explicit and implicit commitments and promises.

Responsibility—this involves accepting the consequences of our marketing decisions and strategies.
- We will make strenuous efforts to serve the needs of our customers.
- We will avoid using coercion with all stakeholders.
- We will acknowledge the social obligations to stakeholders that come with increased marketing and economic power.
- We will recognize our special commitments to economically vulnerable segments of the market such as children, the elderly and others who may be substantially disadvantaged.

Fairness—this has to do with justly trying to balance the needs of the buyer with the interests of the seller.
- We will clearly represent our products in selling, advertising and other forms of communication; this includes the avoidance of false, misleading and deceptive promotion.
- We will reject manipulations and sales tactics that harm customer trust.
- We will not engage in price fixing, predatory pricing, price gouging or "bait and switch" tactics.
- We will not knowingly participate in material conflicts of interest.

Respect—this addresses the basic human dignity of all stakeholders.
- We will value individual differences even as we avoid customer stereotyping or depicting demographic (e.g., gender, race, sexual) groups in a negative or dehumanizing way in our promotions.
- We will listen to the needs of our customers and make all reasonable efforts to monitor and improve their satisfaction on an on-going basis.
- We will make a special effort to understand suppliers, intermediaries and distributors from other cultures.
- We will appropriately acknowledge the contributions of others, such as consultants, employees and co-workers, to our marketing endeavors.

Openness—this focuses on creating transparency in our marketing operations.
- We will strive to communicate clearly with all our constituencies.
- We will accept constructive criticism from our customers and other stakeholders.
- We will explain significant product or service risks, component substitutions or other foreseeable eventualities affecting the customer or their perception of the purchase decision.
- We will fully disclose list prices and terms of financing as well as available price deals and adjustments.

(continued)

Citizenship—this involves a strategic focus on fulfilling the economic, legal, philanthropic and societal responsibilities that serve stakeholders.
- We will strive to protect the natural environment in the execution of marketing campaigns.
- We will give back to the community through volunteerism and charitable donations.
- We will work to contribute to the overall betterment of marketing and its reputation.
- We will encourage supply chain members to ensure that trade is fair for all participants, including producers in developing countries.

Implementation

Finally, we recognize that every industry sector and marketing sub-discipline (e.g., marketing research, e-commerce, direct selling, advertising, etc.) has its own specific ethical issues that require policies and commentary. An array of such codes can be linked to via the AMA website. We encourage all such groups to develop and/or refine their industry and discipline-specific codes of ethics in order to supplement these general norms and values.

Source: AMA Ethics Committee (O.C. Ferrell—chair; M. Etzel, G. Findley, G. Laczniak, L. Lee and P. Murphy—members) (2004). Subject to approval by AMA board.

company policy. Why? Because this is the only mechanism to recover a legitimate cost. In contrast, the *when in doubt, don't* rule questions whether padding expense accounts is ever acceptable. (Of course, the company that has such a rule might be viewed as guilty of placing their employees in a "no win" situation, one that could be avoided if a specific provision for tips were included in its expense reimbursement policy.)

Despite such ambiguity, these short maxims can have considerable value. One wonders whether the product manager who permitted the controversial ad (Scenario 2) to continue to be advertised could feel comfortable explaining those actions to the general public on television (i.e., pass the TV test). Similarly, the *professional ethic* can be extremely useful for those subspecialties in business that have a code of professional conduct that covers certain recurring situations. For example, various groups of professional marketing researchers have developed detailed codes of ethics that cover situations commonly encountered by their peer group (see Chapter 2).

Whenever such rules are used, the consensus regarding what constitutes proper ethical behavior in a decision-making situation tends to diminish as the level of analysis proceeds from the abstract to the specific. Stated another way, it is easy to get a group of managers to agree *in general* that a practice is improper; however, casting that practice in a very specific set of circumstances usually reduces consensus. For example, most managers would agree with the proposition that business has the obligation to provide consumers with facts relevant to the informed purchase of a product or a service. However, let's test this proposition in a specific situation:

> A manufacturer sells a cleaning concentrate with instructions calling for mixing one part of the concentrate with four parts of water; this product has been sold in this manner for twenty-five years. Now, assume an issue of *Consumer Reports* indicates, based on several test applications, that the product is just as effective when mixed with one part concentrate to eight parts water. Thus, consumers need only use half as much concentrate. **Does the company have an ethical responsibility to inform customers of this fact?**

Most managers will agree that business has the obligation to provide consumers with facts relevant to an informed purchase. But does such an informed purchase include full disclosure of this *new information*, especially if further product testing in different cleaning situations might produce different results?

THE IMPORTANCE OF ETHICAL THEORY

In order to better structure ethical questions, managers should enhance their ability to reason ethically. What is meant by *ethical reasoning?* It is **the process of systematically analyzing an ethical issue and applying to it one or more ethical standards.** This process will generally consist of three steps:

1. *Definition of an ethical problem.* The first step necessitates determining whether a marketing decision has ethical implications. This requires an assessment of the nature and consequences of the action. This step frames a marketing question as an ethical problem. For example (recalling Scenario 2), is it acceptable to highlight medical benefits and minimize side effects in an advertising campaign?

2. *Selection of an ethical standard.* Various theories of recommended moral behavior exist. While most theories will lead managers to the same solution given similar circumstances, different standards sometimes lead to divergent solutions. The existence of competing moral theories is one reason why well-intentioned managers disagree about what is ethically *proper*. (One goal of this chapter is to elaborate on the major ethical theories.)

3. *Application of the ethical standard.* Once an ethical standard is chosen, it still must be applied to a specific situation. For example, a standard can be applied to a particular ethical dilemma, and the subsequent determination of an ethical choice is the completion of the ethical reasoning process. (Throughout this book we describe various rationales marketing managers use to reason ethically about solutions to ethical problems.)

If marketing managers do not follow this or a similar procedure, ethical discussions too easily degenerate into a clash of personal opinion or preference. For the most part, ethical reasoning ability is grounded in a knowledge of ethical theory. If managers understand ethical theory, they can apply specific principles or rules to guide decision making. Those principles can then be unpacked and examined in order to determine the appropriate choices emanating from an ethical problem. For example, a manager considering marketing a soft drink banned in the United States because of health questions raised by the FDA might consider

1. Sending the product to the foreign market where it can be legally sold
2. Waiting for additional research information that might further validate or invalidate the danger of the substance
3. Exporting the product with a warning label
4. Dumping the product as waste
5. Disposing of the product to a wholesaler at a severely discounted price and letting that independent business firm make its own determination as to what to do with the controversial product

Each of these options raises ethical questions.

How should a marketing manager go about deciding what to do? How does one go about reasoning to an ethical solution? The answer to these questions lies partly in understanding different ethical theories. This response is not without its challenges. As noted earlier, the difficulty in choosing among various theories is that different ethical theories may lead to different conclusions. However, this realization should not be sufficient to dismiss the study of ethical reasoning as a fruitless exercise. Ethical issues regularly stem from "tough cases." Few people maintain that ethics is an easily understood subject. The existence of ethical dilemmas, where different approaches lead to different solutions, should not be a cause of cynicism. Some ambiguity is inherent in grappling with tough ethical problems, whether in marketing or in other realms. The fact that different principles sometimes generate different decisions opens up more options than may have been considered initially. A more optimistic view is that managers should take some satisfaction from knowing that the application of various ethical theories to a particular situation will most often lead to consensus. At minimum, ethical theories will usually not generate unethical solutions. Finally, for those who may be skeptical about the values of ethical theory in marketing, we offer this statement by the classic philosopher Cicero in resolving a conflict between a grain trader and the famine-starved citizens of Rhodes in favor of the latter:

> To everyone who proposes to have a good career, moral philosophy is indispensable. (De Officiis, 44 B.C.)

TWO PSEUDO "ETHICAL" APPROACHES

Many observers of marketing ethics invoke either relativism (situational ethics) or egoism as rationales for discussion. We do not consider them to be comprehensive theories (hence, the quotes around ethical) but they do need to be examined before moving on.

Cultural and Ethical/Moral Relativism

The most prevalent form of this approach is *cultural relativism*. It is a *descriptive* claim that ethical practices differ among cultures; that, as a matter of fact, what is considered right in one culture may be considered wrong in another. Many believe that one should adjust his/her ethical thinking depending on the culture in which the firm is operating.[15] The long-standing phrase "When in Rome, do as the Romans do" captures the essence of this idea. One cannot determine what one ought to do mainly from the fact that some people permit it.

Moral relativism is a stronger claim that advocates what is *really* right or wrong is what the culture says is right or wrong. Relativism, then, presents a challenge to marketing executives, especially in the global marketplace. Managers must adjust to a certain extent to the tastes and needs of diverse consumers. In addition, defenders of ethical relativism argue that there is no better, more valid basis for making ethical judgments because any other conclusion assumes some absolute set of norms that would not be sensitive to situational factors. Nonetheless, managers who act solely on the basis of ethical relativism run both legal and reputational risks, especially in an era of worldwide communications. For marketing managers, relativism would guide them to engage in bribery if that was the norm in a certain country. However, for U.S. based firms, bribery is effectively prohibited by the Foreign Corrupt Practices Act.

Several traps brought on by relativist thinking should be avoided. The first trap is that we should be careful not to hold ethics to too high a standard of proof. If we start with the assumption that ethical judgment must be proven as absolutely certain and beyond doubt, then ethics assuredly will fail to meet this standard. The second trap involves confusing the fact that there is wide disagreement about values, with the conclusion that no agreement is possible. The fact of disagreement provides no reason for concluding that all of these diverse opinions are equally valid. A third trap involves confusing values such as respect, tolerance, and impartiality with relativism. Respect for other people is a fundamental ethical value. Part of what it means to respect someone is to listen to his or her opinions and to show tolerance for opinions that differ from our own. But tolerating diverse opinions and values is not the same as ethical relativism.[16]

Managerial or Organizational Egoism

Egoism is a philosophy which asserts that individuals act exclusively in their own self-interest. Consequences are judged only as they affect "me." The late twentieth century saw manifestations of egoism in phrases such as the "me generation" or "looking out for Number 1." Thus, *egoism* holds that executives should take those steps that most efficiently advance the self-interest of themselves or their divisions or firm. An example of individual egoism might be the product manager who postpones making needed improvements to a mature product, because she knows already that she will be promoted in the next year to a new division and she is interested only in next quarter's financial performance. An instance of organizational egoism would be a firm ordered to install pollution abatement equipment because of illegal discharges that delays until the deadline date so that interest earned from cash-on-hand can be maximized. Obviously, a problem with such a philosophy arises when pursuing organizational goals conflicts with their impact on other stakeholders. Often managerial egoism is used in conjunction with a legalistic approach—the adage that the fiduciary duties of management boil down to "obey the law" and, beyond that, to the view that "the business of business is to maximize profits." Presumably, other required controls over unacceptable behavior will be provided by the invisible mechanisms of the marketplace, competition, reactions by customers, and so forth.

Several problems arise with managerial egoism. First, some moral philosophers do not see egoism as a philosophy at all. Why? An egoist has problems "universalizing" egoism as a guiding philosophy for others, because if the egoist advocated that everybody acts in their own self-interest that prescription itself would *not* be in the self interest of the egoist. A second problem is that some see egoism as being incompatible with the human tendency to be concerned for others in addition to oneself. Finally, there are obvious potential conflicts between individual and organizational egoism. However, philosophical semantics aside, managerial egoism does not stand up to scrutiny for other reasons.

Many questionable marketing practices seem to illustrate the egoistic approach. For example, until recently, public accounting firms were enthusiastic about developing codes of ethics, driven by the belief that these would allow them to continue to bid on audit and consulting contracts despite past scandals. It is also clear that the marketplace does not always provide a fair and level playing field for business organizations and consumers. Furthermore, early growth in the dot-com industry was often characterized by "bending the rules" and "get rich quick" mentalities, ignoring investor and larger industry interests. Responsibilities are owed to stakeholder groups other than shareholders, and these groups may not hold a primary interest in seeing the maximization of short-term return on investment. Insofar as the long-term goals of the managerial egoist are often limited to economic considerations, the long-term interests of the organization are not necessarily best served

EXHIBIT 1-4   Managerial Egoism at Enron

Because Enron believed it was leading a revolution, it encouraged flouting the rules. There was constant gossip that this rule breaking extended to executives' personal lives—rumors of sexual high jinks in the executive ranks ran rampant. Enron also developed a reputation for ruthlessness, both external and internal. [Enron CEO, Jeff] Skilling is usually credited with creating a system of forced rankings for employees, in which those rated in the bottom 20% would leave the company. Thus, employees attempted to crush not just outsiders but each other. "Enron was built to maximize value by maximizing the individual parts," says an executive at a competing energy firm. Enron traders, he adds, were afraid to go to the bathroom because the guy sitting next to them might use the information off their screen to trade against them. And because delivering bad news had career-wrecking potential, problems got papered over—especially, says one former employee, in the trading operation. "People perpetuated this myth that there were never any mistakes. It was astounding to me."

Source: Bethany McLean, "Why Enron Went Bust," *Fortune* December 24, 2001, from www.fortune.com, accessed January 13, 2002.

using this approach.[17] A disastrous example of taking the short-term view is Enron. The quote in Exhibit 1-4 recounts that ethical egoism appeared to be the dominant ethical theory guiding the top management of that firm.

Having addressed the "pretender theories" of relativism and egoism, we now briefly present four general categories of ethical theory—utilitarianism (i.e., consequence-based theories), duty-based approaches (i.e., deontological theories), contract-based perspectives, and virtue-based ethics.

COMPREHENSIVE ETHICAL THEORIES

Unless a manager operates in a completely intuitive manner (and some do), the ability to reason about ethical questions requires some familiarity with the principal theoretical frameworks that have come to dominate the field of moral philosophy. The aforementioned major categories of ethical theories are now presented along with a discussion of how they relate to marketing decisions.

Consequences-based theories

Consequences-oriented theories are sometimes called *teleological*, from the Greek word *telos*, meaning end or purpose. That is, a marketing decision is judged as ethical or unethical depending on the *outcome*. Hence, if the

foreseeable consequences of a decision are positive, then the decision is ethical. The major category of theory that falls within the consequences approach
is utilitarianism.

Utilitarianism

Probably the most widely understood and commonly applied ethical
theory is *utilitarianism*. In an organizational context, utilitarianism basically
states that a decision concerning marketing conduct is proper if and only if
that decision produces the *greatest good for the greatest number* of individuals.
"Good" is usually defined as the *net benefits* that accrue to those parties
affected by the choice. Thus, most utilitarians hold the position that moral
choices must be evaluated by calculating the net benefits of each available
alternative action. It is important that *all* of the stakeholders affected by the
decision should be given their just consideration. As mentioned earlier, teleological theories deal with outcomes or end goals. The often-stated declaration, "the end justifies the means," is one classic expression of utilitarian
thinking.

Several formulations of utilitarianism exist. Their differences harken
back to the original writers on the topic, nineteenth-century philosophers
Jeremy Bentham and John Stuart Mill.[18]

One major school of thought, *act utilitarianism*, focuses on the *action* that
has been taken, analyzing it along the lines of whether the selected action
produces more good than bad consequences. For example, a pharmaceutical
company may operate by the principle that it will release any Federal Drug
Administration approved drug with some side effects, as long as it helps
more persons combat a particular disease than the number troubled by a
minor side effect. For another example, Scenario 2 discusses a new drug
product dealing with weight gain advertised using two short commercials,
one part that introduces the product and a second part that touted its benefits. However, the side effects are not discussed. If the benefits are sufficiently
great and the problems with the side effects sufficiently limited, then the
action of the pharmaceutical in Scenario 2 is justified on act utilitarian
grounds.

A second formulation, *rule utilitarianism*, looks at whether the option or
choice conforms to a *rule* that attempts to maximize the overall utility. Some
have criticized act utilitarianism on the grounds that it often gives the wrong
ethical answer when evaluating individual actions. To use an example from
banking, suppose a banker is considering whether it is right to foreclose on
the mortgage of a widow and her children. To consider that action in isolation,
it is fairly easy to show on act utilitarian grounds that foreclosure would cause
more pain than not foreclosing. However, suppose we had a rule that said that
banks should not foreclose whenever the action of foreclosing would cause

more harm than foreclosing. If that rule were adopted, then banks would be reluctant to lend money. Thus, the rule permitting foreclosure on widows is better for society than a rule that forbids such foreclosure. Rule utilitarians, then, focus on the rules for acting rather than on individual actions themselves. For a rule utilitarian a rule is morally correct when it provides more social good than any alternative rule. For act utilitarians rules are just rules of thumb. For rule utilitarians rules are determinate of right and wrong.

Business executives commonly embrace such consequentialist approaches to ethical problems, because they are so compatible with traditional business thinking. Why? Just as this results-based theory seeks to maximize happiness or *the good,* business executives often hope to maximize profit, return on investment, or share price. If a businessperson draws the broader conclusion that the greatest good is equivalent to the highest profitability and this situation produces the most benefits for society, it is easy to see how these two systems, both oriented to optimum results, are philosophically compatible.

Consequence-Oriented Philosophy and Marketing Management

A strong appeal of the utilitarian approach is its *cost-benefit* character. Marketing managers regularly weigh the pros and cons of alternative economic and managerial actions. This approach to solving business problems is a staple of most MBA programs and therefore is ingrained in the psyche of many administrators. Business executives appreciate the fact that most utilitarians recognize that not everyone will benefit from a particular action. Hence, the emphasis in utilitarianism is upon the *net* utility of the set of outcomes resulting from a decision being considered. Marketing managers, of course, also realize their business decisions must often be placed in the context of a "win-lose" situation. That is, the consequences of a business action are seldom singular; rather they are multiple and may "cut both ways." For instance, in mature markets, the only way to *gain* market share is for at least one competitor to lose share. Or the only approach to increasing long-term shareholder value is to sacrifice near-term profits (and perhaps management bonuses) in favor of future product or market development expenditures.

Another reason marketing managers are so accepting of utilitarian thinking lies in its flexibility in response to differing situations. Utilitarianism accommodates complex circumstances more easily than other, more absolute, philosophical approaches. The factors considered in a utilitarian framework can be conveniently varied from the short term to the long term, or from financial to nonfinancial criteria. While conflicting stakeholder claims *can* be recognized, managers typically weigh business owner or stockholder goals associated with corporate profitability as more important than the goals of

other groups such as employees or the community. **Do you think this weighting is proper?**
For example, in a situation involving the distribution manager of the supermarket chain sending lower quality cuts of meat and vegetables to lower profitability stores in disadvantaged neighborhoods, one can see how this approach *might* be defended. The manager rationalizes that as long as the meats and vegetables are above some minimally acceptable quality level, it is in the best financial interest of the supermarket chain to take whatever action it can to enhance overall operations. With respect to units located in the least affluent areas of the city, economic advantage is maximized by systematically discriminating against these less profitable units. Alternatively, management may also calculate (quite reasonably) that the marginal value of the inner city store can only be maintained by offsetting the impact of higher insurance and security costs and lower sales volume per square foot with other cost-cutting measures. This reasoning may also be combined with recognizing the need to provide higher quality to customers in more affluent areas which may also present the greatest threat from competitors. When compared with the alternative of closing an otherwise unprofitable store (with the external costs of unemployment and less service to that neighborhood), the current practice *may* be the most ethical in a utilitarian sense.

Limitations of Utilitarianism

Consequentialist approaches to ethical reasoning are obviously not without their problems. Perhaps the most evident concern, which applies to almost any formulation of utilitarianism, is the question of who decides what "the greatest good" is. Indeed, usually many opinions exist as to what constitutes the nature of the actual benefits of a particular action. When this is the case, *who* is it that decides which perception of what "good" shall prevail? Is it the CEO, the vice president of marketing, the product managers, or a panel of customers? Second, it appears that utilitarianism is a philosophy where ends sometimes may justify otherwise unacceptable means. That is, just because the outcome of a particular action produces a "net good" for a corporation, or, for that matter, the whole of society, should that necessitate a penalty or expense for some parties? Should any product be permitted in the market if it causes a significant and lasting health problem for a minority of users? Those who practice most forms of utilitarianism recognize that one *cannot* cause great harm to certain others in order to achieve a desirable or noble end. This seems to be the point that animal-rights activists stress in advocating a ban on the use of animals in safety testing such products as cosmetics. In fact, one of the greatest ethical precepts (mentioned earlier) is *never knowingly do harm*. But, the definition of what constitutes "a harm" or a significant harm is subject to debate.

Third, those marketing managers who adopt a primarily economic interpretation of utilitarianism must answer whether such an approach is compatible with the concept of justice. The transformation of utilitarian theory into economic utilitarianism is somewhat understandable, in the sense that a business organization is primarily an *economic* enterprise. But just because an action is economically beneficial, does this mean it is just and proper? For instance, because the market demands sexually explicit Internet pornographic material—and pornography is profitable to most of the parties involved in its production and consumption—is it ethical to market such material? Even though a particular action has produced the greatest economic good for the greatest number, that still does not *prove* that the action is just and proper when both production and consumption are seen to victimize some participants and, arguably, the consumers as well in other than economic terms.

In short, the utilitarian principle to act in a way that results in a greatest good for the greatest number is a popular method of ethical reasoning used by many marketing managers which also presents problems in some circumstances.

Duty-Based Theories

A second category of ethical theories are classified by philosophers as *deontological,* the term coming from the Greek word *deon,* "duty." This impressive sounding word basically indicates that actions are best judged as "good," standing alone and without regard to consequences. Thus, the inherent rightness of an act is *not* decided by analyzing and choosing the act that produces the best consequences, but rather according to the premise that certain actions are "correct" in and of themselves because they stem from fundamental obligations. Intentions or motivations then determine whether a marketing decision is ethical or unethical.

Perhaps the most famous duty-based theory was developed by the Prussian philosopher Immanuel Kant.[19] Kant contended that moral laws took the form of categorical imperatives—principles that defined behavior appropriate in all situations and that should be followed by all persons as a matter of duty. Kant proposed three formulations of the categorical imperative as follows:

1. Act only on maxims that you can will to be universal laws of nature. (Universality)
2. Always treat the humanity in a person as an end, and never as a means merely. (Never treat people as means to an end)
3. Act as if you were a member of an ideal kingdom of ends in which you were both subject and sovereign at the same time. (Moral community)

The first formulation argues that there are universal moral standards. For example, could any society universalize customer shoplifting? The answer is no. Similarly, bribery of government officials by marketers is unethical following the first formulation. The second formulation is concerned with treatment of all stakeholders as persons. Application of this principle in marketing is to never treat customers as means, manipulating their behavior to attain company goals. One of the controversial areas of marketing that might violate this formulation is sex appeal advertising. Exhibit 1-5 reports on a variation of this issue in a European context. The third formulation views any marketing organization as a moral community. Managers, then, should respect the humanity of all workers in the firm and employees should try to achieve common goals and shared ends.[20] In a larger sense, a market, including suppliers, competitors, and customers, constitutes a relevant moral community.

For business, duty-based approaches to ethics have important implications. This theory suggests, among other things, that cost-benefit analysis is inappropriate to the evaluation of some situations. Why? Decisions that produce good corporate outcomes but significantly hurt other stakeholders in the process are not morally acceptable using this line of reasoning. If marketers have a special obligation to vulnerable consumers, for example, the elderly, children, or less educated who are unable to resist advertising appeals that more sophisticated consumers receive with skepticism, those advertising appeals violate that obligation. Also, it suggests that the goal of seeking the maximum *net* consequences of an action may include intermediate steps, which could be judged as morally inappropriate. Why is this so? Because *means* as well as *ends* should be subjected to moral evaluation. Thus, an implication of duty-based theories is that sometimes business executives must take actions that do *not* produce the best economic consequences. To do otherwise could be morally wrong. That is, some actions might violate the basic duty to treat everyone fairly. For example, reflection indicates that the customers of the low-income stores, where the poorest cuts of meat and vegetables are sent, have been used merely as a *means* to obtain a satisfactory economic *end*. For Roche, in Scenario 2, certain overweight consumers have been unjustly discriminated against to the benefit of others. A similar judgment might be applied to the use of fear appeals in promoting certain financial service products. Finally, buzz marketing (Scenario 1) is probably unethical from a duty-based perspective because the intention is to mislead consumers.

Like utilitarianism, duty-based theories are controversial in part because there are many different deontological theories. Various moral philosophers have compiled different lists of basic obligations or duties. While the lists overlap, they are not identical. Second, duty-based theories represent the antithesis of modern relativism (i.e., the notion that the context of particular situations determine the rightness of decisions). Hence, they are viewed by some as not being well suited to our complex, multicultural, and global marketplace, because they emphasize the development of *universal* rules. The very nature

EXHIBIT 1-5   The "Porno-Chic" Advertising Controversy*

France, known for its liberal positions toward provocative advertising, has taken the initiative to lead the European protest against indecent and offensive marketing campaigns. The "phenomenon" at the center of the controversy has been termed "porno-chic." For a time, porno-chic was the marketing basis for several European fashion gurus. A far cry from conservative US marketing standards, the objection of the French (and many other European nations) to porno-chic comes not to its use of nudity. "Nude women in advertising don't pose any problem," says a female official in the Employment Ministry. "It's the violence and degradation that offends people."[1]

So what exactly is porno-chic? Porno-chic is a "naked woman, caressing herself into a state of ecstasy" posted over hundreds of Paris bus shelters. Porno-chic is "women who are bruised, bullied, even consorting with animals."[2] Recently ordered out of Italian advertising was an ad for Cuban beer that featured: "a sultry model kneeling in black bikini with a bottle of Tinama beer between her legs." The tagline: "Have yourself a Cuban."[3]

It is not only the French who have found these types of ads to be degrading and humiliating to women, but also Italy, Germany, and even the European Union have discussed the implementation of more rigid advertising guidelines in both print and television. Although ad agencies cannot be forced to comply with new rulings, most are expected to withdraw press and poster ads if asked to do so. Governments have urged citizens to take action and voice their objection to messages that are "degrading and humiliating" to women. In doing so, authorities maintain that it is not nudity in and of itself ("Bare breasts are used to promote everything from pullovers to Parmesan cheese in continental Europe.") that is under attack; "it is the use of nudity" that is being questioned.[4]

With a market seemingly overrun by attractive naked women, European marketers have been forced to look beyond what has traditionally been considered "bold and sexy." In doing so, they have ignited a moral controversy.

The French government released a report condemning a new breed of ads that were perceived as degrading and humiliating to women. Finally, France's Truth in Advertising Bureau issued new standards on what is acceptable when the human body is portrayed as a means to sell products. These regulations come as a result of a governmental report issued in July.

---

* Prepared by Diana Laquinta under the supervision of Professor Patrick E. Murphy.
[1] Stephen Baker and Christina White, "Why 'Porno Chic' Is Riling the French," *Business Week*, July 30, 2001, 47.
[2] Ibid.
[3] Alessandra Galloni, "Clapdown on 'Porno-Chic' Ads Is Pushed by French Authorities," *Wall Street Journal*, October 25, 2001, B4.
[4] Ibid.

of such absolute approaches includes certain problems that are inherent in the development of categorical imperatives. Among them are the following:

1. *There are always contingencies that seem to complicate real-world situations.* For example, suppose a sales organization has an absolute rule against the practice of providing gifts to customers. Now suppose, further, it enters a new international market where gift giving is a common and expected practice. Now also consider the prospect that success in this market will determine whether the firm can survive. Should the universal rule be violated or changed to accommodate these contingencies? Other examples also might be explored. What about the prospect of dire consequences if one tells the truth? Are duties to customers or employees conditioned by their comparative vulnerability?

2. *Universals also do not take into account the ethical character of the formulator of the universal principle.* That is, if the morality of the person formulating the principle is flawed, it is possible that the principle itself will be deficient. For example, one might take issue with the universal maxims formulated by egoistic managers who see business as merely a game, the sole purpose of which is the accumulation of personal wealth.

3. *There may not be a mechanism for resolving conflicts among two absolute moral duties.* Managers clearly have a fiduciary responsibility to their shareholders and a duty of fidelity to their employees. What happens when action requires a trade-off between these duties? Which duty takes precedence? Is one universal more absolute than another? What about the duty of motherhood for a female employee versus loyalty to the job and company?

Contract-Based Theories

Social contract theory is based on the most fundamental considerations for maintaining social order and harmony, that is, that individuals must generally agree to abstain from preying on each other and that, to ensure that this does not happen, rules and a mechanism to enforce them are required. For marketers, social contract theory (SCT) has special implications for relationships among competitors and for transactions with less powerful or vulnerable buyers and sellers, especially those who are dependent on a marketer as either a customer or supplier. By implication, social contract theory demands obedience to laws and adherence to the provisions of business contracts.

Rawlsian Theory

One contemporary theory, which is contract based in its approach, was formulated by the late Professor John Rawls.[21] Central to Rawls' thesis is the *original position,* from which one can make impartial, moral judgments. This position should not be influenced by social status, educational opportunities, class position or physical and intellectual abilities. He therefore proposes to cast a *veil of ignorance* on a person's life situation so that the reasoning on the principles of justice is not influenced by those circumstances. Rawls also proposed two principles of justice, which, like Kant's categorical imperative, are not to be violated. These principles are the liberty principle and the difference principle.

The *liberty principle* states that each person is to have an equal right to the most extensive basic liberty compatible with a similar liberty for others.

The *difference principle* states that social and economic equalities are to be arranged so that they are to the greatest benefit of the most disadvantaged.

The liberty principle is fairly understandable in light of the American political tradition. It implies that people have inherent rights, such as freedom of speech, to vote, to due process of law, to own property, and that they have a right to exercise these liberties to the extent that they do not infringe upon the fundamental liberties of others. The Patient's Bill of Rights (incorporated in the McCain-Kennedy Bill) represents a good illustration of the liberty principle. All patients have the right:

- To choose their own doctor
- To independent, external reviews of medical decisions made by their health plan
- To sue their health plan in state court for medical decisions that result in injury or wrongful death
- To sue their health plan for up to $5 million in punitive damages over decisions resulting in injury or death

The difference principle is a bit more complicated. Basically, it states actions should not be taken that will further disadvantage those groups in society that are currently the least well off. In other words, corporate actions should be formulated in such a way that their social and economic effects are of most benefit to the least advantaged. This somewhat controversial principle is basically a call for *affirmative action* on behalf of the poor and politically underrepresented groups in society, comparable to the *preferential option for the poor,* enunciated in recent papal pronouncements.[22] Over time, it is an egalitarian principle that should make those least well off, better off. The difference principle also emphasizes that it would be unethical to exploit one group for the benefit of others. In the example of the public relations firm considering whether to accept a foreign government with a questionable civil rights record as a client, discussed earlier, the difference principle would suggest the agency should forgo that opportunity because the implementation of a public relations campaign could add legitimacy to the (presumably corrupt) ruling foreign government. Furthermore, it might exacerbate the position of a worse off group, namely, citizens in a country where human rights are systematically violated. More generally, it suggests that marketers have superordinate duties to consumers who are illiterate in the workings of the marketplace.

Integrative Social Contracts Theory

A hypothetical social contract takes into account ethical standards developed by groups through real social contact and based on their mutual interest in supportive or, at least, benign interaction. In other words, managers both desire and expect that there be ethical rules to govern their marketplace transactions. They envision global humanity coming together to work out a rational arrangement for ethics in economic life. The rational humans at this global convention would recognize that moral rationality is bounded in the same way that economic rationality is bounded. Thus, T. Donaldson and T. Dunfee, two chief advocates of the SCT approach, conclude that business communities or groups, including managers, should have moral free space because they want to keep their moral options open until they confront the full context and environment of a decision.[23]

In theory, there may be norms that condone murder as a method of enforcing contracts or that endorse racial or sexual discrimination. As a consequence, it can be assumed that the vast majority of people would want to *restrict* the moral free space of communities by requiring that, before any community norms become ethically obligatory, they must be found to be compatible with hypernorms. Hypernorms (the norms by which all other norms are to be judged) entail principles so fundamental to human existence that we would expect them to be reflected in a convergence of religious, philosophical, and cultural beliefs. A list of hypernorms would surely include

- An obligation to respect the dignity of each human person
- Core human rights, such as personal freedom, physical security and well-being, the ownership of property, and so on
- Equity, the fair treatment of similarly situated persons
- Avoiding unnecessary injury to others

The notion that "acceptable standards" of business or industry practice cannot violate hypernorms is one of the basic contributions of integrative social contracts theory. It "establishes a means for displaying the ethical relevance of existing norms in institutions as dissimilar as the European Community, the Sony Corporation, the international rubber market, and Muslim banks."[24]

Virtue-Based Ethics

Virtue Ethics

A final comprehensive theory of ethics is referred to as *virtue ethics*. It has a long tradition and is currently receiving renewed support. In part, virtue ethics is a contemporary reaction to the rampant relativism wherein

society seems to lack a way of reaching moral agreement about ethical problems. The relativistic approach to morality seems to be based on the strength
of persuasive appeals and intuitionism, whereby, when interests collide, one
opinion is as good as another. It is almost a one-person, one-vote method to
establishing what is ethical. Virtue ethics has been resurrected to counteract
modern relativism.

What exactly is virtue ethics? Its key criterion is seeking to live a virtuous life. In many ways, it is a renaissance of the Greek ideal suggesting that
the guiding purpose of life should be the quest for goodness and virtue. In
philosophical circles, one of the most prominent proponents of this position
is Alasdair MacIntyre of the University of Notre Dame. MacIntyre basically
defines virtue as acquired human qualities that enable persons to achieve
"the good" in their chosen vocations, that is, the development of personal
character.[25]

Virtue ethics differs from the consequences, duty, and contract-based
ethics in that the focus is on the individual and not the decision to be made
or the principle to be followed. As such, virtue ethics is fundamentally different from the other theories. Advocates of virtue ethics suggest that one
problem with contemporary organizations is that when they do look at situations with ethical implications, they are preoccupied with what the public
thinks. Put another way, today's corporations may be entirely too reactive,
wondering at times whether their actions will be perceived as "opportunis-
tic," "exploitative," or in "bad taste" by the general public. This may be a
misdirected effort that can be rectified through virtue ethics. Thus, organizations should instead focus on questions such as "What kind of organization
should we be?" and "What constitutes the ideally ethical organization?"
Companies that know what they stand for and then embody these beliefs in
a company credo or values statement are following this approach to ethics. In
short, the virtue ethics perspective seems to imply that the question of *understanding* virtue precedes the discussion and development of rules of conduct. Once management understands the nature of a virtuous organization,
ethical decision rules are much easier to develop.

Believers in this approach find much value in the writings of Aristotle.[26]
While the essence of virtue ethics cannot easily be captured in a few sentences, there are some key elements that reflect this mode of thinking. First,
virtues are essentially good habits. In order to flourish, these habits must be
practiced and the uninitiated managers in the organization must learn these
virtues. This point has powerful implications for managers, including the
notion that (a) firms can only become virtuous by engaging in ethical activities and (b) organizations have to teach managers precisely what the appropriate virtues are. In other words, companies have the responsibility to foster
ethical behavior. Wharton Professor Thomas Donaldson says, "Aristotle
tells us that ethics is more like building a house than it is like physics. You
learn to be an ethical manager by managing, not by reading textbooks on

philosophy." Professional philosophers sometimes view the practice of business ethics as a theoretical pursuit, continues Donaldson. "It's not. It is an art. It can't be reduced to a science." For an Aristotelian, it's impossible for a company to be too ethical.

A second dimension of virtue ethics is that admirable characteristics are most readily discovered by witnessing and imitating widely acclaimed behavior. Aristotle, while focusing on the individual rather than the organization, listed such virtues as truthfulness, justice, generosity, and self-control as characteristics to which the noble person should aspire. In the theory of virtue, much attention is placed on role models. The insight here is that to be an ethical person is not simply an analytical and rational matter. It takes virtuous people to make right decisions, and virtue is learned by doing. Put another way, the ultimate test and source of ethical conduct is the character of the actor. Aristotle often discussed the lives of obviously good Athenians in order to teach ethics. One learned the right thing to do by observing good people and by doing what they did. Such lessons reinforce the importance of top management serving as role models in the formation of an ethical corporate climate.   **Who has been a mentor or role model in your life?**

Companies that are acclaimed for their ethical corporate culture most often can trace their heritage back to the founder's intent on developing an organization that respected human dignity and insisted on a humane way of life. Founders of such companies as Johnson & Johnson shaped their organization so that they embodied the values and virtues that proved personally rewarding. The way of life in the company was not a result of an abstract code of conduct, but rather such statements were later used to spell out exactly what was at the heart of the existing corporate culture. For example, the top management of Levi Strauss has recently put forth four guiding values/virtues—empathy, originality, integrity and courage. (For a complete discussion, visit levistrauss.com.)

Third, a key to understanding virtue ethics and the discipline it requires is based on the *ethic of the mean*. Applied to virtue ethics, the mean is an optimal *balance* of a quality that one should seek. An excess or deficiency of any of the key virtues can be troublesome, as Aristotle effectively argued.[27] For example, an excess of truthfulness is boastfulness. A deficiency of truthfulness is deception. Both of these outcomes (the excess or the deficiency) are unacceptable. (See Exhibit 1-6 for a discussion of the "golden mean.") The Swedish language has a word, *lagom*, that means "not too much, not too little, but just enough." The virtuous marketing manager, then, strives for a balance among the qualities it takes to be an effective manager. For example, she should not be so directive as to be authoritarian, nor so easygoing as to abdicate her leadership role. Golfers may appreciate the analogy that one's goal in the sport is to stay in the fairway and out of the rough. This is the way a marketing manager should behave, by not going to extremes.

EXHIBIT 1-6   Aristotle's Golden Mean

It is in the nature of moral qualities that they are destroyed by deficiency and excess, just as we can see . . . in the case of health and strength. For both excessive and insufficient exercise destroy one's strength, and both eating and drinking too much or too little destroy health, whereas the right quantity produces, increases and preserves it. So it is the same with temperance, courage and the other virtues. The man who shuns and fears everything and stands up to nothing becomes a coward, the man who is afraid of nothing at all, but marches up to every danger, becomes foolhardy.

Source: Aristotle, *Ethics* (London: Penguin Books, 1976), 94.

Obviously, there is disagreement about exactly which characteristics should appear on a list of virtues to which an organization should aspire. Over the years, different philosophers have compiled many different lists. Business executives and professors have enumerated virtues (Exhibit 1-7) that they feel are most important for international marketing.[28] Whether a particular corporation elects to foster those virtues is another issue.

However, let's assume for a moment that an organization accepts the virtue ethics approach to corporate conduct. In other words, they subscribe to the belief that an organization should be "all that it can be" in an ethical sense. Then, with regard to the scenarios discussed earlier, one might conclude that (a) the virtuous organization has no need to provide gifts to purchasing agents in order to secure product orders; (b) the virtuous organization should be totally truthful; therefore, it has no problem with disclosing a change of components, as well as updating consumers with regard to the reliability of all their brands; and (c) the virtuous organization will not stoop to fear-generating emotional appeals to sell its products—manipulation is wrong; thus, almost all fear appeals would be inappropriate.

One logical objection to the application of virtue ethics in an organizational context is that it would sometimes be very difficult to agree on what, in fact, constitutes "the good." What virtues should an organization emulate and how should those virtues be operationalized in company policy? The contemporary philosopher MacIntyre and other recent proponents of virtue ethics seem to deal with this situation in the following way. First, they recognize a great diversity of virtues exists in society. However, in many cases, particular organizations are self-contained. It is within the context of individual companies that the notion of appropriate virtues should be explored.

EXHIBIT 1-7   Virtue Ethics for International Marketing

Virtue	Definition	Related virtues	Applications to marketing
Integrity	Adherence to a moral code and completeness	Honesty Moral courage	Conveying accurate and complete information to consumers
Fairness	Marked by equity and free from prejudice or favoritism	Justice	Selling and pricing products at a level commensurate with benefits received
Trust	Faith or confidence in another party	Dependability	Confidence that salespeople or suppliers will fulfill obligations without monitoring
Respect	Giving regard to views of others	Consideration	Altering products to meet cultural needs and refusing to sell unsafe products anywhere
Empathy	Being aware of and sensitive to the needs and concerns of others	Caring	Refraining from selling products to consumers who cannot afford them

Source: Patrick E. Murphy, "Character and Virtue Ethics in International Marketing," *Journal of Business Ethics* (January 1999), 113.

Second, consistent with Aristotle, they assume these virtues will be "other directed" (i.e., undertaken for the good of the community rather than in a self-serving manner). Third, this theory assumes people aspire to a higher level of ethics. Unfortunately, we know that this is not always the case. Hence, virtue ethics is sometimes criticized as being too idealistic.

It is important to note that we find the corporation among the more controlled communities in modern society. Each corporation has its own *corporate character*, often rooted in religious values (discussed next). It is within the context of corporate culture that a particular firm can seek virtues appropriate for that organization. All of this, of course, underscores the importance of developing an ethical corporate culture that facilitates appropriate managerial behavior. The idea of a corporate culture rooted in ethics follows from the "shared community" worldview discussed in the Introduction. The steps necessary to do this are a topic of this book's concluding chapter.

RELIGIOUS MODELS OF MARKETING ETHICS

The various ethical schools of thought presented previously are properly characterized as mostly *secular* or *civic*. They are the product of moral reasoning, based on human experience, and can be viewed as applying to and derived from nature or the world as opposed to any religious or sectarian source. While these ethical theories have, directly or indirectly, been embraced over time by religious teachings and traditions, it is important to recognize their independence from them.

However, it is also relevant to recognize the extent to which religion contributes to the ethical standards observed in the world. Because of the historical importance of trade, both within and between communities, it was natural for people to seek moral guidance from religious sources, and for religious leaders to provide such guidance as representing divine instruction. In particular, the Judeo-Christian, Confucian, Jewish, Islamic, and Buddhist religions have ethical precepts at their core. All have supported a variation of the Golden Rule for centuries. (See Exhibit 1-8.) Although the religious perspective is sometimes expressed as opposing business institutions, the world's religions have much to offer in terms of ethical guidance to marketers. In recognizing cultural influences over human behavior, regardless of their own religious heritage, students of marketing (particularly global marketing) are well advised to become familiar with such primary rules and principles from religious sources. They continue to be a dominant force in the development and maintenance of social norms.

Religious leaders have often preached that the answers to the majority of moral questions, business-related or otherwise, could be found in the Bible. There has also been considerable debate about the level of guidance generated by religious principles. Proscriptions like "thou shalt not steal" are fairly unambiguous. On the other hand, many situations that the contemporary corporate manager is faced with are exceedingly complex and defy the simple application of biblical precepts. Despite the difficulty of applying religious teachings, often rooted in centuries-old social conventions, to contemporary marketplace problems, to ignore them would be a serious omission. (We discuss a sample of religious traditions below and use Catholic Social Thought as our example of Christianity, knowing several prominent [and fairly compatible] Protestant approaches also exist.)

Roman Catholic Social Thought

Beginning in the late nineteenth century, in a belated response to the challenges posed by the Industrial Revolution, popes and bishops of the Roman Catholic Church began to seek scriptural wisdom and to interpret it in light of modern circumstances. One notable attempt to inject moral values

EXHIBIT 1-8   The Golden Rule Across Religions

Judaism and Christianity   *You shall love your neighbor as yourself.*
(Old Testament)   Bible, Leviticus 19.18

Judaism   *When he went to Hillel, he said to him, "What is hateful to you, do not do to your neighbor: that is the whole Torah; all the rest of it is commentary; go and learn."*
Talmud, Shabbat 31a

Christianity   *Whatever you wish that men would do to you, do so to*
(New Testament)   *them.*
Bible, Matthew 7.12

Islam   *Not one of you is a believer until he loves for his brother what he loves for himself.*
Forty Hadith of an-Nawawi 13

Confucianism   *Try your best to treat others as you would wish to be treated yourself and you will find that is the shortest way to benevolence.*
Mencius VII.A4

Tsetung asked, "Is there one word that can serve as a principle of conduct for life?" Confucius replied, "It is the word shu—reciprocity: Do not do to others what you do not want them to do to you."
Analects 15.23

Hinduism   *One should not behave towards others in a way which is disagreeable to oneself. This is the essence of morality. All other activities are due to selfish desire.*
Mahabharata, Anusasana Parva 113.8

Buddhism   *Comparing oneself to others in such terms as "Just as I am so are they, just as they are so am I," he should neither kill nor cause others to kill.*
Sutta Nipata 705

African Traditional   *One going to take a pointed stick to pinch a baby bird*
Religions   *should first try it on himself to feel how it hurts.*
Yoruba Proverb (Nigeria)

Source: Adapted from Tom Dalla Costa, *The Ethical Imperative: Why Moral Leadership Is Good Business* (Reading, MA: Addison-Wesley, 1998), 141–42.

into the marketplace was the pastoral letter authored by the American Catholic bishops.[29] Drawing upon scripture and Catholic social teaching, this document attempted to derive propositions with useful current applications. For example, among the ethical precepts implied by this document are the following:[30]

> When considering trade-offs between labor and technology, managers have the responsibility to give special weight to human resources because of the *primacy of labor over capital* doctrine.
>
> When making strategic marketing decisions, managers have a special duty to consider the effect of those actions upon economically vulnerable members of the community because of the *preferential option for the poor* doctrine.
>
> When making business decisions that may negatively impact the physical environment, managers have a special obligation to strongly consider possible external costs upon the ecological environment because of the *stewardship* doctrine.

Jewish Ethical Tradition

The Hebrew Torah also offers substantial guidance to marketers.[31] One business executive publicly proclaimed that his Jewish faith led him in 1995 to continue paying his employees after a disastrous fire destroyed his operations facility.[32] A Halakic Code of Ethics has been formed by the Center of Business Ethics and Social Responsibility in Israel. Among the stakeholders specifically mentioned in this code are investors and executive officers, employees, customers, competitors, suppliers, investors, and the community. Two specific statements relate directly to customers and marketing:

> *Pricing.* We will not charge customers for the goods we are selling or the services we are providing by any amount greater than its market value, unless customers are aware of the additional benefits they are receiving in paying a higher price. Care will be taken not to exploit any short-term difficulties encountered by our customers. To not act in this manner would be in breach of *ona'ah* (price oppression).
>
> *Selling Practices.* Our firm does not accept the principle of "buyer beware." Instead, we will ensure that the buyer has accurate and full information regarding the nature and quality of the goods sold or services provided, without any concealment of defects or deficiencies. All goods sold or services provided will be according to those specified in the contract or as advertised.

Islamic Ethical Tradition

The Islamic religious tradition has received much closer examination after the tragic events of September 11, 2001. In fact, the mainstream Muslim religious tradition is rich in the moral precepts it espouses. Muslim business executives have followed several axioms of Islamic ethical philosophy for centuries. Muslims observe the values of *equity* and *justice*. Among the most prominent are *unity, equilibrium, free will, responsibility,* and *benevolence.*[33] These axioms are defined and related both to marketing ethics and the traditional philosophical ethical theories in Exhibit 1-9. **What, in your opinion, are the most significant items of ethical advice from this exhibit?**

Confucian Ethics

The Confucian conception of business ethics is most closely akin to virtue ethics. *Trust* and *trustworthiness* are central to the Confucian ethos.[34] An early Confucian philosopher, Mencias, noted three interrelated concepts are key to what virtue is all about. These three notions are *extensions* (t'ui or ta), *attention* (ssu), and *intelligent awareness* (chih). Virtue is actualized by individuals when they learn to extend knowledge from one situation to other similar ones. From a marketing standpoint, product and advertising managers should learn the appropriate ethical norms in their dealings with advertising agencies and other external consultants. For the attention concept, Mencias pithily commented: "If one attends one gets it; if one does not, one does not." Thus, ethical training depends on the individual perceiving clearly, identifying corresponding actions, and responding only after careful reflection. Finally, intelligent awareness is expressed by the middle way between two extremes: "[I]ntelligence should guide our actions, but in harmony with [the] texture of the situation at hand, not in accordance [only] with a set of rules or procedures."[35]

Buddhist Ethical Imperatives

Trade and industry are viewed as comparatively recent developments in those nations where Buddhism is a prominent religious tradition. Nonetheless, the writings attributed to the Buddha address a number of issues that are relevant to marketers, particularly at the macrolevel.[36] Among these are the need to provide for basic needs (in the context of a simple lifestyle); the need for agricultural/rural development (as opposed to concentrating development efforts in urban areas); respect for the preservation of the resource endowment and beauty of nature; encouragement of private enterprise, self-reliance, and economic freedom; and the personal and social value of full employment with a living wage (certain business enterprises are also frowned on such as those involving armaments, intoxicating drink, poisons, animal slaughter, gambling, and slavery). There are five Buddhist principles that cannot be broken while working: (1) one cannot cause harm to another, (2) one may not cheat, (3) one may not lie, (4) one cannot promote intoxication, and (5) one cannot engage in sexual exploitation.

EXHIBIT 1-9   Axioms of Islamic Ethical Philosophy

Axiom	Definition	Relationship to Marketing Ethics	Similarities to Other Ethical Theories
Unity	Related to the concept of *tawhid*. The political, economic, social, and religious aspects of man's life form a homogeneous whole, which is consistent from within, as well as integrated with the vast universe without. This is the vertical dimension of Islam.	Muslim business executives will not: • Discriminate among stakeholders on issues of race, color, sex or religion • Be coerced into unethical practices	Kantian/Duty Based Ethics 2nd Formulation
Equilibrium	Related to the concept of *adl*. A sense of balance among the various aspects of a man's life mentioned above in order to produce the best social order. This sense of balance is achieved through conscious purpose and is the horizontal dimension of Islam.	• A balanced transaction is equitable and just • Islam attempts to curb a business executive's propensity for covetousness and love for possession • Will seek a moderate profit	Virtue Ethics (Very similar to "ethic of the mean")
Free Will	Man's ability to act without external coercion within the parameters of Allah's creation and as Allah's trustee on earth.	• Muslim executive has freedom to make a contract and either honor it or break it • Muslims do choose a code of conduct (either ethical or unethical)	Social Contract
Responsibility	Man's need to be accountable for his actions.	• Business executive bears ultimate moral responsibility for one's actions • All obligations must be honored unless morally wrong	Kantian/Duty-Based Universality
Benevolence	Ihsân or an action that benefits persons other than those from whom the action proceeds without any obligation.	• Kindness is encouraged by Islam • Responsibility to less fortunate • Modest profit, debtors should have time to pay, return policies	Virtue Ethics (Similar to empathy)

Source: Adapted from Rafik Issa Beekun, *Islamic Business Ethics* (Herndon, VA: International Institute of Islamic Thought, 1997).

Hindu Ethics

The Hindu religion also contains directions for spiritual fulfillment. The Hindu scripture give insights into how to balance priorities to attain true success:

> Generating wealth (*artha*) is to be pursued within the larger priority of contributing to the well-being of society (*dharma*). Satisfying desires (*Kama*) is to be pursued within the larger priority of spiritual fulfillment (*moksha*). In accord with the wisdom of these spiritual teachings, we can see that business success naturally emphasizes contribution to society and spiritual fulfillment. When traditional measures of business success—shareholder return, market share, industry power, and so on—are subordinate to these higher priorities, wealth can be generated and desires can be satisfied while naturally promoting well-being rather than harm, service rather than greed, and an uplifted spirit rather than unscrupulous competition.[37]

A practical example comes from Isaac Tigret, the founder of Hard Rock Café. One of his objectives was to open an "absolutely classless" (aiming at all social classes) restaurant in London. While on a spiritual pilgrimage in India, he heard the saying, "Love All, Serve All." To him, it embodied the ultimate goal of life: to love people and to serve from that place. That became the spiritual source of the company culture:

> *All I did was put spirit and business together in that big mixing bowl and add love. I didn't care about anything but people . . . just cherish them, look after them, and be sensitive to them and their lives.*[38]

OTHER THEORETICAL DEVELOPMENTS IN MARKETING ETHICS

Because of the difficulty of applying general theories and principles to specific case situations, a number of scholars have begun to investigate what particular factors account for ethical marketing decisions. In an effort to aid their investigations, some of these researchers have begun to formulate *models* that stipulate the factors contributing to ethical decisions.

The Moral Development Model

The concept of moral development is mostly derived from the work of educational psychologist Lawrence Kohlberg, who studied moral development in adolescents.[39] Kohlberg postulated that, over time, individuals develop moral systems that are increasingly complex, although there is no guarantee that any particular individual evolves beyond the initial and most fundamental stage of moral development. Essentially, he saw three broad levels of cognitive moral development. These are

1. *The preconventional stage.* At this stage the abiding concern of the individual would be to resolve moral situations, with the person's own immediate interests and consequences firmly in mind. An individual at the preconventional level gives strong weight to external rewards and punishments. Normally, this stage includes a strong emphasis upon literal obedience to rules and authority, because of the penalties attached to deviation.

2. *The conventional stage.* Individuals at the conventional stage have progressed to a level where their ethical decision-making mode takes into consideration the expectations of significant reference groups and society at large. This mostly reflects what we have come to term *enlightened self-interest*, that is, a recognition of the longer term and indirect effects of actions that may injure others or otherwise depart from social norms. What constitutes moral propriety follows a concern for others, but is still influenced most directly by explicit, especially organizational, rules. Observance of rules is often tempered by keeping loyalties and doing one's duty to society.

3. *The principled stage.* This is the highest level of moral development. Individuals who reach this level solve their ethical problems in a manner that goes beyond the norms and laws applicable to a specific situation. Proper conduct certainly includes upholding the basic rights, values, and legal contracts of society, but beyond that, such individuals seem to subscribe to universal ethical principles that they believe all members of society should follow in similar situations. It is significant that principled actors are typically less bound by procedural rules when circumstances call for a response that may, when rules and principles conflict, violate those rules.

The moral development model implies that the ethical sophistication of managers can increase over time with maturity and experience. The major difference among the various stages of moral development is that, as managers advance to higher levels of moral development, they are able to take more factors into consideration, especially those that go beyond personal self-interest. Two significant implications of the moral development model are

1. Some managers are less sophisticated than others in terms of the considerations they bring to bear upon a decision with potentially moral consequences. Some managers still operate at the most basic level, almost totally from the standpoint of egoistic self-interest.

2. Interventions such as training programs, particularly in combination with organizational sanctions (related to continuing employment, compensation, and advancement opportunities) can be brought to bear that may compel managers toward higher levels of moral development, assuming this is a goal seen to be in the company's interest.

This model has spawned significant academic and applied research. Among the most pertinent to marketing managers and students is the work of Narváez and Rest.[40] They have proposed a model that leads to "acting morally." It has four components:

Moral Characteristic	Ability	Most Important Virtue
Moral Sensitivity	To interpret the situation in terms of how one's actions affect the welfare of others.	Empathy
Moral Judgment	To formulate what a moral course of action would be; to identify the moral ideal in a specific situation.	Fairness Social Responsibility
Moral Motivation	To select among competing value outcomes of ideals, the one to act upon; deciding whether to try to fulfill one's moral ideal.	Altruism Integrity
Implementation	To execute and implement what one intends to do.	Persistence Character

For an illustration of characters in fiction, politics and movies that are strong and weak in these components, see Exhibit 1-10. Marketing managers should strive to be strong in each, but may need mentors, superiors, and even subordinates to support them on dimensions where they are not as strong.

Ethical Behavior in Marketing

Against the background of a growing literature in marketing ethics, mostly devoted to the application of teleological, deontological, and other normative models to marketing problems, Shelby Hunt and Scott Vitell proposed a behavioral or positive model of ethical behavior that has been extensively tested.[41] This complex model takes into account, in sequence (1) such environmental factors as the industry and organizational environment; (2) the recognition of an ethical problem, optional solutions to the problem, and the likely consequences of the various solutions—and their desirability and probability; (3) deontological norms that might "trump" any of the solution alternatives; (4) an ethical judgment based on these steps; (5) the formation of intentions; and (6) actual behavior. The separation of these components recognizes the prospect that, while the components are connected, they are distinct and, for example, an ethical judgment may still be followed by an unethical act. The Hunt-Vitell model also provided for

EXHIBIT 1-10 **Real and Fictional Characters
That Represent the Four Components of Moral Action**

Component	Strong in Component	Weak in Component
Moral sensitivity	Mother Teresa Ralph Nader Bill Moyers The Tin Man (*Wizard of Oz*)	Archie Bunker Mr. Spock Bart Simpson
Moral judgment	King Solomon The Scarecrow (*Wizard of Oz*)	Snow White Homer Simpson Lucy (*I Love Lucy*)
Moral motivation	The Biblical Paul Don Quixote Eleanor Roosevelt	Joseph Stalin Saddam Hussein Osama Bin Laden Mr. Burns (*The Simpsons*) Ebenezer Scrooge
Implementation	Moses Hercules John Wayne characters Dirty Harry Scarlett O'Hara	Many Woody Allen characters Garfield Cathy

Source: Partially adapted from D. Narváez and J. Rest, "The Four Components of Acting Morally," in *Moral Development: An Introduction,* ed. W. M. Kurtines and J. L. Gewirtz, 385–99 (Boston: Allyn and Bacon, 1995).

experiential feedback or learning such that the consequences of an act might inform future assessments and actions.

IDEAS FOR ETHICAL MARKETING

The call to apply a specific ethical theory to a particular marketing situation is easier given than implemented. Philosophers who study moral theory and reasoning regularly argue among themselves about what constitutes the *best* way to analyze and solve ethical issues. Once again, ethics is not an easy area to understand or control. Although ethical theory for its own sake is important, theory in action is what makes for ethical marketing practice. Thus, marketing managers can vitalize ethical reasoning in their organizations by the following:

1. Identify the issues most likely to lead to moral or ethical conflict in your firm.
2. Develop a list of questions that reflect various ethical theories which can aid managers in determining whether a particular contemplated action or decision is unethical.
3. Recognize that there are sometimes conflicts among the various ethical principles that imply different (sometimes contradictory) decisions. Moreover, realize that these conflicts increase as the number of relevant stakeholders in a decision increases.

These points can be elaborated on.

First, a sequence of questions to improve ethical reasoning should be asked. One approach to deal more normatively with ethical issues is to require managers to proceed through a sequence of questions that tests whether an action they are contemplating is ethical or has possible ethical consequences. A battery of such questions might include the following:

Question 1 (the legal test):   Does the contemplated action violate the law?

Question 2 (the duties test):   Is this action contrary to widely accepted moral obligations? Such moral obligations might include *duties of fidelity,* such as the responsibility to remain faithful to contracts, to keep promises, and to tell the truth; *duties of gratitude,* which basically means that special obligations exist between relatives, friends, partners, cohorts, and employees; *duties of justice,* which basically have to do with obligations to distribute rewards based upon merit; *duties of nonmaleficence,* which consists of duties not to harm others; and *duties of beneficence,* which rest upon the notion that actions should be taken that improve the situation of others—if this can be readily accomplished.

Question 3 (the special obligations test):   Does the proposed action violate any other special obligations that stem from this type of marketing organization? (For example, the special duty of pharmaceutical firms to provide safe products, the special obligation of toy manufacturers to care for the safety of children, and the inherent duty of distillers to promote responsible drinking are all special obligations of this sort.)

Question 4 (the motives test):   Is the *intent* of the contemplated action harmful?

Question 5 (the consequences test):   Is it likely that any *major* damages to people or organizations will result from the contemplated action?

Question 6 (the virtues test):   Does this action enhance the ideal of a moral community, and is it consonant with what the marketing organization wants to be?

Question 7 (the rights test):   Does the contemplated action infringe upon property rights, privacy rights, or the rights of the consumer (the right to information, the right to be heard, the right to choice, and the right to remedy)?

Question 8 (the justice test):   Does the proposed action leave another person or group less well off? Is this person or group already a member of a relatively underprivileged class?

The questions outlined need not be pursued in lockstep fashion. If none of the questions uncover any potential conflicts, clearly the action being contemplated is quite likely to be ethical. However, if the sequence of queries does produce a conflict, this does not necessarily mean that the action being proposed is unethical per se. Unusual intervening factors may be present that would still allow the action to ethically go forward. For example, suppose it is determined that the contemplated action is a violation of the law. Perhaps the law is unjust, and thus, there could be a moral impetus for an organization to transgress the law. Some companies use a decision-making model somewhat similar to this one. Exhibit 1-11 shows the ethical decision approach bp (British Petroleum) expects employees to follow in its far-flung operation. For example, bp has acquired Amoco and ARCO in the United States, along with several other oil companies and Russian oil fields. The model combines both rights and virtues in its commitments statement, as well as a number of the same ethical questions that we listed.

Second, the stakeholder concept should be linked to marketing ethics. As the earlier sections illustrate, several comprehensive theories can be utilized to guide the reasoning of managers as they try to reach moral conclusions. The difficulty, of course, is applying these theories to specific marketing situations and then resolving conflicts among principles. Sometimes, these conflicts will take the form of two competing duties owed to different stakeholder groups. For example, there is a fiduciary responsibility on the part of managers to render to stockholders a fair return. At times, this might involve taking steps that are clearly counterproductive to another stakeholder group, such as employees. This may occur in the case of a plant closing. The judgmental difficulty then is deciding which of the two duties takes precedence. Utilitarianism, and the cost-benefit analysis it often implies, is an extremely useful tool if one looks at a problem only from the standpoint of one or two stakeholder groups. However, when multiple stakeholders are introduced into the situation, the use of consequence-based theories is complicated considerably. In different instances, we would expect marketing managers to draw from various and multiple ethical theories.

Similarly, duty-based or virtue ethics approaches are also complex. There are often contradictory duties, such as in Scenario 2, where management has the right to point out their truthful strategic competitive advantage (i.e., benefits of weight loss drug), while at the same time perhaps violating the duty not to unfairly manipulate the receivers of their promotional messages by using incomplete information. Frequently, however, most conflicts between stakeholders can be resolved through compromise or by broadening how the problem is framed. The existence of competing claims suggests

EXHIBIT 1-11   BP's Decision Model

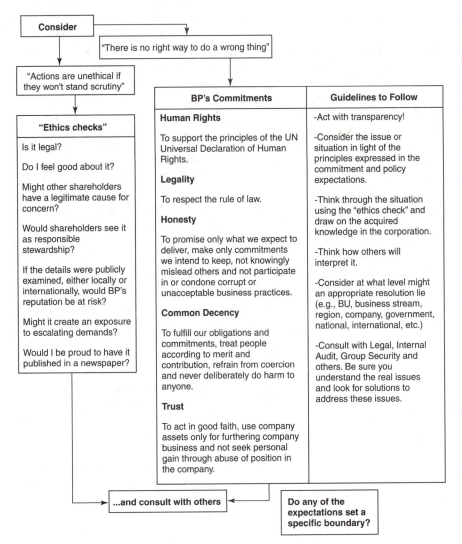

Source: bp, Ethical Conduct Policy: Guidelines on Business Conduct, 2000, 6–7. Reprinted with permission.

management must face up to the challenge of creating new alternatives that result in a better balance of obligations.

CONCLUDING COMMENT

In the end, weighing the concerns of multiple stakeholder groups becomes the essence of appropriate ethical decision making. Multiple claims on the organization are at the root of the complexity of such decision making. The stakeholder concept, and the multiple responsibilities it implies, provides the necessity for sensitizing managers to ethical implications and teaching them to reason from the standpoint of moral theory. In the final analysis, ethics still requires considerable prudential judgment that comes from the intuition of the marketing manager (hopefully, grounded in virtue ethics), but it is tempered by a knowledge of ethical theory as well as corporate, industry and societal standards.

Chapter Two

Ethics in Researching and Segmenting Markets

Scenario 1

The International Franchise Association ran a nationwide newspaper ad touting a poll conducted by the Gallup Organization. They attempted to show how satisfied franchise owners are. The headlines read "Gallup Survey: 92 Percent of Franchise Owners Successful."

The survey, which involved only franchises still operating and not those that failed, found that 92 percent of owners considered themselves either "very successful" or "somewhat successful."[1] **Might this survey or the advertising based on it be biased or unethical?**

Scenario 2

A research supplier estimates that a study will cost $20,000 plus or minus 10 percent. The client agrees that this price is reasonable. But when the study is completed, the research supplier submits a bill for $25,000, claiming that the cost increased because of changes the client wanted made during the course of the study. The client, while acknowledging that certain unplanned changes were made, argues that such changes should have cost no more than an additional $2,000. **How should this problem be resolved?**

Scenario 3

"We're conducting a survey," reads a letter from the XYZ Survey Research Company. The (online) survey will be e-mailed to 10 million homes this year. The questionnaire asks for the respondents' preferences on consumer products plus demographic and personal information such as names, addresses, telephone numbers, occupations, and family income. To improve respondent cooperation, the sponsoring company offers free samples of various consumer products. What is not said is that the personal information as well as product choices that are collected will be compiled onto disks and sold to other marketers so they can promote their products. **Is this ethical?**

As these three scenarios show, a range of ethical dilemmas confront marketing research practitioners. The questions posed at the end of each vignette are not easy to answer. For example,

- How should cost overruns be handled between a research supplier and the client?
- Should the public receive information about the technical details of how a widely disseminated poll was conducted?

Possible ethical difficulties flowing from market research practices involve technical, managerial, and societal issues. Researchers must also decide how to treat the respondent, client, and the general public fairly in discharging their duties. We return to these scenarios in developing this chapter.

PROFESSIONALISM AND ETHICS

Within the marketing profession, researchers generally receive more academic training, especially in methodological and statistical techniques, than other marketing professionals. Presumably, a higher degree of professionalism exists within the research field, because the scientific method and objectivity are two of its hallmarks. However, ethical issues do arise in marketing research for two reasons. First, marketing research often involves contact with the general public, usually through the use of surveys, which are increasingly being conducted online. Because this activity relies so heavily on information from the public—often including sensitive personal information—marketing research is open to abuse or misuse. For example, as survey research has migrated online, researchers have accumulated easily transferable files concerning consumers' usage and satisfaction with products and services such as movie rental records, sexual performance aids (e.g., Viagra), and financial services (e.g., bankruptcy counseling). Obviously, this evolving environment of marketing research techniques places consumer privacy in greater jeopardy than in the past. Second, most marketing research is conducted by commercial (i.e., for profit) firms as either independent research agencies or departments within corporations. The emphasis on the profit motive may cause researchers, their managers, or clients to occasionally *compromise* the project's objectivity or precision. Throughout the chapter, we deal with some instances where such compromises might occur.

Concern for ethics can benefit marketing research practitioners in several ways. Most important, an ethical approach enhances the profession through the increased public acceptance of the marketing research process. (This principle follows the "Beneficial" B within the ABCs discussed in Chapter 1.) If marketing research is to be successful, the research community needs candid and accurate responses from the public. Another benefit is that the thoughtful study of ethical problems can help improve researchers' sensitivity and professionalism. Finally, voluntarily maintaining high ethical standards can forestall negative publicity and restrictive government regulation concerning data gathering. For instance, the expanding use of computerized, random dialing for telephone calling along with computer-assisted questioning is intrusive and/or offensive and raises ethical questions.

DUTIES AND OBLIGATIONS OF RESEARCHERS

The dominant philosophical perspective used in evaluating marketing research ethics is *absolute obligations* (i.e., the duty-based approach from Chapter 1). Since marketing research is ideally built on a foundation of professional conduct, this field is rooted in a set of obligations. In addition to the obvious duties to one's client and respondents, the researcher also has a professional responsibility to uphold the integrity of the research process. The major professional associations (American Marketing Association—AMA—www.marketingpower.com, Marketing Research Association—MRA—www.mra-net.org, Council of Survey Research Organizations—CASRO—www.casro.org, European Society for Marketing and Opinion Research—ESOMAR—www.esomar.org) have developed codes for marketing research that contain normative guidelines for researchers. Among others, these include the duties to avoid misrepresentation of research methods and to identify a survey's sponsor.

Other approaches focus on the *rights of subjects* in the research process and the obligations of researchers, clients, and others involved in the research process. Kant's categorical imperative holds that rules of conduct should be applied universally. Marketing researchers ideally try to implement this approach. Al Blankenship, one of the pioneers of marketing research, offered the following rationale for rejecting a more pragmatic utilitarian approach to marketing research: "Too often, we have taken the position that if our efforts don't really damage the consumer (respondent), they aren't really all that bad. . . . Let's be honest with ourselves; that is merely saying that the end justifies the means." A recent survey about marketing research practices suggested that researchers are primarily duty oriented. "One major finding is that deontological considerations (the inherent rightness/wrongness of an actor's behavior) underlie marketing professionals' research ethics judgment."[2]

Another philosophical perspective refers to the *stakeholders* that must be considered. They include respondents, clients, research firms, employees, and the general public. If one or more of these groups is harmed by the research process, the whole field of marketing research suffers. For example, some political polling results reported in major newspapers likely mislead the voting public and harm the credibility of the research profession.

The balance of this chapter examines in detail researchers' duties to their various stakeholders and the ethics of market targeting. We begin with ethical concerns emanating from the relationship of the researcher with the respondents and then move to interactions with clients. We also examine the researcher's responsibilities to the general public. Then, we discuss the competitive intelligence gathering process. Finally, we address vulnerable markets and propose several ideas for ethical marketing aimed at enhancing the ethics of researching and segmenting markets.

What Researchers Owe Respondents

Several ethical concerns arise in the relationship between the respondent and researcher. A *respondent* could be an individual answering questions via a telephone, e-mail, postal survey, personal interview, or as a subject in experimental research. Exhibit 2-1 lists the most prevalent activities in this context that raise ethical questions. Dubious research tactics fall into three categories: deceptive practices, invasion of privacy, and lack of concern for respondents. *Deceptive practices* occur when the researcher misrepresents the purpose of the research, the investigative procedures, or the use of the results. An entire volume of a recent publication was devoted to deception in marketing research and practice.[3] Two selections directly addressed the application of major theoretical perspectives to deception in marketing research (see Exhibit 2-2). *Invasion of privacy* is a sensitive issue and one that is becoming more complex with the growth of sophisticated technology. This concern has grown in importance because of heightened use of research on the Internet. As a result, most Web sites now include a "privacy policy" statement that discloses what information might be gathered and how it will be used by the site sponsor or host. The practices listed under *lack of concern for the respondent* in Exhibit 2-1 do not raise as serious a set of ethical concerns as the other two categories, but

EXHIBIT 2-1   Ethical Concerns in the Researcher-Respondent Relationship

Deceptive Practices

Unrealized promise of anonymity
Falsified sponsor identification
Selling under the guise of research
Misrepresenting research procedures
Intrusive questionnaire or interview length
Possible follow-up contacts
Unspecified purpose of study
Questionable use of results
Undelivered compensation (premiums, summaries of results)
Nondisclosure of research procedures (sample, follow-up, purpose, response rate)

Invasion of Privacy

Observation studies without informed consent
Use of controversial qualitative research techniques
Use of "cookies" in online research
Merging data from several sources
Overly personal questions and topics

Lack of Concern for Subjects or Respondents

Contacting respondents at inconvenient times
Incompetent or insensitive interviewers
Failure to debrief after deception or disguise
Research producing a depressing effect on respondents
Too frequent use of public in research and opinion polling
Misrepresentation of time commitment

Source: Professor Kenneth Schneider, St. Cloud State University, personal communication with the authors (January 2002).

they represent a long-term threat as they shape public opinion toward marketing research. They demonstrate a lack of sensitivity/empathy for the respondent. Exhibit 2-3 depicts some of the ethical challenges that occur in conducting marketing research in several countries.

EXHIBIT 2-2   Ethical Theory and Deception

(A)

Ethical Drawbacks to the Use of Deception. The crux of the typical moral argument against deception in research is the contention that regardless of the anticipated research ends, it is always wrong to mislead research participants because deception represents a clear violation of the individual's basic right to informed consent and it shatters the trust inherent in the implicit contractual relationship between the researcher and participant.

This argument attacks at the very heart of the utilitarian justification for using deception in research contexts, which holds that beneficial scientific ends sometimes justify the use of means that would necessarily infringe upon individual participants' rights or general welfare.[1]

(B)

Intentional deception in a research setting is wrong from a rule-utilitarian perspective because it violates ethical rules that are generally accepted in Western society, including the right of self-determination within the law (the right of informed consent in a research setting) and the obligation of people whose roles in a given relationship imply power or authority (researchers) to protect the welfare of those who are in less-powerful positions (participants). Viewed through the lens of rule-utilitarianism, [a] deceptive research practice must have very substantial benefits at all levels of society to justify the intentional violation of these ethical rules.[2]

---

[1]A. J. Kimmel, "Deception in Marketing Research and Practice: An Introduction," *Psychology and Marketing* (July 2001): 668.
[2]D. Toy, L. Wright, and J. Olson, "A Conceptual Framework for Analyzing Deception and Debriefing Effects in Marketing Research," *Psychology and Marketing* (July 2001): 711.

The Duty Not to Engage in Deceptive Practices

Exhibit 2-1 also lists four major types of deceptive marketing research practices. The first involves *unrealized promises of anonymity*. Most survey research is predicated on the presumption that the respondent will remain anonymous and therefore can give his/her candid opinion. The use of "cookies" and other tracking devices to trace specific respondents without their explicit consent is considered to be unethical and unprofessional among most marketing research associations.[4]

A second concern revolves around *falsified sponsor identification*. This happens when the researcher believes that the respondent's knowledge of

EXHIBIT 2-3   **Marketing Research Across the World**

Country	Dominant Research Method	Ethical Challenges	Response
Argentina	Field survey (personal interviews) (only 60% have phones)	Interviewer's safety (robbery)	Interviews in daytime only
Israel	Telephone (95% have phones)	Political/social tension and violence (makes people unwilling to participate) Religious/ethnic sensitivity	Steer clear of sensitive political questions Use interviewers who know multiple languages
China	Personal interview (because of low literacy rates)	Do not understand the "idea" of brands	Greater instructions and respondent hand holding
Saudi Arabia	Personal interview	Questions about alcohol must be left out of surveys	Use local experts
Northern Ireland	Personal interview	Accent identifies interviewer as nationalist Catholic or unionist Protestant People nervous about doorstep interviews so more is being done in public areas	Use only Northern Ireland-based interviewers

Source: Alison Maitland, "The Word on the Street Is 'Danger,'" *Financial Times,* March 5, 2003.

the sponsor may bias the results. For example, would the users of radar detectors respond honestly to a survey conducted by the state highway patrol? What some researchers do is to create fictitious names (like U.S. Research Inc. or Public Opinion Institute) to mask the identity of the firm doing the research. Most marketing researchers and marketing executives approve of this practice. Even though this is a common and accepted practice in industry, it does raise ethical questions. A better approach, and one that the public finds more acceptable, might be to hire an external consultant to conduct the research for the sponsor using the consultant's name.

A third area of potential respondent deception is *selling or fund-raising under the guise of research*. In the trade, these techniques are called "sugging" and "frugging," respectively. Such tactics have received much criticism in the consumer sector over the years, and in 1996 the United States passed the Telemarketing and Consumer Fraud and Abuse Prevention Act. This act makes sugging and frugging illegal. In the business-to-business sector, both telephone and personal interviews are used to generate leads for follow-up sales presentations. Also, mail surveys and even focus groups are sometimes utilized for this purpose. In recent years, fund-raisers for nonprofit organizations and political parties have also borrowed this technique. Researchers need to be aware of this practice and realize that it is not only unethical but also illegal as well.

The fourth type of possible ethical concern between researcher and respondent in Exhibit 2-1 falls under the general title of *misrepresenting research procedures*. Part of the research challenge is selling the idea of participation to potential respondents. If deception or false pretenses are used to gain their cooperation, several problems can occur. For example, if the researcher seriously understates the time it will take to complete the interview or survey, respondents are being purposely misled. At minimum, interviewers may get irritated or become uncooperative. Similarly, other forms of deception (e.g., false promises about follow-up contact or lying about the true purpose of the study) can undermine the integrity of the research. The researcher, who cannot disclose some of this information (because it may bias the results), should say nothing rather than lie to the respondent. Promises regarding respondent compensation should always be kept.

The Duty Not to Invade Privacy

The right to privacy involves the respondents' ability to decide for themselves how much they will share with others about their thoughts, feelings, and the facts of their personal lives. Exhibit 2-1 also depicts several research practices that have privacy implications. A number of privacy laws in the United States, Europe, and elsewhere protect individual privacy in data collection and storage. Personal privacy is an issue that is likely to stay in the international limelight and continue to place pressure on researchers who violate this right.[5]

One topic pertaining to respondent privacy is *observational studies without informed consent.* The general rule of thumb is that observation studies conducted in public places (e.g., retail stores or supermarkets) are acceptable. When the behavior is observed in private or semiprivate settings, ethical problems arise. For instance, it is generally considered to be unethical to videotape someone in a department-store dressing room to prevent shoplifting. Examples of questions with less clear answers are:

- Is it *ethical* for researchers to sort through collected consumer trash to measure the household consumption of liquor or other products? (Legally, this is pemitted in most jurisdictions.)
- Should researchers use information collected by "cookies" to make decisions about Web preferences of consumers?

The *use of qualitative or projective research techniques* also raises privacy issues on occasion. A projective technique is an indirect method of measuring an individual's personality characteristics, underlying motivations, or basic value structure. An example of such a research method would be having consumers fill in open-ended sentences. Sometimes researchers want to seek knowledge about a respondent's purchasing behavior that can only be gained through the use of projective techniques. Why? Because some consumers have difficulty expressing the reasons why they buy some products, toiletries for instance. In this way, unconscious buying motives can be uncovered.

In the marketing research profession, the following ethical standard seems operative: If there is no psychological or physical harm to the respondent, the research is considered acceptable. This has been labeled the "no harm, no foul" approach. It does require strict attention to anonymity and confidentiality, but does not demand informed consent. Essentially the perspective is that one's privacy cannot be invaded if one is unaware of the invasion and/or it causes no "harm." This conclusion does not, however, extend to observational studies in dressing rooms or other private locations. Nor should it extend to information gathered on the Web without consumer permission. Another principle is to protect privacy with confidentiality. In other words, names, addresses, and telephone numbers should never be given to clients by research firms although selective audits to verify that the research was actually done would be permitted.

The *merging of data from several sources* has become a more important concern because of the extensive use of computerized databases and lists for direct marketing purposes. Some firms copy lists of especially good prospects from other sources of names. The Direct Marketing Association has developed a code of conduct to cover this practice (see www.the-dma.org), and some of the largest mail order firms such as L. L. Bean and Lands' End (now part of Sears) subscribe to a service that detects when their lists have been surreptitiously copied. Credit bureaus and credit card companies are also criticized for assembling and selling personal information. American Express, however, has a strict policy against sharing its vast data on cardholders because the firm views this information as a big asset. The Web also has facilitated stored information to the point that, for very little cost, anybody can learn almost anything about anybody.

The issue of *overly personal questions and topics* remains a sensitive topic especially in light of the privacy concerns discussed. Researchers studying social problems such as drug abuse and AIDS are caught between the right to privacy on the one hand and the need for good data and honest opinions on the other. Financial institutions and marketers of highly personal products and practices (e.g., feminine hygiene products, condoms) must also be aware that any questions about their offerings may be perceived to be too personal by some respondents.

The overall issue is one of freedom of information versus the right to privacy. Researchers must be more cognizant of potential privacy abuses in the future and establish and enforce acceptable marketing practices regarding privacy. One observer over a decade ago insightfully commented that all the discussion about privacy may:

> stir thought within the professional community about how important the respondent-researcher relationship is and how it may be jeopardized by the unethical use of information under the guise of new and better technology. And with that thought, there may come a plan for merging the miracles of modern machinery with some good old-fashioned morals if not for goodness' sakes, for business sake.[6]

The Duty to Manifest Concern for Respondents

The list of ethical concerns for this category (Exhibit 2-1) does not demand as much attention as some of the other issues examined earlier. Most of these areas fall under the commonsense notion of "good business practice." The failure to debrief respondents may lead to individuals becoming suspicious of all research and, as a result, they may refuse or even attempt to subvert future research projects. Furthermore, confusing questions, poorly trained interviewers, hard-to-read questionnaires, and other factors that place an unnecessary burden on respondents should be avoided. When respondents agree to give the researcher their time, the researcher's responsibility is to minimize their burden.

As a summary point on the researcher-respondent relationship, several avenues exist to approaching these potential problem areas, so that the research can be conducted ethically. The choice is not to be either unethical or abandon the study. Rather, what should be done is to identify "ethical alternatives to questionable research practices and urge their immediate adoption."[7]

WHAT RESEARCHERS AND CLIENTS OWE ONE ANOTHER

The relationship between the researcher and the client presents a number of potential ethical issues. Exhibit 2-4 shows three categories where ethical abuse may occur: in the research design, in the researcher's responsibility to the client, and in the client's responsibility to the researcher.

EXHIBIT 2-4   **Ethical Concerns in the Researcher-Client Relationship**

Abuse of Research Design or Methodology or Results

Conducting unnecessary research

Researching wrong or irrelevant problems

Use of unwarranted shortcuts to secure contract or save expenses

Misrepresenting limitations of research design

Inappropriate analytical techniques

Lack of sufficient expertise to conduct required research

Overly technical language in research report

Overstating validity or reliability of conclusions

Researcher Abuse of Researcher-Client Relationship

Overbilling the project

Failure to maintain client confidentiality

Failure to avoid possible conflict of interest

Client Abuse of Researcher-Client Relationship

Inappropriate use of research proposals

Disclosure or use of the researcher's specialized techniques and models

Cancellation of project (or refusal to pay) without cause

Conducting research solely to support *a priori* conclusions

Failure to act upon dangerous or damaging findings

Source: Professor Kenneth Schneider, St. Cloud State University, personal communication with the authors, January 2002.

Forthright Research Designs

Ethical issues may arise at any stage of the research design. Problem definition is the first stage in the process. It is often an arduous undertaking in many marketing research situations, and the researcher has an ethical obligation to help clients to define precisely the problem they hope to solve. One result may be that research is unnecessary. For example, the researcher may suggest to a fast-food client that a survey is needed when secondary information (like a simple traffic count already compiled by a regional planning authority) might suffice. For more guidance on the topic of protection from unnecessary research, see also Exhibit 2-5.

Another common problem is that the research method may cost more than the client wants to pay. Similarly, implementation of the research may be more expensive than originally proposed. What should the researcher do? Too often, the researcher scales back the design, sometimes to the point where it is methodologically suspect. In other words, the redesigned project doesn't meaningfully answer the research question. For instance, reducing the sample size or number of interviews by one-half to meet budgetary restrictions may result in findings that do not meet the client's accuracy requirements. Similarly, not using proper respondent verification procedures or not adequately pretesting a new questionnaire are other common shortcuts.

EXHIBIT 2-5   What about Unnecessary Research?

Researchers are frequently requested to engage in a specific research project that is unrelated to the underlying problem, has been done before, or is economically unjustified. The researcher can often benefit from such an activity. This gain will frequently exceed whatever goodwill might be generated by refusing to conduct unwarranted research. **Should the researcher accept such assignments?**

This issue is not addressed in the American Marketing Association code of ethics. However, it seems that the researcher has a professional obligation to indicate to the client that, in his or her judgment, the research expenditure is not warranted. If, after this judgment has been clearly stated, the client still desires the research, the researcher should feel free to conduct the study. The reason for this is that the researcher can never know for certain the risk preferences and strategies that are guiding the client's behavior.

Source: Professor Del Hawkins, University of Oregon, personal communication with the authors, June 2002.

We believe that the researcher should try to convince the client to spend more in the first place or admit to the client at the earliest opportunity that it will cost more to do the study right. Researchers should not wait until the project's completion, as was discussed in Scenario 2. If the client is informed of the impact of scalebacks on the project's validity *and* the research provides the best possible project for the price, the ethical concern is probably satisfied. Alternatively, the researcher might be prepared to sacrifice some profit to do the project right, much as physicians do when they treat low-income patients at lower rates, especially if they view the client as a source for repeat business or the potential for an ongoing relationship with the firm.

Other points in Exhibit 2-4 deal with the expertise of the researcher. A client hires a researcher to secure professional expertise. Thus, issues regarding limitations of certain research designs (e.g., although experiments can best measure cause and effect, they may be too artificial) and use of sophisticated analytical techniques often present researchers with ethical dilemmas. For instance, researchers must make judgments on how much methodological and analytical detail to share with clients. One area where researchers may let monetary considerations cloud their professional judgment pertains to a situation where they lack the expertise to conduct the required study. For example, a firm specializing in focus groups may take on a client who would best be served by telephone interviews rather than referring that client to another research provider. In addition, researchers should *not* try to "snow" clients with excessively technical jargon in the project report and presentation. Ultimately, such tactics usually backfire because clients may get the impression that the researcher is trying to hide other inadequacies in the research (even if none exist).

A final ethical issue in research design is the *overstatement of conclusions.* To please the client (and possibly secure future contracts), the researcher sometimes presents conclusions in the most positive light. For example, a consumer satisfaction study might report the fact that 70 percent of the respondents viewed the product favorably, while downplaying the 20 percent of the users who were *strongly* dissatisfied with the product. Therefore, researchers should avoid the impression that they are "puffing" the results. Some researchers may indicate that certain findings are significant at the .10 level. To unsuspecting managers this may appear to be important, whereas most researchers know that acceptable statistical significance is at the .05 level or lower.

Researcher Responsibility to Clients

The second section of Exhibit 2-4 lists three areas where researchers may abuse their relationship with the client. One practice is *overbilling the client.* This questionable practice can be contrasted with the two usual forms of pricing by research firms—cost-plus pricing and market pricing. Most research agencies utilize the first type of pricing where the costs allocated to a particular study are determined and a percentage markup is added for administrative overhead and profit. The market-oriented method attempts to determine the market value of the research to the client; thus, more critical studies are pegged to going market price, and researchers bid for these studies at a higher level. Overbilling for research, however it is done, is somewhat analogous to "price gouging" (see discussion in Chapter 4). A number of specific practices fall into this category, including building in extra overhead, charging for senior researchers' time when the work is done by junior staff, falsifying hours worked, and adding an override to subcontractors' work. These activities are unethical because overbilling is not tied to either costs or potential payoffs to the client.

Confidentiality and *conflict of interest* are two other concerns that marketing researchers must commonly address. The identity of a sponsoring firm should not be divulged to respondents or other existing or potential clients, unless the firm allows it. For instance, letting a respondent or another client know who is funding the study is a breach of the researcher's professional ethics and is covered in most codes (see Web sites of organizations described earlier). Conflict of interest is a growing concern especially with the increasing specialization of some marketing research firms. Certain researchers are now such specialists focusing exclusively on narrow topics such as political polling, hospital-patient satisfaction surveys, or image studies for financial institutions. These specialized firms must take great care, especially in this era when there are fewer potential clients because of mergers, that they do not work for two competing companies or else fully disclose the fact the firm has worked for competitors.

A temptation to inappropriately use one client's methodologies for another's project is sometimes present. Similar survey instruments might be used (as long as each client is not charged for instrument development), but research firms must be careful not to seek out direct competitors for their services. For example, a northeastern advertising and research agency that worked with Lotus software solicited Microsoft with the following: "You probably haven't thought about talking to an agency in Boston. . . . But since we know your competition's plans, isn't it worth taking a flier?" They went on to say that several of their employees had worked on the Lotus account at another agency and were familiar with Microsoft's competitive software product. Microsoft shared this information with Lotus, which won a restraining order barring the agency from revealing trade secrets and pitching any other competitors.

The Client's Responsibility to the Researcher

This issue represents the reverse of the previous discussion. Clients also have a responsibility to act ethically in dealing with research suppliers. Soliciting proposals from several suppliers just to get free advice on the solution to a particular problem or to combine multiple approaches to develop an in-house study constitutes unethical behavior by the potential client. Exhibit 2-4 lists additional areas where clients may abuse their relationship with the researcher. Clients should not disclose or try to use proprietary techniques that are not their own. Furthermore, delaying payment for services or canceling standing contracts can cause serious financial and organizational problems for the research firm.

The misrepresentation of findings by the client can also lead to problems for the researcher. For example, Scenario 1 at the beginning of the chapter discusses the misuse of a survey conducted by the Gallup Organization. The heated response by Gallup to the International Franchise Association was as follows: "They traded off our reputation to try to get people to invest in franchises. . . . And that's a violation of our rules," says Gallup lawyer Steve O'Brien. "We turn down a thousand requests (for surveys) a year. This year, it should have been a thousand and one."[8] As the quote indicates, the reputation of the research firm can be damaged when its name is used in the advertising, if the message misleads the receiver. Situations like these do happen and have ramifications not only within the researcher-client relationship but also with the public at large.

WHAT RESEARCHERS OWE THE PUBLIC

The general public is also a relevant secondary stakeholder in the practice of marketing research. Much so-called research is disseminated to the public through advertising (e.g., via slogans such as "three out of four doctors recommend"), political polling results (e.g., exit interviews), and other "pseudo polls" (e.g., 900 number telephone voting). Inaccurate use of marketing research can lead to false impressions by the public. For example, numerous Internet votes, often precipitated by TV news or sports programs, are nonscientific, convenience samples without generalizability, but they create impressions about issues and products among the public simply because they are well publicized.

Marketing research practices that deceive the public undermine ethical research practices. The negative consequences (one of the Cs in ABCs) of unethical research to the general public and policy makers are captured in the three points below. Such inaccurate or untrue market research:

- Impairs legitimate research activities by diminishing the public's willingness to participate in survey research. This affects response rates, statistical reliability, and ultimately response quality.
- Distorts policy makers' perceptions of public opinion and business-related issues. Dangerous feedback can result if policy makers misread consumer sentiment because of invalid research procedures.

• Confounds the public's ability to distinguish valid from invalid research findings. Deceptive polls as well as the inconsistent and contradictory results that they provide may render the public indifferent, confused, or distrustful of what they read, see, or hear from survey research. At best, this results in widespread miseducation.[9]

Specific manifestations of these practices involve incomplete and misleading reporting and nonobjective research.

Incomplete Reporting

When a researcher leaves out relevant information in a report circulated to the general public, problems can occur. For example, some companies conduct test markets and publicize these results in the trade press. What is sometimes omitted is that certain firms choose to conduct test markets in areas where their distribution or reputation is particularly strong. Therefore, the results of the test market are probably skewed in the favorable direction.

Actions mitigating questionable research practices may lead to less incomplete reporting in the future. For instance, we applaud the practice of major publications to provide, via a boxed insert, information with their polling results on how the sample was drawn and respondents contacted. Although many readers may consider this information superfluous, it provides those interested with a basis to judge the limitations and scientific validity of the poll. Furthermore, the Public Affairs Council of the Advertising Research Foundation (ARF) has published *Guidelines for the Public Use of Market and Opinion Research* that covers the origin, design, execution, and candor of the research conducted (available at www.marketinginfo.com/arf/pdf/guidelines.pdf).

Misleading Reporting

This practice involves presenting research results in such a way that the intended audience will draw an unjustified conclusion. Misleading reporting sometimes happens when research findings are used in promotional campaigns and can be a particular problem in comparative advertising. For instance, a recent ad campaign for Lowe's (the do-it-yourself superstore) advertised that its prices were 20 percent lower than Home Depot (its main competitor). Does this mean all or just some prices are lower at Lowe's? The presentation of results likely misled a substantial portion of the public. The ARF guidelines can guard against this type of potentially misleading reporting.

Nonobjective Research

In many instances the general public is not in a good position to judge whether research is conducted objectively. Understandably, they rely on overall percentages and often read only the ad's headlines rather than studying how the research was conducted. A potentially serious problem is using *leading questions* and then promoting the results to the public. For example, Burger King once used the responses to the following question to justify the claim that its method of cooking hamburgers was preferred over McDonald's: "Do you prefer your hamburgers flame-broiled or fried?" Another researcher asked a rephrased question on the same topic ("Do you prefer a hamburger that is grilled on a hot stainless steel grill or cooked by passing the raw meat through an open gas flame?") and found McDonald's to be preferred over Burger King. The upshot is that who you ask and how you phrase the question often determines the results. Viewers of commercials that make claims often assume a research objectivity that doesn't exist.

The researcher, then, has an obligation to warn management in advance of any presumed nonobjective aspects of a proposed research project, especially if the results are disseminated to the public. In the final report, the researcher should also clearly stipulate any effects of research bias. For instance, there may be some question about undersampling certain minority groups. Managers should then use these data cautiously.

COMPETITIVE INTELLIGENCE GATHERING

"One is legal, one is illegal. One's ethical, one is unethical." This statement by Leonard Fuld, a leading spokesperson and CEO of a market research agency, contrasts the illegal activity of industrial espionage to the acceptable, and universally used, practice of competitive intelligence (e.g., utilizing salespeople to monitor competitors' public actions or checking competitor's Web pages). Competitive intelligence (CI) entails gathering information about competitors, rather than consumers. Much greater attention was placed on intelligence gathering as domestic and global competition heated up in virtually all industries during the 1990s. There is a joke about the extensiveness of CI: 50 percent of the largest American firms do CI, 60–80 percent of European firms do CI, and 150 percent of Japanese and Korean firms do CI. While the last percentage given reflects the punch line of the joke, the greater emphasis on competitive intelligence gathering by European and Asian headquartered companies has put the issue of CI front and center in the U.S. marketing research community. Furthermore, given the growth of marketing information systems (MIS), massive amounts of data about consumers and company performance are stored on computerized databases, including records of sales, number of employees, plant dollar volume, and so forth. These records can be stolen, illegally purchased, or "hacked" by unethical competitors.

The whole area of intelligence gathering has earned a bad name because of certain dubious and even illegal tactics employed by some firms. For instance, a well-known computer company has bought their competitors' garbage from the trash hauler in order to sift through it for morsels of pungent information. (Some call this practice "waste archeology.") Other marketers stage phony job interviews to pump information from competitors' unsuspecting employees. Still others have instructed executives (using disguised names or positions) to take tours of their competitors' plants to get details of manufacturing processes and outputs or to sign up for job interviews with competitors. The Society for Competitive Intelligence Professionals (SCIP at www.scip.org) has an eight-point code that its 7,000 members in 50 chapters around the world are expected to follow. Many companies have instituted formal intelligence programs and some, like Motorola, have won awards for ethical CI. In the United States, the Economic Espionage Act was passed in 1996 to curb stealing trade secrets and other egregious CI activities (see Exhibit 2-6).

Very legitimate reasons exist for corporate intelligence gathering. First, executives should take advantage of information that is publicly available so as not to neglect their fiduciary duty to shareholders and other stakeholders. For example, virtually all companies have Web sites. It is the responsibility of competitors to monitor them probably at least monthly. A second reason for gathering competitive intelligence is as a basis for strategic planning. Companies find, sometimes the hard way, that strategic planning cannot be conducted in a competitive vacuum. Gathering accurate information about competitors is now a must for devising a good strategy. This heightened interest spawned an industry of corporate intelligence consultants, seminars, and Web sites. The dirty tricks even invaded the snoopers themselves when one intelligence seminar director found a competitor who conducted similar seminars enrolled in his course under an assumed name. On another occasion his lecture notes and source book were stolen.

Third, corporate intelligence is necessary in order to be successful against global competitors. As the earlier joke suggests, Asian companies have long been acknowledged as expert intelligence gatherers. North America lags significantly behind Europe and Asia in the area of CI. With the end of the Cold War in the 1980s, many former European intelligence officers turned to corporate espionage services in order to continue practicing their expertise. And while North American firms have been debating the ethics of CI, their competitors in Japan, Sweden, Israel, and Germany just kept using it. Most of these countries have an innate advantage in CI, since

EXHIBIT 2-6   United States Economic Espionage Act of 1996

- Definition: A federal law providing domestic and foreign protection which defines—for the first time—a trade secret as:
  - Something a business has taken reasonable effort to keep secret
    - which derives its value from being secret
    - which is not easily developed by the public
    - which is not protected by patents or copyrights
  - Any form or type of financial, business, scientific, technical, economic or engineering information, including patterns, plans, compilations, program devices, formulas, designs, prototypes, methods, techniques, processes, procedures, programs, or codes, whether tangible or intangible, and whether or how stored, compiled or memorialized, physically, electronically, graphically, photographically, or in writing.
- Passage: October 1996 . . . Economic Espionage Act (EEA). The EEA makes stealing or obtaining trade secrets by fraud a U.S. federal crime.
- Penalties: Up to 15 years in prison and $10 million in fines.
- Cases: Twenty-six cases from '96 to '03. (See www.usdoj.gov/criminal/cybercrime/eeapub.htm.)
- Enforcement: The U.S. Justice Department/Criminal Division's Computer Crime and Intellectual Property Section (CCIPS) has grown from five attorneys in January 1996 (prior to the passage of the EEA) to 40 attorneys now.
- Reality: Light sentences handed down thus far.
- Suggested Alteration: Allow companies to file civil suits to win compensation and perhaps triple punitive damages.

Source: Partially adapted from Sylvia Long-Tolbert and Patrick E. Murphy. "Competitive Intelligence on the Net: A Multinational Perspective on Ethical Practices," Paper presented to ESOMAR Net Effects[4] Conference, February 12, 2001, Barcelona, Spain.

their national cultures value information and intelligence and they operate in a more collectivist manner. Many U.S.-based firms, imitating their Japanese and European counterparts, are now more routinely disassembling or "benchmarking" competitors' products.

Fourth, intelligence gathering can be quite useful in the introduction of a new product. For example, by tracking the expected product introductions of related products by competitors, a firm can either create a window of exclusivity for their own product launch or use their introduction to blunt the competition's grab at market share.

Competitive Intelligence on the Web

The Internet, with the explosion of company Web sites, chat rooms, and search engines, has produced a gold mine of information for those seeking to scoop the competition. A plethora of information is now available at one's desk about the plans and strategies of competitors. In fact, one well known CI Web site (www.fuld.com) lists sources of information about entire industries. Since the Internet is global, it is easy to get information about a far-flung competitor. Similarly, most newspapers are available on the Web so searching for information about a company's activities in its hometown newspaper is also very easy. A number of search engines, including AltaVista, Google, Anonymizer, and Netsol, facilitate this search. The bottom line regarding CI on the Web was summarized recently: "The good news is that your competition's kimono is more open than ever. . . . The bad news is, so is yours."[10]

The information-rich Web has spawned new and more sophisticated CI firms that combine their analysis with custom searches to produce more useful information. One firm tracks companies in the same fashion that consumers are tracked with electronic cookies. Another consultant assists companies who believe others are violating their trademarks or copyrights via the net. In the post-9/11/01 world, many firms have become more security conscious: "The same kind of spying techniques used to cull intelligence on competitors can also pick up possibly threatening comments or behavior that might bear closer investigation in today's more security-conscious environment."[11]

How to Discourage CI

Companies cannot prevent their competitors from getting some information about them. However, they can guard against "loose lips" and inadvertent slips that may divulge confidential data. Corporate training programs should emphasize the importance of confidentiality and specify the types of information that are considered classified. All employees, including Web designers, secretaries, and even summer interns, should receive such training. Furthermore, corporate codes should spell out company policies for this area. The IBM and United Technologies codes explicitly deal with the unintentional disclosure of proprietary information.

Stories are legion concerning recruiters from competitors finding out valuable information from workers because the current or former employees did not know they should *not* be talking about certain things. Furthermore, buyers, purchasing agents, scientists, and engineers should be instructed that certain subjects are "off limits" when they attend trade shows, seminars, and professional meetings. Companies should consider *not* posting some job openings on their Web sites so as to make it more difficult for competitors to ferret out plant openings and new product development. On the other hand, employees should be advised about what *not* to do in obtaining competitor information. The rule of thumb is that deception should never be used (i.e., trying to coax information from a competitor without identifying yourself). The watchword for companies concerned about CI issues is *education* of all employees.

How to Do CI Ethically

Exhibit 2-7 shows a list of traditional and new technology sources of competitive information. They are ranked in terms of their ethical and legal ramifications. These are good lists for companies to follow, because they give explicit guidance on what activities are acceptable. One source of public information not listed is help wanted advertising or postings on Monster.com. These ads can offer a wealth of information on competitors' intentions, strategies, and sometimes even planned products. For example, sales reps also should be trained to seek out competitive information as part of their daily activities. Regarding the Web, companies should be diligent in both studying competitors' information and even going into message boards and chat rooms to find out what is being said about their firm. Other technical staffers such as engineers and scientists need to be alert to publicly available competitive information at professional meetings or in scientific journals. The bottom line here is that the strategically competent organization must gather such information, but do so from an ethical perspective. Deception should not be part of the corporate intelligence gathering process. The practices listed in the lower two-thirds of Exhibit 2-7 are arguably inappropriate and sometimes illegal.

What ethical strictures are being violated by some corporate intelligence gathering practices? The Golden Rule and other simple maxims can guide managers. We believe that the principles of honesty/integrity and fairness are two important ethical precepts that companies engaging in these practices tend to ignore. Furthermore, playing the intelligence game fairly is one of the absolute obligations of ethical marketing executives. We also would urge marketers to evaluate intelligence-gathering efforts using a virtue ethics perspective (recall Chapter 1). That is, managers should decide what their organization *should be* and whether its corporate intelligence gathering is consistent with the underlying values of their firm and what it claims to be.

TARGET MARKETS: SOME SPECIAL ETHICAL CONCERNS

One of the basic precepts of marketing is to take the information gathered in marketing research and use it to initially segment and then target markets

Exhibit 2-7   An Index for Judging Traditional and New Technology
Sources of Competitive Information

Traditional Sources

Ethical

1. Published material and public documents (court records).
2. Disclosures made by competitor's employees, and obtained without subterfuge.
3. Market surveys and consultant's reports.
4. Financial reports and brokers' research reports.
5. Debriefing the sales force and others in the field.
6. Analysis of competitor's products.
7. Legitimate employment interviews with people who worked for competitor.

Arguably Unethical

8. Camouflaged questioning and "drawing out" of competitor's employees at a technical meeting or trade show.
9. Not wearing a name tag at trade show when visiting competitors' booths.
10. Direct observation under secret conditions.
11. Conducting phony negotiations for a license or franchise to gain insider information.
12. False job interviews with competitor's employee (i.e., where there is no real intent to hire).
13. Hiring a professional investigator to obtain a specific piece of information.
14. Hiring an employee away from the competitor, to get specific know-how.

New Technology Sources

Ethical

1. Information posted on the company Web site—annual reports, company and product descriptions, and employment information.
2. Tracking hits the competitors' Web site receives.
3. Job postings by the firm on Web sites dedicated to employment opportunities.
4. Product reviews by independent organizations.
5. Product reviews or reactions in chat rooms or message boards.

Arguably Unethical

6. Employees contacting the competition anonymously to ask information without disclosing the purpose for the contact.
7. Instructing student interns to contact competitors online and telling them to state they are doing research for a class.
8. Flooding a competitor with e-mails.
9. Spreading rumors about the shortcomings of a competitor's products in chat rooms.
10. Using Web crawlers to harvest customer data or pricing information from competitor Web site.

(continued)

Illegal

15. Trespassing on competitor's property.
16. Bribing competitor's supplier or employee.
17. "Planting" your agent on competitor's payroll.
18. Eavesdropping on competitors (e.g., via wire tapping).
19. Theft of drawings, samples, documents, and similar property.
20. Blackmail and extortion.

Illegal

11. Stealing passwords of competitors' employees.
12. Breaking into databases or voice-mail system of competitors.
13. Paying current or former employees to gain access to a firm's private electronic information.

Sources: Adapted from several sources, including Sylvia Long-Tolbert and Patrick E. Murphy, "Competitive Intelligence on the Net: A Multinational Perspective on Ethical Practices," Paper presented to ESOMAR Net Effects[4] Conference, February 12, 2001, Barcelona, Spain; Terri L. Rittenberg, Sean R. Valentine, and James Faircloth, "The Ethics of Competitor Intelligence," Working paper, University of Wyoming (2002); and Worth Wade, *Industrial Espionage and Mis-Use of Trade Secrets* (Ardmone, PA: Advance House, 1965).

with the organization's products (i.e., goods, services, and ideas). Well-known target markets include affluent consumers for luxury automobiles, African Americans for the hair care treatment with Johnson Products (which specializes in this market segment), and college students for their consumption of fast food.

While marketing practitioners and academics generally believe that the "idea" of targeting markets is ethical, a recent book coauthored by a well-known philosopher calls into question this notion. He says, "Insofar as the customer remains an 'object' or the 'target' of marketing, such talk is wildly off the mark and self-defeating."[12] From our viewpoint, the ethical questions surrounding target marketing occur when companies focus on "vulnerable" populations. A target market of consumers can be vulnerable in four ways: physically (due to safety considerations), cognitively (they are lacking in ability to process information), motivationally (they cannot resist ordinary temptations or enticements), and socially (there is extreme pressure on them to conform).[13] In the section below, we examine several vulnerable markets that imply ethical implications for marketers.

Children

The target market sparking the most controversy over the years is children. The reason companies aim some of their efforts toward children is that kids represent an obvious market (over $24 billion annually in the United States) for many products such as toys, sugared cereals, candy/sweets, and video games. Though parents are presumed to make the decision for their children, marketers know that children can influence product selection and brand choice (another $500 billion) even from a very young age.[14] Hence, companies target children with advertising and increasingly by Internet messages (including ads and engaging games—see Exhibit 5-1).

Critics believe that the commercial socialization of children and the fact that marketers view them as "consumers in training" call into question the ethics of targeting this market. Many public and consumer interest groups (such as the campaign for Tobacco Free Kids and Mothers Against Drunk Driving [MADD]) have noted marketing's unique responsibility in protecting children. For younger children (less than eight years old), it is a question of understanding the difference between advertising and the program or Web site content. The use of cartoon characters as product spokespersons is generally discouraged. Still, there is a strong relationship between toy companies and many cartoon shows. The authors still remember GI Joe action figures being sold on a program that held that name. Two of the authors recall their sons wanting all the toys advertised on the *Ghostbusters* cartoon show (proton packs, firehouse, ambulance car, etc.). Some critics argue that such shows were actually 30-minute commercials—"program length commercials" (PLCs)—and were attacked by those who believe that these shows manipulate impressionable children. Congress passed the Children's Television Act (CTA) that prohibits PLCs among its provisions.[15]

Other issues that are raised with respect to marketing and advertising to children have to do with violence and product safety. Among the questionable products aimed at older children are violent video games. For example, the video game series Grand Theft Auto (GTA), currently very popular with adolescents, is a particularly brutal game. The game player might score points by running over people, stealing cars, and conducting assassinations. While this game cannot be legally sold to anyone under 17, it seems to find its way to a substantial market of younger male gamers. (Such "point and shoot" video games have been criticized by journalists, activists, and scholars.[16]) Product safety also has long been a concern of most stakeholders (parents, consumer advocates, policy makers, and marketers) regarding children's products from tricycles to BB guns to playground equipment. We examine product safety in more depth in the following chapter but raise it here to indicate that marketers are held to a higher standard on safety when children are involved in using their products.

The Children's Online Privacy Protection Act (COPPA; U.S. 112 Stat. 2681) was passed in October 1998 because of concerns regarding online marketing practices aimed at children. Both COPPA and the CTA "raised the bar" (recall Chapter 1) for marketers by making questionable acts illegal. FTC research released in June 1998 found low industry compliance with its Fair Practice Principles, which require Web sites to include information practice statements (e.g., "kids, get your parents' permission before you give out information online") and privacy notices, as well as parental notification. The FTC report also indicated that personal information such as age/birth date, sex, hobbies, interests, and hardware/software ownership was collected more from children than from adults. A particular concern with these findings has to do with the limited cognitive abilities of children, which suggests that kids may be more motivated by the incentives intended to get their information (e.g., trading cards, freebies) than by the cautionary and self-protective information provided in the privacy statement.

Basically, COPPA prohibits the collection of personally identifiable information from children 13 years of age and younger on Web sites *unless* the children obtain verifiable permission from their parents. Still, questions continue about the protection and safety of youth when they are using the Web. For example, there are practical difficulties in verifying a child's age and obtaining parental consent, along with the FTC's limited ability to enforce these requirements.[17] (For more information on COPPA and how the FTC expects companies to comply with it, see www.ftc.gov/bcp/online/pubs/buspubs/coppa.htm.)

Recently, the FTC announced a COPPA settlement with the Ohio Art Co., manufacturer of the Etch-A-Sketch drawing toy. The FTC alleged that the company's Web site collected the names, mailing addresses, e-mail address, age, and date of birth from children who wanted to qualify to win an Etch-A-Sketch toy on their birthday. The FTC charged that the company merely directed children to "get your parent or guardian's permission first" and then collected the information without first obtaining parental consent as required by COPPA. In addition, the FTC alleged the company collected more information from children than was reasonably necessary for children to participate in this "birthday club" activity and that the site's privacy policy statement did not clearly or completely disclose all of its information collection practices or make certain disclosures required by COPPA. The site also failed to give parents the opportunity to review the personal information collected from their children and to inform them of their ability to prevent the further collection and use of this information, the FTC contended.[18]

Tweens

A new target market that has received substantial marketing and public attention is labeled "tweens" because of its life-cycle status between early childhood and the teenage years. Professor Elizabeth Moore, a colleague who studies this group, says that "tweens are not developed enough psychologically to know how to be skeptical about advertising."[19] These preteen individuals represent a huge market for many products. They want to be like teenagers and, therefore, are subject to extreme peer pressure to "be cool." Young girls seem especially sensitive to the marketing efforts particularly when the promotions are linked to female entertainers who wear provocative clothing styles (scantily clad and/or bare midriffs). One marketer that has actively cultivated this group is Abercrombie and Fitch, which marketed thong underwear to preteens and has long utilized a blatant sex appeal approach with its company catalogs.

Teens

Teenagers are another potentially vulnerable segment, although they may not think they are. Many products are properly targeted to this group, such as movies, clothing, fast food, and soft drinks. Where their vulnerability comes into play is when "adult" products target them with both products and advertising. Alcoholic beverages are discussed in other chapters, but the targeting of teens appears to be a continuing problem. "While many factors may influence an underage person's drinking decisions, including among other things, parents, peers and the media, there is reason to believe that advertising also plays a role."[20] Sex-oriented products and messages aimed at teens have increased with the popularity of *Friends*, Britney Spears, and *Lara Croft: Tomb Raider*. The pervasiveness of sex appeal encompasses many products, including movies, magazines, music, and, as mentioned earlier, video games and clothing. Tobacco and its promotion have long had a stigma of targeting youth. **What is your view of marketers' ethical responsibility to teenagers?**

Older Consumers

This market is projected to grow substantially as baby boomers age. Until the last decade or so, the elderly were often ignored or stereotyped by marketers. Now, seniors are not only living longer, but also more of them are affluent and engage in active lifestyles. For example, Sun City, Arizona, and the many retirement villages in Florida are a testament to the vibrancy of this market. Active living (and, therefore, active spending) has made the elderly particularly good targets for financial services, travel packages, and full-service restaurants. Also, some older, less active seniors use television as a companion and get much of their news and product information from this source, which raises special ethical issues about TV advertising directed to the elderly segments. Marketers need to reexamine their ethical responsibilities to this growing market, not only in the United States but around the world.

More complete disclosure of purchase-related information, accurate pricing, easier to use product designs, and larger print in promotions are but a few areas to consider when targeting this age segment.

Market Illiterates

The demographic features of this market are low income, low education, and a naive understanding of economies. The burgeoning number of immigrants over the last two decades, including undocumented residents, probably means that the size of this segment has grown substantially. Two groups of consumer make up this category: the functionally illiterate and those that don't understand how the market works. In their purchasing habits, market illiterates are generally more national brand loyal, more likely to buy home remedy health care products (possibly because they can't afford to see a physician), and are not as nutritionally conscious.[21] Furthermore, "functionally illiterate consumers display a predilection for what we call *concrete reasoning*—focusing on a single perceptible piece of information such as a price or a product attribute or ingredient, size, when engaged in shopping decisions."[22]

Responsibility for aiding market illiterates should be shared among government, education, the health care community, and companies. Market illiteracy is a significant long-term ethical problem if these individuals are being misled by marketers or if the marketing strategy used in targeting exacerbates their social problems. One particular issue that has surfaced within this community is check cashing/"payday" loan outlets and "subprime lending schemes." Basically, these are lending practices that seek to extract user and rates of interest from consumers who are desperate for cash advances or quick financial services. Several well-known banks and financial services marketers have been engaged in one or more of these practices.

These five target markets are special cases for marketers, but they are not the only ones. Special responsibilities are also inherent when selling to minorities, the physically and mentally disabled/handicapped, and even college students (e.g., the extensive marketing of credit cards and "easy financing" comes to mind). It appears that large companies and especially advertising agencies have a special obligation, given their considerable influence, to look out for the needs of these special groups who are at an inherent disadvantage in the marketplace. For example, toy and cereal producers should examine closely how they are socializing children's consumption patterns. In other words, they should ask themselves: What values are we fostering by our selected advertising? The use of fear appeal advertising directed toward the elderly should be avoided wherever possible because of their particular vulnerability to such messages or their possible lack of understanding. Fast-food and snack-food marketers should consider using information rich and easily understood product messages when they are

Exhibit 2-8 Types of Targeting Strategies[1]

PRODUCT

	Less Harmful	More Harmful
Low Vulnerability	e.g., Low-fat hamburger to above-average income consumer target	e.g., High-interest rate credit card to suburban consumer target
TARGET	Strategy 1	Strategy 2
	e.g., Low-nicotine cigarette to black consumer target[2]	e.g., High-alcohol content malt liquor to less than high-school educated consumer target
High Vulnerability	Strategy 3	Strategy 4

[1]References to product harmfulness and target vulnerability are to the perceptions of these factors. Also, both in reality could be conceived as having a continuum; however, for our purposes, each is divided into two categories.

[2]Some people never would consider cigarettes to be in a less harmful category because of the strong evidence of the harmful nature of smoking. However, we note that cigarettes can differ in their levels of harm (e.g., through a reduction in benzo(a)pyrene, the cancerous compound in tobacco smoke) and hence some types can be considered "less harmful."

Source: N. Craig Smith and Elizabeth Cooper-Martin, "Ethics and Target Marketing: The Role of Product Harm and Consumer Vulnerability," *Journal of Marketing* (July 1997): 4. Reprinted with permission.

targeting market illiterates. Exhibit 2-8 shows how target market vulnerability might be combined with specific harms associated with the product.

IDEAS FOR ETHICAL MARKETING

First, marketing researchers should establish ground rules and let these ethical research standards be known to the people and firms with which they deal. To counteract many of the potential problems between researcher and client, it is essential that both sides understand each other. One researcher offered the following advice to maintain and increase integrity in the marketing research profession.

> Put things in writing.
>
> Don't be afraid to face up to clients with issues and cost problems.
>
> Try to maintain open communication and promote regular feedback to the people with whom you interact.
>
> Don't be an ostrich. We are members of a profession, and we owe it to that profession to support ethical behavior by its practitioners.[23]

These sage words emphasize the necessity of researchers and clients to use formal contracts that spell out details of the research. However, the contract should not be viewed as a straightjacket; mechanisms should be put in place to alter or amend it with the agreement of both parties.

Regarding the client's responsibility to the researcher, most of the same principles hold. If clients abuse their relationship with research suppliers, it will damage their reputation in the research community and may even preclude their finding reputable research firms to work with them in the future. To guard against such abuses, the Council of American Survey Research Organizations has developed a set of guidelines that should be used to evaluate research proposals (see www.casro.org). We suggest that clients inform prospective research firms that they will follow these guidelines *before* research proposals are submitted.

Second, researchers should treat respondents, clients, competitors, and the public using ethical, not just legal or competitive, criteria. Most marketing researchers understand that it is in their best interest to treat these stakeholders fairly. What sometimes happens in the pressures of day-to-day activities is that researchers use the "everyone else does it" excuse to condone ethically debatable behavior (e.g., creating a fictitious research name when calling customers). Or they trot out the age-old argument that "if it is legal, it must be okay." We believe that researchers need to be held to high professional standards. Therefore, ethical criteria should be used in evaluating researchers. For instance, in focus group research a mutual trust should exist among the moderator, the client, participants, and the research sponsor. Furthermore, the moderator and participants should treat each other in an honest and straightforward manner. Regarding online research, one report advised: "If you are a member of a national or international industry group, you should place the name (with a hyperlink) in your text-based email invitation and the logo on your privacy page and on the first page of your Web survey. The recommended wording is 'XYZ company is a member of IMRO, the Interactive Marketing Research Organization [see Exhibit 2-9 for IMRO's code of ethics—www.imro.org], and we subscribe to the privacy policies and code of research ethics published by that group.'"[24]

Exhibit 2-9   Interactive Marketing Research Organization (IMRO) Code of Ethics

As a means of achieving and implementing ethical research practices, the IMRO endorses the following Code of Ethics:

The use of interactive and Internet research technologies provides an unprecedented communication mechanism for the exchange of ideas on a worldwide basis. These same tools also have the potential for misuse, particularly in consideration of the privacy rights of individuals. The Interactive Marketing Research Organization is founded on the principles of upholding the highest standards of both ethical and professional conduct in the use of research technologies.

Over and above normal standards of research, our professional activities shall be conducted with particular respect for the individual's right to privacy, both in terms of confidentiality of information collected during the marketing research process and the right to be free from unsolicited and unwanted contact.

Rights of Confidentiality

By default and design, confidentiality shall be granted for all information collected from customers and individuals and will be used for the clearly stated and intended purposes only. All personal data will be secured against access by third parties and/or unauthorized individuals or organizations.

Rights of Privacy

The right of the individual to be free from unsolicited contact is duly recognized. By default and design, customers and individuals will have the right to opt out of the research process. Specifically, IMRO members will abstain from the following types of surreptitious sampling and unsolicited or unethical recruitment techniques, known collectively as "spamming":

Surreptitious Sampling can include but is not limited to the following:

- Collection of respondent e-mails from Web sites, portals, Usenet or other bulletin board postings without specifically notifying individuals that they are being "recruited" for research purposes;
- The use of Spambots, Spiders, Sniffers or other "agents" that collect personal information without the respondents' explicit awareness;
- The purchase of bulk e-mail addresses from sources that have not provided verifiable documentation that the individuals on the list have opted for contact for the purposes of research; and/or
- The use of client customer lists that have been assembled without the express consent of the individual for future contact via e-mail.

Unsolicited/Unethical Recruitment (Spamming) can include but is not limited to the following:

- Unsolicited e-mail recruitment of potential respondents;
- Misleading or off-topic newsgroup postings designed to "trick" a potential respondent into participating in research;
- Junk mail sent in bulk to recruit for studies or panels;

(continued)

- Scamming, which refers to the practice of recruiting under false pretenses (e.g., recruitment for research that is in reality a sales or contribution solicitation pitch);
- Spoofing, which refers to the practice of putting in a false or missing return e-mail address; and/or
- Chain or "buddy" letters aimed at recruiting respondents' friends, relatives, or colleagues for studies or panels.

In all cases, the purpose of research conducted by IMRO members will be clearly and accurately stated along with the limitations of the use of personal information gathered. Individuals will have the right to be removed from potential research respondent lists and given a clear and simple way of communicating such a decision. Members will not willingly and knowingly mislead respondents as to the parameters of the research process including length of survey, incentive, use of data, etc. IMRO members will at all times conform to the 1998 Children's Online Privacy Protection Act (*COPPA*) and not collect personal data from children under the age of thirteen without the express approval of their parents or guardians. IMRO members pledge to comply with the local, national, and regional laws and regulations regarding the use of all modes of data collection including both interactive and traditional channels of communication in the countries where research is being performed.

Source: www.imro.org/code.htm.

Third, the increased **professionalization** *of marketing research is imperative.* We end this chapter as we began it—discussing marketing research as a profession. There are several reasons why the practice of conducting marketing research can be considered a profession. First of all, there are association endorsed codes of ethics; there is a recognized body of market research knowledge; and there is the use of the scientific method and the presumed objectivity of researchers. All these characteristics are hallmarks of a profession. However, enough issues have surfaced in the preceding pages that might cause one to wonder. A strong statement on this topic by the executive director of a major marketing research professional organization reads:

> The U.S. research industry is working with the FTC and the Federal Communications Commission to address abuses by research pretenders and to document that we enforce our mandatory codes of standards and ethics. We're also working together with other associations to ensure that our ethical codes are consistent with each other, particularly as we expand them to cover the Internet and other research methodologies that may be created. Our research image and identity must be clearly defined and consistent across national boundaries. We all must use the same words to describe ourselves and what we do, if we ever hope to create a better public understanding and appreciation of research and thereby increase respondents' willingness to participate in the research process.[25]

We would like to advance three proposals to further enhance professionalism in marketing research. We first advocate the designation of *certified public researchers* (CPRs), analogous to CPAs or CFAs. These CPRs would audit the validity and accuracy of marketing research numbers used in public forums (e.g., in advertising claims, political polls reported in the media, or in legal/regulatory proceedings). This idea was proposed by a prominent member of the research community several years ago. Two reasons were given why such verification is needed: (1) the public is being asked, more and more, to accept the accuracy of marketing research, and (2) there are a substantial number of managers (especially in the government and nonprofit sectors) who know little about the validity of marketing research but are using the results for important policy and decision making. Although the issue of certification is controversial, it is worth exploring.[26]

Major marketing research professional organizations should also work together in revising their codes to make them more useful for their members. It is our understanding that such a joint effort among the marketing research practitioners of the Advertising Research Foundation, American Marketing Association, Council of American Survey Research Organizations, European Society of Marketing and Opinion Research, Marketing Research Association, and Qualitative Research Consultants of America has begun. They hope to come out with baseline recommendations on a model code that is useful for all these associations.

There are a couple cautionary notes we want to voice concerning codes. Revisions to the code should follow the guidelines elaborated upon in Chapter 7. And enforcement is essential. Unless sanctions exist—even if they simply consist of publicizing questionable behavior—the efforts at enhancing professionalism in marketing research will be in vain. Another factor revolves around the realization that the research community is not a homogeneous group. There are many different types of researchers, from the junior corporate analyst to the high-level consultant who only interacts with CEOs. Their ethical concerns regarding research are varied. Thus, professional associations should try to tailor not only the code, but also related programs on ethics they might sponsor for their divergent constituencies.

A third recommendation is that education in marketing research should place a higher priority on professionalism. Both at the university level and within the vast continuing education empire, teachers of research methods need to stress the importance of a strong ethical posture so that researchers view themselves as professionals and not "hired guns trying to arrive at a preordained conclusion." If those educated in market research had the feeling they were truly professionals and embraced the concomitant responsibilities of professionalism, many of the problems discussed earlier would cease to exist.

Our final idea for ethical marketing is *target markets must be selected and served in an ethical manner.* We only reviewed a few instances of markets that may be vulnerable. Some of these targeting efforts have elsewhere received extensive treatment and scrutiny. However, other vulnerable markets exist that need much more investigation by marketers. We advocate both a duty-based and social-contract approach to these target markets. Special obligations on the part of marketers should be accepted and adherence to norms would likely make marketing efforts more ethical.

CONCLUDING COMMENT

This chapter captures some of the many and varied ethical issues facing practicing marketing researchers. As discussed, researchers have distinct obligations to respondents, clients, and the public. Likewise, clients also owe potential researchers a sense of fairness. Obviously, not all situations are covered here, but the research firm conscious of its ethical posture should establish appropriate ground rules and ethical standards for their firm. We also examined the responsibilities of marketers to vulnerable target markets. In the next chapter we turn our attention to ethical issues in product management, which presents another specific set of challenges.

Chapter Three
Product Management Ethics

Scenario 1

Curry, a British electronics retailer, manufactures and sells a *private brand* line of electronic products (e.g., televisions, VCRs, audiotape recorders) that it assembles from components made around the world. The brand name for these products is HATSUI. The motto for the product line is "Japanese technology made perfect." The product symbol is the rising sun—similar to that featured on the Japanese flag. Curry is not a Japanese company or subsidiary. The vast majority of components used in the HATSUI products are not made in Japan. To add a further twist of irony to the entire endeavor, Hatsui is the name of a Japanese war criminal responsible for atrocities in China during the Second World War. Curry defends itself by saying that it never claimed that it was a Japanese company, that it has legal copyright for the brand name HATSUI, that the firm did not intend to mislead or offend anyone. Rather, the company managers "made the name up" because it was "a bit mystical and foreign sounding." **Is the consumer being misled by this brand-name scheme?**

Scenario 2

Paul Klug is the president of a successful consumer electronics firm that specializes in the manufacturing of car telephones, compact disc/tape players for automobiles, and citizen's band radios for trucks. The company is cash rich, and President Klug asked his vice president of marketing, Sue Simmons, to suggest a product acquisition. Sue suggests acquiring the Acme Corporation, a small producer of radar detection equipment branded the "Cop Buster." The rationale contained in a written report is basically the following:

1. Radar detectors are very compatible with our existing lines.
2. Trends show that this product has been rapidly increasing its sales among young drivers.

In addition, Simmons points out that, as women have become a more important part of the workforce, their purchases of radar detectors have been increasing dramatically. In summary, she recommends acquisition of the company along with an advertising campaign aimed toward young female drivers. President Klug responded, "As far as I can tell the only purpose of such a product is to circumvent the posted speed-limit laws. Aren't we advocating law-breaking by adding such a product to our existing line?" **What do you think?**

In reviewing these scenarios, some of the ethical issues that emerge in the area of product management begin to crystallize. For example, what *degree of disclosure* does a product manager owe consumers who will be using the organization's branded product? What responsibilities do product managers and retailers have related to the *social ramifications* of their products? While there are some aspects of the scenarios that could be questioned on legal grounds, none of them are illegal per se. A major point of debate then is: Do they represent unethical product practices? Do they cross the boundaries of proper and expected business conduct? This chapter provides guidance in grappling with such questions.

As this chapter unfolds, we discuss several major ethical questions inherent in product management. We cover a range of issues: those that have legal implications, such as product safety and product counterfeiting; and those that are mostly left to managers to confront on the grounds of ethics or social responsibility, such as products perceived to be in bad taste; products that are environmentally incompatible; and products, such as tobacco and alcohol, that have been challenged in terms of their social acceptability.

PRODUCT SAFETY

Many ethical concerns in product management pertain to the safety of products offered to the market. Safety is a fundamental ethical responsibility rooted in the adage that marketers should *never knowingly do harm*. Nonetheless, the examples of transgressions of this rule that regularly occur have many manifestations. For example, one of the longest running and most controversial issues is that of toy safety and the extent to which toy manufacturers market unsafe products. Each Christmas season, various consumer advocacy groups identify and publicize toys that are potentially dangerous to young children unless used with extreme care or under adult supervision. For example, a recent holiday season brought its usual array of unsafe products: those that easily break apart exposing sharp or jagged edges, others designed for young children that contained small pieces that could lead to chokings, and some that fired projectiles of various sizes and shapes. A general ethical principle, widely accepted in the industry, is that toy manufacturers have a special responsibility to their consumers, because children are a particularly vulnerable group. Despite the general acceptance of this principle, analysts of the toy industry are somewhat amazed that some unsafe toys reach the marketplace each year. The Toy Industry Association prepares an annual fact book that includes a chapter on various ethical obligations concerning safety that its members accept.[1]

There are alternative perspectives on this issue. The first is that if users are sufficiently warned about a product's potential hazards, the liberty principle (see Chapter 1) would suggest that no further regulatory steps should be taken, because consumers have been explicitly warned about possible negative outcomes. Also, product safety can be valuable when marketers promote it as a benefit of their products.

While safety issues pose ethical concern (and, it may be added, elicit a public response that may adversely affect sales and profits), product safety is also governed by common and statutory law and regulated by a variety of government agencies. As we shall see in other chapters devoted to strategic topics in marketing, ethical duties go beyond legal responsibilities. However, the minimal obligation of marketers in the area of product safety is clearly specified in law. In the paragraphs below, we look at some of these areas of codified responsibility, including warranties, product liability law, and some federal agencies having responsibility for product safety. We review these legal constraints because many charges about the unethical marketing of unsafe products are really criticisms of illegal activity.

Warranties

The first guarantee a consumer has of product safety is the *warranty*. There are two types of warranties. The first is that written document that sometimes accompanies a product when it is purchased, called the *express* warranty. This sets forth any specific obligations sellers accept concerning product performance. A second kind of warranty is *implied*, so labeled because it need not be expressed or stated. An implied warranty indicates that goods (or services) are "merchantable" (i.e., worthy of sale and fit for the ordinary purpose for which the goods are used). Thus, in common law, there are certain minimum product performance expectations the seller can never legally avoid. This, among other things, means the product will perform safely. The net effect of the implied warranty is that, in summary, a warranty is an assurance given by the seller to the buyer. To the extent it is "expressed," the seller takes on additional obligations beyond those included in the implied warranty.

Express obligations may also be utilized as *promotional warranties.* Examples of this type of warranty are the "7 year/70,000 mile" or "10 year/ 100,000 mile" guarantees on major repairs given by some automobile manufacturers or the Cross pens "lifetime guarantee" on its writing instruments. Such express warranties, which extend coverage beyond customary experience, may also be provided by retailers or manufacturers who guarantee extra service (e.g., free repair and parts service for four years on a vacuum cleaner or free replacement of tools or tires in the case of failure irrespective of the absence of any defect). These promotional warranties are an attempt to attract buyers to a particular brand, store, or chain.

An advertising executive recounted to one of the authors that he developed a campaign for a camera company—"Guaranteed for ten years or your money back." His position was that the consumers would forget and never ask for their money back. **Is this ethical?** The U.S. Magnuson-Moss Warranty Act, however, does not allow for a manufacturer to disclaim implied warranties by virtue of restrictions written into the express warranty. But this legislation does permit the seller to limit the express warranty to a specific time period. The key point, though, is that the fitness for intended purpose, including the fundamental safety of the product, can never be renounced.

Product Liability Law

The law of warranties suggests a product's performance will be of a certain basic quality. However, additional protections are afforded to the consumer if a product does *not* perform as intended, to the extent that the consumers (or users, passengers, etc.) are injured or economically disadvantaged by this product failure. Such protection stems from the law of torts.[2] *Tort law* consists of principles developed as part of common law; it is fundamentally rooted in the *theory of negligence.* See Exhibit 3-1 for a more complete discussion of negligence.

The theory of *strict liability* was established and adopted in the 1960s by many states. It is now applied, in varying degrees, throughout the United States. This has placed a higher burden of responsibility upon the seller as a firm may be held liable for injuries caused by its product if it was in defective condition and unreasonably dangerous. The fact that the seller knew in

EXHIBIT 3-1   **Negligence: Legal and Ethical Implications**

Negligence is a central component of tort law. As the word suggests, negligence involves a type of ethical neglect, specifically neglecting one's duty to exercise reasonable care not to harm other people. . . . What duties, exactly, do producers owe to consumers?

One can think of possible answers to this question as falling along a continuum. On one extreme is the contractarian answer: Producers owe only those things promised to consumers in the sales agreement. At the other extreme is something closer to strict liability: Producers owe compensation to consumers for any harms caused by their products. In between these extremes are a range of answers that vary with different interpretations of negligence. We have already suggested why the strict contractarian approach is not convincing. . . .

Negligence can be characterized as a failure to exercise reasonable care or ordinary vigilance that results in an injury to another. . . . People have done an ethical wrong when they cause harm to others in ways that they can reasonably be expected to have avoided. Negligence includes acts of both commission and omission. One can be negligent by doing something that one ought not (e.g., speeding in a school zone) or by failing to do something that one ought to have done (e.g., neglecting to inspect a product before sending it to market).

Consider a case that received a good deal of media attention a few years ago. In 1992 a 70-year-old women was severely burned when a cup of coffee she had just purchased at a McDonald's drive-through window spilled on her lap. She apparently held the cup between her legs and tried to pry off the lid as she drove away. The coffee was hot enough (185 degrees) to cause third-degree burns which required skin grafts and long-term medical care. A jury awarded this woman $2.86 million, $160,000 for compensatory damages and $2.7 million in punitive damages.   **Should McDonald's be held liable for these injuries?**

Source: Joseph DeJardins, *An Introduction to Business Ethics* (New York: McGraw-Hill, 2003), 143.

---

advance that the product was dangerous does *not* have to be established. The development of theory of strict liability has ushered in an era of major customer litigation against manufacturers. As the burden of proof on plaintiffs was reduced, both the number of suits against manufacturers and the size of damage awards to injured parties has increased dramatically. Of special note have been some spectacular cases involving products alleged to have caused serious and permanent injury to many consumers. During 2000–2001, Ford Motor Company and Firestone were subjects of numerous lawsuits attributing injuries and deaths from rollover accidents to Explorer sport utility vehicles equipped with Avenger and Wilderness tires.

Many corporations have responded by purchasing product liability insurance. After several large damage awards, however, the insurance premiums became so high in some industries (e.g., athletic equipment such as football helmets) that this form of protection is either unaffordable or has dramatically increased the cost of the product and, accordingly, the price charged to all consumers. Companies that continue producing these products knowingly become higher risk economic endeavors. Business organizations were, thus, put on notice that if they marketed unsafe products which cause injury, courts are likely to award damages (possibly including punitive damages) that could substantially impact the organization's financial position.

Regulation by Federal Agencies

The federal government also regulates many products to ensure their safety, quality, and performance. In the United States, this oversight is provided by various agencies with jurisdiction over different product categories. These include the *Consumer Product Safety Commission, Food and Drug Administration, Department of Justice, Department of Agriculture,* and *Department of Transportation.* Brief sketches of the responsibilities of these agencies are provided below.

The **U.S. Consumer Product Safety Commission** (CPSC) is the agency with the strongest and most encompassing mandate to oversee product safety. Established by Congress in 1972, this independent regulatory commission was charged to protect the public from unreasonable risks associated with consumer products (except automobiles, alcohol, tobacco, firearms and prescription drugs, regulated by other agencies as noted below). The commission also (a) develops product safety standards, (b) conducts research on products that have led to injury, illness, or death, and (c) takes other needed steps to assist consumers in making product safety evaluations. Other safety-related legislation passed earlier was also placed under CPSC jurisdiction, for example, the Flammable Fabrics Act and the Federal Hazardous Substance Act, regulating products such as fireworks. To date, safety standards have been written for such products as power lawnmowers, bicycles, and match books. The commission also has the power to order manufacturers to disclose product testing information, to secure company files related to consumer injuries and/or complaints, and to order products withdrawn from the market. An example of the CPSC in action is presented in Exhibit 3-2.

The **United States Department of Agriculture** (USDA) oversees agricultural products, including meat, poultry, eggs, fruits, and vegetables. The agency has the right to inspect manufacturing and processing facilities as well as take action against manufacturers and distributors when such

EXHIBIT 3-2   All-Terrain Vehicles

A product category that has attracted significant recent attention is all-terrain vehicles (ATVs), small motorized vehicles with wide tires that people ride "off road" for fun and recreation. The product is potentially dangerous because ATVs are regularly driven over rough terrain in areas with no enforceable operating rules (a fact that also endangers the natural environment of wilderness areas where ATV usage is common). Many riders, especially youths, suffer injuries such as paralysis or even death when ATVs crash or roll over.

Designed in the late 1960s by Honda, ATVs were introduced in the United States in the early 70s. The first ATV was designed in a three-wheel tricycle-like configuration, the standard design until the late 1980s. Shortly after Honda's first ATV was released, other manufacturers introduced competing vehicles. Unfortunately, the increased popularity of the vehicles brought an alarming number of accidents, prompting the United States Consumer Product Safety Commission (CPSC) to launch an investigation into their safety. In 1986 the CPSC issued a report in which the agency determined that there were approximately 2.4 million ATVs in use in the United States—and that nearly 600 deaths and over 239,000 injuries were associated with their use. Shortly after the CPSC report was issued, the U.S. Justice Department filed a lawsuit alleging that ATVs and their manufacturers violated the Consumer Product Safety Act. In 1987, the various ATV manufacturers agreed to discontinue producing "three-wheelers" as expert testimony had identified the three-wheel ATV design as one of the primary flaws of the original ATVs (but did not require manufacturers to recall the 2.4 million in use). Today's ATVs are manufactured utilizing a four-wheel design that helps stabilize the vehicle. Recently, the CPSC ordered recalls for twelve different models of ATVs, involving six manufacturers, alleging a variety of safety-related defects, and a number of states have developed licensing requirements limiting use to operators over sixteen years old.

Source: http://www.cpsc.gov/cgi-bin/recalldb/model.asp. Accessed July 15, 2003.

products are judged to be adulterated. The USDA also administers a voluntary "grading system" for these regulated products, which is used for many meat, poultry, and dairy products.

The **Food and Drug Administration** (FDA) is responsible for overseeing drugs, medical devices, and cosmetics. The central responsibilities of the FDA is to approve new drugs and applications, to monitor quality controls at pharmaceutical manufacturing plants, and to certify drugs as being "safe and effective" based on clinical tests. The length of this certification process and the requirements to establish such safety have been a source of controversy in recent years with pharmaceutical firms charging the drawn-out process stifles new product innovation and increases the cost of bringing new medications to market, with significant pricing implications. The FDA also oversees the safety of drugs, cosmetics, and nonprescription medical devices. If it finds these products create an unreasonable risk of harm to the consumer, the FDA has the ability to seize the products via a court order.

The **Department of Justice** (DOJ) now has jurisdiction for alcohol, to-bacco, and firearm products (ATF—www.atf.gov). Its unique responsibilities include protecting the public and reducing violent crime. ATF enforces the federal laws and regulations relating to alcohol and tobacco diversion, firearms, explosives, and arson. (Until late 2002, ATF was a law enforcement agency within the U.S. Department of the Treasury. The revenue collection function was retained while the ATF functions were moved to DOJ as part of the Homeland Security Act of 2002.) These products raise a number of ethical and social questions, and some of these aspects are treated later in this chapter.

The **Department of Transportation** (DOT) is charged with regulating automobile safety in the United States. A DOT subsidiary, the **National Highway Traffic and Safety Administration** (NHTSA), conducts the much publicized "crash testing" program that results in guidelines for injury-reducing automobile design. For example, automobile bumpers must pre-vent certain levels of damage at prespecified crash speeds.

NHTSA has jurisdiction over the controversial issue of rollovers for sport utility vehicles (SUVs). One issue being debated is roof testing. A U.S. estimate is that roof crush is a factor in 26 percent of the rollover deaths and injuries (over 26,000) with about 3,700 of these people wearing seat belts. Europe has mandated stricter tests than the United States (See Exhibit 3-3 for details.) European affiliates of the big three U.S. auto makers—GM's Saab, Ford's Volvo, and Daimler Chrysler's Mercedes Benz—subject their vehicles to tougher roof tests because they say the benefits are clear.[3]

The size of vehicles involved in crashes is another concern of NHTSA. Some auto industry advocates and consumers claim larger SUVs and pickup trucks are safer than most cars. Size does matter when really big vehicles crash into much smaller ones. However, "new studies show not only that drivers of pickups and SUVs are killed at a higher rate than drivers in, say, Toyota Camrys, but also that a higher mileage fleet could actually reduce overall deaths."[4] According to experts, it is technically feasible and poten-tially economical to improve fuel economy without reducing vehicle weight and size. Another positive safety development is the trend to making lower riding SUVs and pickups.

Based on the existence of express and implied warranties, product lia-bility law, and the various federal product category oversights, we conclude that product safety is guaranteed by law in addition to being an ethical

Exhibit 3-3 How United States and European Auto Roof Tests Differ

U.S. government-mandated tests:

- Require only a "static" test in which pressure is forced downward by a metal plate at a 25 percent angle along the roofline. Critics say the load forces are too low and the angle too narrow to replicate the sideways force on a roof in a rollover.
- Examine a vehicle with the windshield in, though critics say that in real-world rollovers windshields often break out, which they say reduces the strength of the roof support by as much as 40 percent.
- Apply only to vehicles with a gross weight of up to 6,000 pounds, which excludes the heaviest SUVs.
- Don't require crash-test dummies, so occupant-protection measures are not evaluated.

Voluntary steps used by European auto makers:

- Dynamic tests in which a vehicle is dropped or rolled over. Volvo hurls vehicles off moving dolly; Mercedes-Benz hoists them upside down and drops them. A Saab test simulates a head-on collision with a moose.
- Some dynamic tests include crash-test dummies.
- Use stiffer materials on roofs and roof-support pillars so they resist crushing. Volvo uses boron pillars in its new SUV. Mercedes uses a boron tube in the pillar of its new E-Class sedan.

Source: Milo Geyelin and Jeffrey Ball, "How Rugged Is Your Car's Roof?" *Wall Street Journal,* March 4, 2002, B1.

responsibility. Still, there remain ethical questions regarding safety that must be asked:

- How safe should a product be?
- How safe is safe enough?

For example, studies have shown that air bags save lives in automobile crash tests, but consumers were often unwilling to incur the extra cost to voluntarily equip their new car with airbags beyond those mandated by law. (Even after all automobiles had seat belts, it took legislation in most states requiring their usage to get even a majority of consumers to comply.) Of course, the airbag question is further complicated by the record of injuries of small children associated with the deployment of these devices. Since 1990, virtually all car and truck models are equipped with driver and front passenger air bags as standard equipment. Early in the twenty-first century, the debate regarding this device was mostly over whether to install rear seat and side airbags and under what circumstances these may be disengaged. A current safety issue is the placement and crash resistance of auto, SUV and truck bumpers. Should these manufacturers be required to have stronger and similar weight bumpers on all vehicles? Thus far, attempts to answer such questions have used mostly utilitarian type analyses, that is, weighing costs of additional safety features against the number of deaths and injuries expected to be prevented. **Can you think of other examples where product safety issues may not be covered adequately by current regulations?**

PRODUCT COUNTERFEITING

Product counterfeiting involves the unauthorized copying of patented products, inventions, and trademarks or the violation of registered copyrights, for example, manufacturing look-alike branded products of market leaders. While often discussed as an unethical product practice, many forms of product counterfeiting are an outright violation of U.S. and other governments' laws. Counterfeiting has become a major concern to American businesses as bogus products cost legitimate organizations $450 billion worldwide each year in lost sales. In 2002, the International Anti-Counterfeiting Coalition estimated that 750,000 U.S. jobs have been eliminated because of these foreign-made counterfeit products.[5] Among the many products copied are medical equipment, auto parts, compact disks, sunglasses, basketball shoes, liquor, and various pharmaceutical products. Some of the more sensational examples of product counterfeits are Rolex watches (readily available in East Asian and Mexican markets), knock-off Levi jeans (especially popular in Eastern Europe), and illegally pirated video- and audiotapes (China).

Product counterfeiting is unethical and (in most of the world, including the United States) illegal. Why? Because it amounts to one company's attempt to capitalize on the goodwill the originating company has generated for its own branded product via product quality and advertising; in effect, it is theft. The key ethical issue is: When does imitating the design, packaging, or other brand images violate patents and/or confuse the consumer? When such knockoffs steal sales, market acceptance, and profits from the original product producers, damages are incurred by the originator and transferred to the imitator with neither compensation nor permission. In response to such practices, the brand name, known as a *trademark*, has been given specific legal protection. Brands are especially important to the firm, because they provide a shorthand device for customers to identify and recall the attributes of a particular product offering. Internationally recognized brand names such as Pizza Hut, Coca-Cola, Nike, Volkswagen, and Sony convey quality and dependability the product counterfeiter hopes to exploit.

A *trademark*, according to the Lanham Act of 1946, is defined as any "word, name, symbol, device, or any combination thereof adapted and used by the manufacturer or merchant to identify his goods and distinguish them from those manufactured by others."[6] Trademarks (or brand names) can be registered in law, and such action provides certain legal rights. Those rights increase after the trademark has been used in commerce for five consecutive years, thereby preempting the practice of simply having organizations secure the rights to names that they will not use. The key clause of the Lanham Act, section 43(a), also protects brand and packaging images that the public has come to identify with a single source. For example, McDonald's golden arches and the Mercedes logo would be protected under this clause. Because of wide-scale counterfeiting emanating from foreign markets, Congress passed the 1984 Trademark Counterfeiting Act, which provides for steep penalties (up to a quarter of a million dollars and five years in prison) for those who knowingly traffic in counterfeit products. It also allows plaintiffs to sue for triple the damages or an amount equal to the profits the counterfeiter has made from the illegal product (whichever is greater).

As suggested earlier, much of counterfeiting today relates to international producers, based in developing countries, that either do not recognize patents or copyrights or fail to enforce them by imitating well-advertised U.S., European, and Japanese brands. For example, when Yao Ming (the 7'6" Chinese basketball player) signed with the Houston Rockets, he also entered into a contract with Nike. The firm's Yao shoe retails for $125 in China, but down the street from the store in Beijing, a knockoff pair of "Nike" shoes goes for $31.[7]

A specific form of counterfeiting is the competitor making its product appear similar to the known brand by duplicating packaging, colors, or shapes. For instance, in Europe a supermarket chain introduced its store brand "Fizz Up" lemon-lime soft drink in a green can. A similar tactic was taken by two other retailers who introduced American Cola and Classic Cola in red cans with "cola" written in script similar to Coca-Cola. The copyright law seems to indicate that these practices are legal in Europe, **but are they ethical?**

Legal protection for trademarks is somewhat better within domestic markets. Current legal interpretations of the Lanham Act now assist manufacturers in establishing their investments in product and market development and branding without having to prove another organization intended to deceive the consumer. This makes it somewhat easier for marketers to protect their trademark rights. Since trademark law is such a complicated area, marketing managers are well advised to seek intellectual property counsel when attempting to establish brand rights and protect their brand development investments from violations by other sellers. However, litigation is expensive, damages are difficult to establish, and outcomes never certain. Moreover, a casual tour of drugstore and supermarket aisles in the United States will disclose many examples of "knockoff" products by the package color and shape, that is, private and secondary brands taking advantage of demand generated by others. Irrespective of the legal environment of trademark protection, product counterfeiting obviously remains an important ethical issue in marketing.[8]

SOCIALLY CONTROVERSIAL PRODUCTS

Many consumers question the social value of certain categories of products such as cigarettes, alcoholic beverages, and firearms. Marketing Professor Kirk Davidson added gambling and pornography to this list in his book on "sin" products.[9] The most strident critics of these products maintain they should not even be permitted to be sold to the general public. Other, less severe critics feel that the inherent danger associated with certain products calls for restrictions concerning their marketing. The nature of commodities such as tobacco and alcohol seems to require special responsibilities by marketers.

Cigarettes

The (legal) product receiving the greatest amount of criticism concerning its social utility is surely cigarettes. Other tobacco products (e.g., chewing tobacco and cigars) have also fallen under this judgmental cloud. Cigarettes are different from other socially questionable products, because it seems that, based on scientific evidence, cigarettes cause damage to users' health *when they are used as intended.* In addition, secondhand smoke appears to affect the health of others—coworkers, family members, and servers in eating and drinking places, who cannot avoid it. This situation differs from the circumstances associated with the use of alcoholic beverages and firearms (for hunting and target shooting) where the negative impact generally occurs with abuse or misuse.

Should cigarettes be banned? Both sides of this controversy have made impassioned pleas defending their positions. The six largest tobacco companies spent over $11 billion in 2001 on the advertising and promotion of their products in the United States alone. Since 1970, when cigarette advertising was banned from U.S. television, national advertising for tobacco products has increased from $64 million to over $358 million in 2001.[10] In addition, huge amounts of money were shifted to billboard advertising, sales promotions (including the *free* distribution of new brand samples—now prohibited), and sponsorships of sporting and entertainment events (also no longer permitted). Another recent marketing development is the addition of new "discount" cigarette sales outlets in some markets.

The U.S. Public Health Service estimates cigarette-related deaths in this country at about 350,000 per year,[11] more than the total number of Americans who die annually in automobile accidents and by fire, murder, and suicide combined. (This statistic is a good example of the consequences "C" from the ABCs discussed in Chapter 1.) Direct medical costs resulting from smoking-related illnesses are estimated at $22 billion a year, excluding problems caused by secondary smoke inhalation. Canadian Marketing Professor Rick Pollay has been particularly critical of cigarette advertising over the years, both because of its health-oriented content in the past ("Got a cold? Smoke Kools?" and "Nine out of ten doctors smoke Camels") and its apparent targeting to younger people[12] and minority groups.[13] Yet the Tobacco Institute (the trade association and lobbyist group for the manufacturers), which also claims the mortality rate from smoking is only somewhat more than 200,000 per year, argues cigarette advertising should not be banned because it does not cause smoking any more than soap causes people to bathe or detergent advertising causes people to wash their clothes. The institute insists tobacco promotion is quite appropriate as it consists of information disseminated about a *legal* product and is protected under the First (Freedom of Speech) Amendment to the U.S. Constitution.

However, the constitutional protection of commercial speech may not be as complete as the tobacco industry insists. In 1980, the Supreme Court (in the *Central Hudson* case) ruled that commercial speech can be restricted when it affects a substantial government interest and the intervention is not more restrictive than necessary.[14] The health and medical costs to society apparently resulting from cigarette smoking appear to constitute a "substantial interest." Furthermore, a promotional ban on cigarettes probably causes fewer complications than completely outlawing the product. Thus, a complete advertising ban may be legally justifiable in the United States. Canada, Sweden, New Zealand, and, most recently, the European Union have comprehensive promotional restrictions, and the United Kingdom has now banned all cigarette advertising. The World Health Organization proposed a "tobacco control treaty" that will clamp down on tobacco advertising and sponsorship, require prominent health warnings on cigarette packets, and promote tough measures on passive smoking, tobacco taxes, labeling, and smuggling.[15]

Because the most controversial issue is the targeting of promotion to young people, that is, encouraging socially vulnerable nonsmokers to take up a destructive habit, efforts to ban copy and media most likely to include youthful audiences may be most acceptable in the current public policy climate. **Do you recall the controversy over "Joe Camel"?** (He was more recognizable to a six-year-old than Mickey Mouse in the early 90s, and R. J. Reynolds stopped using the character in 1997.)[16]

The argument for restricting tobacco advertising can also be made from an ethical perspective. Recall our discussion in Chapter 1 of duty-based ethics. One could argue that restrictions on tobacco manufacturing and promotion are appropriate because of failure by tobacco producers to exercise their *duty to investigate* and their *duty to inform*.[17] Several major advertising agencies that have cigarette accounts allow employees who have philosophical objections to remove themselves from working on promotional campaigns for tobacco products. Exhibit 3-4 tells the story of arguably the most memorable (and effective) advertising campaign for a single cigarette.

Specifically, with regard to the *duty to investigate,* one can argue businesses have a responsibility for the consequences of using their products. The outcomes of cigarette smoking should have led tobacco manufacturers to realize the damage inflicted on users and society by continued production and promotion of this product. Various attempts by cigarette manufacturers to reduce tar and nicotine and even to produce smokeless or "safer" cigarettes indicate recognition of the hazards inherent in their products. Similarly, the *duty to inform* evokes the obligation that business organizations make known any potential risks to product users. Tobacco manufacturers, of course, would argue that the warning labels on cigarette packages meet this obligation. From the public policy perspective, one would argue that society has the *duty to interdict* when a firm has failed to exercise its obligations. It is then that the social institution (i.e., government) overseeing the subsidiary institution (i.e., business) should exercise its option to intervene.

A final footnote to this discussion relates to aggressive moves by the tobacco industry, in the face of mounting public controversy in North America, to market their products overseas, especially in less developed nations where legal restrictions are fundamentally weak.   **Is this ethical?**

Alcohol Products

Marketers of alcoholic beverages are not as vulnerable as tobacco manufacturers, because it is the *abuse* rather than the *use* of alcoholic beverages that seems to be associated with most problems. Alcohol-related illnesses and accidents caused by drunk drivers remain a major public concern, but these problems flow from some users' inability to control their alcohol consumption, possibly because of addiction. A troubling recent trend is the rise in "binge" drinking both by students and other consumers. The general controversy, however, has not been lost on marketers of alcoholic beverages. Bacardi Rum has advertised itself as the spirit that mixes with everything—except driving. Anheuser-Busch, the largest brewer in the United States, has had a long-running advertising campaign with the theme line "Know when to say when." Miller Brewing (now part of South Africa Distillers and Brewers) once launched a "think before you drink" advertising campaign. Most major brewers now have nonalcoholic beers in their product portfolio. Diageo, the British company and world's leading spirits marketer, announced that it will voluntarily provide U.S. consumers with information on alcohol content, serving size, macronutrients, carbohydrates, and calories for its products.[18]

EXHIBIT 3-4   **Excerpt from "Marlboro Mirage" Chapter in** *Ashes*
to Ashes

Thirty years later, even though restricted by law to print media only, "Marlboro Country" survived as one of the longest-running and most successful advertising campaigns ever devised. Its enduring appeal was an overworked metaphor that generated its resonating power in direct proportion to the distance from the reality in which most smokers dwelled and by the passionate attention to deal with which the imagery was rendered. "Marlboro Country" seemed to beckon Americans to an earlier, simpler, morally unambiguous time, to the frontier irretrievably lost to the encroachment of thronged modernity. In the final third of the twentieth century, the nation too often found its cities increasingly blighted and violent, its suburbs sterile and conformist, its offices glazed and hermetic boxes, its work programmed and dehumanizing, its government inept when not corrupt, its faith bereft of nobler instincts, and life in general more alienating than fulfilling. . . . "Marlboro Country" transported them past smug suburbia and the cloying sweetness of Norman Rockwell's small towns, out beyond the tidy Arcadia and pastoral prettiness pictured in the Salem and Newport ads, to an immense, indeed limitless, landscape, awesome in its rugged yet serene beauty, where the menaces of nature were ultimately manageable, the mountain streams pure, the chuckwagon fare hearty and unfattening, and the skies were not sooty all day. . . .

And there was the correlative appeal of the Marlboro cowboy himself, as far a cry as possible from Woody Allen with all his urban hang-ups and psychic dysfunction. This ultimate Marlboro Man was a throwback hero, strong, stoic, self-reliant, free (though not without responsibilities), potent—the kind of man women are drawn to—and he never punched a time clock. He was capable of both repose, kneeling pensively beside a campfire, say, while drawing on his smoke with satisfaction, and of action gracefully executed, whether shown heading up a canyon after a thirty-mile ride shaking cattle out of the mesquite, scattering a threatened stampede, or just lugging his saddle past the corral gate. And he was classless, purposely neither a boss nor a hand, though his white hat, confident gait, and effortless handling of his mount tagged him as a leader and no grubby bunkhouse malingerer. He was also an apolitical man of peace who was never armed and had no enemies, a knight errant patrolling his craggy Eden and embodying what Frederick Jackson Turner had termed in writing of the frontiersman, "that dominant individualism . . . that buoyancy and exuberance which comes with freedom." **What is your view of the ethical implications of the Marlboro Man?**

Source: Richard Kluger, *Ashes to Ashes* (New York: Knopf, 1996), 294–97.

The Wine Institute (www.wineinstitute.org) has had a long-standing code and position against targeting underage drinkers. Social pressures to restrict alcoholic beverage advertising have also increased in recent years. For example, the current National Collegiate Athletic Association college football contract restricts the percentage of TV commercials for beer and wine shown during telecasts. Perhaps the most significant development has been the recent precedent-setting legislation requiring warning labels on alcoholic beverages:

> Government Warning: (1) According to the Surgeon General, women should not drink alcoholic beverages during pregnancy because of the risk of birth defects. (2) Consumption of alcoholic beverages impairs your ability to drive a car or operate machinery, and may cause health problems.

Because of the nature of alcoholic beverages as compared with tobacco products, it might be argued that alcoholic beverage marketers are meeting their responsibilities to investigate and inform. Perhaps they have done so reluctantly and only for economic reasons. For example, questions have been raised about the continued production of certain cheap fortified wines that primarily appeal to the street-person alcoholic and the underage drinker. Furthermore, judging from magazine and billboard ads, a disproportionate amount of liquor advertising seems to be targeted at blacks, judging from magazine ads and city billboard placements. Blatant sex appeal and party atmosphere advertising (examined later in the book) also continue to cause controversy for the beer industry.

Environmentally Incompatible Products

Another illustration of negative social consequences is products that create problems for the physical or natural environment. Examples are (a) packaging that is not biodegradable and causes long-term landfill problems; (b) products that use scarce resources such as forest products, for example, paper, or require substantial resource consumption such as large sport utility vehicles that have unusually low fuel mileage; (c) various chemicals and detergents useful for processing or cleaning but that pollute land, air, and groundwater when improperly disposed of; and (d) medical wastes, which sometimes have been dumped into oceans or lakes because the proper disposal of such material is difficult for the institutional user. Product packaging is an especially acute problem for ethical marketers.

The "disposable" lifestyle that many consumers have come to lead (disposable shavers, pens, cans, and even cameras) creates particularly severe waste-handling problems, a residue of convenience. The average American generates approximately four pounds of garbage a day of which 30 percent represents product packaging.[19] As marketers attempt to design products for more attractive display or more efficient handling and storage, they may replace environmentally compatible packaging (or no packaging at all) with less environmentally sensitive materials. Some examples are the polystyrene egg cartons, which replaced the old-fashioned (and easily recyclable) cardboard predecessor, and plastic milk cartons, which superseded waxed cardboard and reusable glass. A positive development is the recycling services (usually for a fee) that exist in most larger U.S. cities. **Does your family recycle? Why or why not?**

The fundamental issue here seems to be one of creating *externalities* (i.e., the cost of handling and disposing of product packaging or the long-run value of scarce resources that may be underpriced in the market) that are not paid for by the original producer or consumer. The stakeholder concept (discussed in Chapter 1) suggests external costs should be foreseen and either paid for or avoided, if that is more efficient, by the manufacturer and, ultimately, the consumer. An additional problem is that the environment is often a "silent" (except for environmental advocacy groups like the Sierra Club) stakeholder. While consumer packaging does not create the front-page headlines associated with major oil spills, the environmental impact of product packaging and disposal has become a significant public policy issue. For example, several states have considered banning the disposal of diapers made with plastic in landfills. And the Federal Trade Commission has asked for information from several companies substantiating the biodegradability claims regarding such products as plastic trash bags (www.ftc.gov). Growing sensitivity to ecological concerns a decade ago prompted consumer groups to call upon U.S. corporations to embrace the Valdez principles (named after the 1989 Alaskan oil spill).[20] They are now known as the CERES principles which encompass the adoption of an ecological ethic that spans product design, use, and disposal. (These principles are listed in Exhibit 3-5.) Organizations such as Wal-Mart, 3M, and McDonald's have made the environmental compatibility of their operations the focus of advertising campaigns.

The practical difficulty of all of this is judging when product packaging is so environmentally incompatible as to require restraint by management. In the most extreme sense, all product packaging raises environmental questions, either because it must be disposed of or because it utilizes scarce resources. The issue then is determining what level of incompatibility are we as a society willing to tolerate? Such judgments have shifted over time. In recent years, communities have enacted bans on nonrecyclable plastics, required deposits on beverage containers, or mandated household organic and inorganic refuse to be separated. These moves typically follow utilitarian evaluation, that is, trade-offs among different cost effects and sources, but it is also accurate to observe that an increasing portion of the population has embraced environmental values. It now appears that *green marketing*, in terms of both design and materials and the truthfulness of claims, has become a major ethical development (see Exhibit 3-6).

EXHIBIT 3-5   **The Coalition for Environmentally Responsible Economies (CERES) Principles**

Protection of the Biosphere

We will reduce and make continual progress toward eliminating the release of any substance that may cause environmental damage to the air, water, or the earth or its inhabitants. We will safeguard all habitats affected by our operations and will protect open spaces and wilderness, while preserving biodiversity.

Sustainable Use of Natural Resources

We will make sustainable use of renewable natural resources, such as water, soils and forests. We will conserve non-renewable natural resources through efficient use and careful planning.

Reduction and Disposal of Wastes

We will reduce and where possible eliminate waste through source reduction and recycling. All waste will be handled and disposed of through safe and responsible methods.

Energy Conservation

We will conserve energy and improve the energy efficiency of our internal operations and of the goods and services we sell. We will make every effort to use environmentally safe and sustainable energy sources.

Risk Reduction

We will strive to minimize the environmental, health and safety risks to our employees and the communities in which we operate through safe technologies, facilities and operating procedures, and by being prepared for emergencies.

Safe Products and Services

We will reduce and where possible eliminate the use, manufacture or sale of products and services that cause environmental damage or health or safety hazards. We will inform our customers of the environmental impacts of our products or services and try to correct unsafe use.

Environmental Restoration

We will promptly and responsibly correct conditions we have caused that endanger health, safety or the environment. To the extent feasible, we will redress injuries we have caused to persons or damage we have caused to the environment and will restore the environment.

Informing the Public

We will inform, in a timely manner, everyone who may be affected by conditions caused by our company that might endanger health, safety or the environment. We will regularly seek advice and counsel through dialogue with persons in communities near our facilities. We will not take any action against employees for reporting dangerous incidents or conditions to management or to appropriate authorities.

Management Commitment

We will implement these Principles and sustain a process that ensures that the Board of Directors and Chief Executive Officer are fully informed about pertinent environmental issues and are fully responsible for environmental policy. In selecting our Board of Directors, we will consider demonstrated environmental commitment as a factor.

Audits and Reports

We will conduct an annual self-evaluation of our progress in implementing these Principles. We will support the timely creation of generally accepted environmental audit procedures. We will annually complete the CERES Report, which will be made available to the public.

Disclaimer

These Principles establish an environmental ethic with criteria by which investors and others can assess the environmental performance of companies. Companies that endorse these Principles pledge to go voluntarily beyond the requirements of the law. The terms "may" and "might" in Principles one and eight are not meant to encompass every imaginable consequence, no matter how remote. Rather, these Principles obligate endorsers to behave as prudent persons who are not governed by conflicting interests and who possess a strong commitment to environmental excellence and to human health and safety. These Principles are not intended to create new legal liabilities, expand existing rights or obligations, waive legal defenses or otherwise affect the legal position of any endorsing company, and are not intended to be used against an endorser in any legal proceeding for any purpose.

Source: www.ceres.org/our_work/principles.htm. Accessed January 8, 2004.

Planned Obsolescence

The term *planned obsolescence* generally refers to a manufacturer building a limited life into a product so that consumers need to replace it sooner than might reasonably be the case. While this topic is often evoked as a possible ethical issue for consumer goods, stiff competition and technological

Exhibit 3-6   "Green Marketing" Around the World[1]

Motivation

Why do companies adopt green marketing practices? Here are several reasons provided by an Australian author:[2]

- Firms perceive environmental marketing to be an opportunity that can be used to achieve its objectives.
- Organizations believe they have a moral obligation to be more socially responsible.
- Government bodies are forcing firms to become more responsible.
- Competitors' environmental activities pressure firms to change their marketing activities.
- Cost factors associated with waste disposal, or reductions in material usage, forces firms to modify their behavior.

Self-regulatory Programs

In addition to the CERES principles shown in Exhibit 3-5, over 30 voluntary programs on green marketing are in place worldwide. Among the most prominent are:

- **Green Seal**—an independent, nonprofit organization that strives to achieve a healthier and cleaner environment by identifying and promoting products and services that cause less toxic pollution and waste, conserve resources and habitats, and minimize global warming and ozone depletion. Green Seal issues a third party seal-of-approval to consumer products that "cause less harm to the environment than other similar products." The Green Seal is available to both U.S. and foreign companies. Since its inception in 1989, Green Seal has certified over 300 products of major companies.[3]
- **Germany's Blue Angel Program**—Germany introduced the Blue Angel program in 1977, making it the first country to implement a national environmental labeling program. The Blue Angel is a voluntary program, designed to allow companies to label the positive features of their products and services. The Blue Angel is a third-party certification program, and relies on information, motivation, and a commitment to the environment from both manufacturers and consumers. Today, approximately 3,700 products and services in 80 product categories bear the Blue Angel seal.[4]

Exemplary Corporate Green Marketing

- **Patagonia**—an outdoor clothing and equipment manufacturer based in Ventura, California. The company's statement of purpose states, "Patagonia exists as a business to inspire and implement solutions to the environmental crisis." At the core of Patagonia's environmental programs is their "1% For the Planet" program. Through this program, Patagonia donates 1 percent of sales, or 10 percent of pretax profits, whichever is greater, to the protection and restoration of the natural environment.[5]

- **Tom's of Maine**—founded in Kennebunk, Maine, by Tom and Kate Chappell in 1970, Tom's of Maine is the leading producer of safe, effective natural care products that work for consumers, the environment, and the community. Tom's products—such as toothpaste, mouthwash, soap, and deodorant—contain no artificial flavors, dyes, or sweeteners, are biodegradable, are packaged in earth-friendly ways, and are tested for safety without the use of animals. For example, its toothpaste comes in a recyclable aluminum tube inserted in a box made from 100 percent recycled cardboard and printed with soy-based inks.[6]
- **Interface**—this is a billion-dollar carpet manufacturer located in Atlanta, Georgia. The founder set out to make his corporation's 26 factories on four continents the world's first environmentally sustainable manufacturing enterprise. The actions they took were to recycle everything possible, release as few pollutants as possible, and sending nothing to landfill.[7]

Sources

[1]Adapted from Patrick E. Murphy and John Commiskey, "Green Consumer Marketing," Paper presented to European Society for Opinion and Marketing Research, May 2004, Berlin, Germany.

[2]Michael Polonsky, "An Introduction to Green Marketing," *Electronic Green Journal* http://egj.lib.uidaho.edu/egj02/polon01.html. Accessed January 6, 2004.

[3]www.greenseal.org. Accessed October 12, 2003.

[4]United States Environmental Protection Agency (1998), "Environmental Labeling Issues, Policies, and Practices Worldwide," B-153–159.

[5]www.patagonia.com.

[6]www.toms-of-maine.com.

[7]Charles Fishman, "Sustainable Growth-Interface, Inc.," in *Fast Company Reader Series: Business Ethics*, ed. Patrick E. Murphy, 47–51 (New York: John Wiley, 2004).

advances have generally lessened the impact of this practice, because there is no guarantee the consumer will again purchase the same brand from the original vendor. (However, the fact that competitive markets may drive certain innovations that are of questionable value raises an important issue in institutional ethics.) Such tactics may take place more often in the business-to-business sector. Product components would be the most likely candidate for such a practice. The availability of substitute items with a longer life and competitive pressures to cut user costs by increasing reliability argue against this practice. Thus, the issue of building technical obsolescence into a product is seldom a major concern, as the threat of competition along with the realization that this is not a wise business practice has usually eliminated any possible economic gain from such efforts. An exception to this conclusion, however, may arise with respect to single source suppliers. An example that has gained attention in recent years is the prospect that computer printer cartridges, generally supplied by the printer manufacturer, do not have the life that it is technically possible to provide. (A converse concern is that manufacturers may hold back new developments in order to protect investments in current product engineering and production facilities.)

A more controversial form of product obsolescence is sometimes referred to as *social (or fashion) product obsolescence.* This practice entails the strategy whereby marketers create brands or styles of products that are usually promoted with substantial upscale advertising. The idea is to position the product as "high status" to a particular (often affluent) segment of consumers. Examples that come to mind are fashion apparel and so-called "upscale" brands such as Rolex watches and Gucci handbags. After a time (often a single buying season), certain styles or models of these trendy brands are consciously replaced by newer versions that, in effect, socially outdate their predecessors. The closets of many consumers are filled with devalued merchandise and effectively wasted material that remain functional. There is probably an ethical *question* associated with this. At the same time, a reasonable response may be that such practices are not unethical because they are often driven by consumers' tastes and preferences.

The notion that people seek status and use the goods that they purchase to help them acquire it is an old idea. It was written about long ago by economists such as Thorstein Veblen who coined the term, "conspicuous consumption."[21] In a free-market economy, most persons see the creation and promotion of such status goods as an expression of consumer individuality that should not be subject to regulatory sanction. While one can question whether the society is better off because every ten years or so there is a shift from wide ties to thin or vice-versa in men's attire, pointing out exactly what damage occurs and to whom because of the existence of such fashion cycles is difficult. Rather, jobs are supported and the economy is more dynamic in offering opportunities for new vendors. Therefore, fashion obsolescence appears to be controversial but not inherently unethical.

Products in Poor Taste

This topic is particularly tricky, as some marketers are regularly accused of crossing the ethical line by selling products that are in poor taste. Illustrations of products that have been publicly pilloried include semipornographic greeting cards, novelties such as plastic excrement, and video games that seem to promote violence among children and teens.

One difficult ethical question, of course, is: who determines what constitutes bad taste? It depends on the audience involved. College students have a reputation for their wide latitude of acceptance in terms of their openmindedness—they are not easily offended. On the other hand, some religious fundamentalists are bothered by many products, including consumption of any alcohol or even coffee. Perhaps an ethical rule of thumb, consistent with duty-based ethics, would be that marketers should be extremely skeptical of any product that either panders to people's darker motivations or is directed at demeaning some group.

Part of the perceptual problem concerning certain products (e.g., feminine deodorant, condoms) is caused by the *spillover effect* of product promotion when the promotional message for a particular item reaches an unintended audience. An ethical solution to problems involving what constitutes *bad taste* can come from management itself or society at large.

Not-So-Healthy Foods

An obvious ethical concern in marketing is that consumers may be misled by some aspect of the marketing mix, for example, pricing, as discussed in the next chapter. Certain products are also open to criticism regarding deception or nondisclosure. In recent years, a heightened interest in health and nutrition has prompted some companies to offer products alleged to contribute to longer lives or an improved quality of life. Nutritional concerns have also put companies with products that are either high in fat or sugar on the defensive. While the prospect of promising more than what is delivered is a complaint that might be leveled at many consumer products, some examples are clearly more troublesome than others. For instance, as is true of many food processors, the Frito Lay division of Pepsico has introduced lower fat versions of its snack foods. However, critics argue the absolute amount of fat in these items is still rather high. As this book is being completed, "low carb" products are being heavily promoted. We suspect that ethical questions will follow this latest product development and promotion craze.

Companies sometimes use descriptive brand names. The use of the word "healthy," in particular (e.g., in "Healthy Choice"), is regulated by the U.S. Food and Drug Administration (FDA).[22] The FDA has guidelines about food content that companies must follow when they use the word in a brand name or a product description. Other words, however, which may connote power or efficacy, such as "force" or "miracle," for example, are less regulated or completely unregulated, allowing them to be used in ways that can mislead consumers.

Equally debatable are fast-food menus featuring product offerings containing high levels of fat, sugar, and/or sodium. Observers point out that a typical combo meal—a quarter-pound hamburger, fries, and shake—involves the consumer ingesting over 1,000 calories, 15 teaspoons of fat, 3 teaspoons of sugar, and 1,400 milligrams of sodium. This is the maximum amount of fat an average person should consume in a day, and some physicians contend current guidelines are already too high. **Are fast-food purveyors being unethical by not disclosing and publicizing the amount of salt, fat, etc.?** McDonald's and other fast food chains have developed healthier menu items (e.g., salads, baked potatoes, chicken breasts, and even "veggie burgers"). A suit brought in early 2003 by several New York overweight teenagers charged

McDonald's with contributing to their obesity. The judge threw out the case, stating that McDonald's was not directly responsible. However, this debate promises to continue. A *Fortune* cover story asked: "Is Fat the Next Tobacco?"[23]

As we discuss in Chapter 5 on advertising, there are legal thresholds that, when crossed, constitute product misrepresentation. However, ethical questions can involve products that do not violate any legal limits. Numerous promotions for weight-loss products, food supplements, and clinics fit this category. These ads often feature very attractive, incredibly fit, young men and women, implying that users of the featured products and equipment can easily shape their own physiques to such dimensions. **Can you think of any other examples of products or services that imply results that few, if any, will attain?**

When do products cross the ethical line and become inherently misleading? Certainly, when products are deceptive to a majority of consumers they cross the line. An example is *slack packaging,* selling product in only partially filled containers. This practice leads most consumers to conclude they are receiving more product than they actually do. Some snack and cereal manufacturers have long been accused of using this technique (i.e., not filling the box completely). This practice is partially explained by material "settling" after the package has been filled. General Mills has wrestled with the fill rate issue and has developed corporate policies to alleviate this problem. A more dubious variation of slack packaging would be coffee manufacturers who sell their product in standard one-pound coffee tins, which are filled with only twelve or thirteen ounces of ground coffee. They contend new roasting methods allow consumers to brew as many cups with thirteen ounces as they previously brewed with sixteen. Is this an acceptable ethical defense?

ETHICAL BRANDING CONCERNS[24]

Together with other elements of the marketing mix, decisions about product quality affect brand equity.[25] Not surprisingly, then, several *brand management* issues fall within marketing ethics. International gray marketing and counterfeiting, the marketing of potentially harmful branded products, and using fear in brand advertising are all branding ethics issues, although they have been examined under other topics, both in this text and elsewhere.

Certain other issues can best be classified under branding ethics. These are issues where the desire to grow or defend brand equity is the primary cause of the issue at hand. Examples include breaking brand promises, abusing brands' ability to create meaning, emphasizing nonsignificant differences between brands, using misleadingly suggestive brand names (as with "healthy," etc., discussed previously), and engaging in questionable behavior in defense of a brand's reputation.

Breaking Brand Promises

The phrase "a brand is a promise" is a common one among marketing practitioners.[26] A brand's identity is made up of a series of brand associations; these can be considered to be a set of promises that the firm makes to current and prospective customers. For example, Volvo's brand associations include leader in safety and security, world-class quality, leadership in environmental care, attractive and distinctive design, pleasure to drive, pleasure to own, and maximized perceived value. Each of these associations can be interpreted as a promise. In the first, Volvo promises a car that is a leader in safety and security. In the second, the company promises world-class quality. In the third, they promise to be among the leaders in environmental care.

When companies take actions that are contrary to their brand identity, they are in breaking a brand promise. Nike's "Just Do It" positioning, for example, suggests brand associations of freedom and personal fulfillment. The Nike brand could therefore be interpreted as promising a contribution toward freedom and personal fulfillment. During the 1990s, Nike as a company was accused of employing child labor in sweatshops and faced a hostile response from consumers.[27] A sweatshop environment is not one that is particularly conducive to personal fulfillment. The intensity of consumers' reactions to such allegations is therefore understandable if Nike is being held to the standards of freedom and self-determination that it appears to be adopting and promoting in its brand associations. In such circumstances, Nike is seen to be breaking a promise.

"A Diamond is Forever," the famous slogan of De Beers diamonds, connotes a promise of persistence or constancy. The product itself creates expectations of beauty. And yet the promises of constancy and beauty stand in sharp opposition to the sometimes shady and violent history of the diamond industry and particularly the role of "conflict diamonds" in fueling civil wars in various African countries.[28] So much so that the De Beers company has attempted to associate its brand with "conflict free" diamonds. It has even gone so far as to create a new firm, a joint venture with the luxury goods firm LMVH, and transfer the De Beers brand name to it. This new firm is responsible for all selling and marketing of diamonds, while the original firm concentrates only on mining.

Abusing Brands' Powers of Meaning Creation

Successful brands offer a combination of functional, emotional, and self-expressive benefits. Emotional and self-expressive benefits tend to be more effective at differentiating brands than functional benefits. Yet they are also more open to abuse, because emotional and self-expressive benefits can serve as meaning creators and validators attempting to fulfill consumers' deeper psychological and spiritual needs. Ethical issues arise when companies do not accept responsibility for the kind of meaning that is created. For example, personalities in the "gangsta rap" music genre are important brands for the major music publishers, and at one time the profits from this genre were credited with the salvation of the music business.[29] Yet such brands promote a "meaning" to life that involves, among other things, drugs and gang rape. It is unlikely that the managers of the music publishing companies in question subscribe to this meaning of life, or think it would be good for anyone else to subscribe to it. Therefore, a question has to be raised as to whether they should be supporting it via the brand message being promoted.

Questionable Behavior in Defense of the Brand's Reputation

Some companies engage in unethical behavior in order to protect their brand reputation. For example, Disney has been accused of having a somewhat high incidence of child abuse committed by theme-park employees and of being particularly uncooperative with law enforcement officers investigating these incidents. Possibly the alleged lack of cooperation arises from a strong desire to avoid negative publicity that will be harmful to the brand.[30]

The use of cause-related marketing to promote a brand also creates ethical dilemmas when the brand's co-opting of the cause is so narrowly self-serving that it provides little or no benefit to the cause itself, except for some publicity of perhaps questionable value. For example, Philip Morris has been criticized for donating $60 million to charitable causes, at the same time spending an additional $100 million to advertise its charitable giving.[31]

Underlying Causes of Unethical Branding

The study of the ethics of branding is a very new one, although, as noted earlier, aspects of it have been studied previously. Most recently, brand management theory has been subjected to direct scrutiny so as to identify if there are aspects of that theory that predispose marketers to unethical action. For example, it has been argued that different approaches to defining and measuring brand equity can bias marketers toward more or less ethical actions.

Specifically, brand theorists argue whether a brand should be defined "additively," as something that is added to a product, or "inclusively," as something that *includes* the product. Yet the additive interpretation of brand, where the brand resides only in the minds of consumers and where the marketer's goal is to create perceptions far from the reality of what the brand is actually delivering, seems more likely to provoke unethical action than the inclusive interpretation, where perceptions and reality are kept more or less constant.

ETHICAL BRANDING PRACTICES

Despite a number of ethical issues raised about products in this chapter, recent years have witnessed several excellent U.S. and international branding practices that make integrity and ethics a central feature. As seen in the business scandals in 2001–2004, when trust in an organization or brand (e.g., Martha Stewart) erodes, the company is likely to experience serious financial consequences. Therefore, firms can use branding and consistent product quality to signal their position on ethical practices.

One illustration is Lego, the Danish "brick" maker. The company has leveraged its brand into new areas, and the Bionicle line is the company's best seller. Each Bionicle kit invites children to create a robot character out of packaged components. The company's brand heritage, grounded in family and ethical values, guides managerial actions. (See Exhibit 3-7 [a].)

A product that has had a 70-year history is the Zippo lighter. Its manufacturer offers a lifetime guarantee without disclaimers for its products. After conducting the needed repairs (and often putting the lighter into "mint" condition), Zippo includes a shiny penny encased in a silver emblem, the back of which reads: "The cent never spent to repair a Zippo product." Employees at the company not only repair over 130,000 lighters a year, but also look for other parts that may need attention and fix them too. The founders' motto is followed religiously at Zippo: "Build your product with integrity . . . stand behind it 100% and success will follow."[32]

A third example is a product introduced in 1999—Honest Tea. Its intrinsic benefits are a healthier, less-sweet beverage (only 9–17 calories per serving vs. 100 for Snapple) made from organic ingredients. The brand name signals a commitment to ethical practices. (In fact, the original brand name did not have a space in it [Honestea] but a threatened lawsuit by a large competitor caused the slight change.) The company philosophy is captured in the short paragraphs shown in Exhibit 3-7(b). Unfortunately, its current distribution is primarily limited to health food stores rather than the larger national supermarket chains; ethical branding sometimes limits markets.

ETHICAL PRODUCT MANAGEMENT

Most of the examples in the foregoing discussion are those where the practice examined is at least questionable on ethical grounds. To be sure, most expositions of applied ethics seem to focus on situations where avoidable harm is

Exhibit 3-7   Ethical Branding

Lego—Play Well

After burning its fingers in the late 1990s, staying true to Lego's brand heritage and founding philosophy is now a priority. But moving further into the software arena while protecting and nurturing its core, brick-based product ranges will require a careful balancing act.

So will staying true to the company's family values in sectors of the market where violent action games now rule. The company was founded by Ole Kirk Christiansen, a Danish carpenter and toy maker in 1932; its name comes from combining the first letters of the Danish words *leg godt*, meaning "play well."

"There are certain things our rivals do that we never would, for ethical reasons," Mr. Ciccolella (senior vice president of corporate development) insists. "Obviously we're not a charity, but profit is a nice side effect of doing things right. We will never compromise our values for the bottom line."[1]

Honest Tea

Honest Tea creates and promotes great tasting, truly healthy, all-natural beverages made the way their cultures of origin intended. We strive to grow our business with the same honesty and integrity we use to craft our products.

Social responsibility is central to Honest Tea's identity and purpose. Not only is the value of our brand based on authenticity, integrity, and purity, but our management team is committed to these values as well.

We will never claim to be a perfect company, but we will address difficult issues and strive to be honest about our ability or inability to resolve them. We will strive to work with our suppliers to promote higher standards. We value diversity in the workplace and intend to become a visible presence in the communities where our products are sold. When presented with a purchasing decision between two financially comparable alternatives, we will attempt to choose the option that better addresses the needs of economically disadvantaged communities.[2]

Sources
[1]Meg Carter, "Building Blocks of Success," *Financial Times*, October 30, 2003, 8.
[2]Honest Tea company documents.

committed, promises are not kept, and profits are achieved at the unwitting expense of others. Yet numerous examples exist where product policies are the result of thoughtful consideration of consumer safety, care for the environment, good taste, and a scrupulous observation of obligations to competitors. And, while it is sometimes said that virtue is its own reward, the evidence is that many companies prosper *because* they project an image of integrity with respect to these values. As cited earlier in this chapter, Volvo automobiles come to mind with the idea of "safe car." Patagonia outerwear has become synonymous with environmental friendliness. **Can you think of other companies or brands whose market success has been based on ethical product policies?**

HOW TO EVALUATE ETHICS IN PRODUCT MANAGEMENT

Intent is an important factor in judging ethical behavior. For example, when marketers sell products as new that are actually used, there is an obvious intent to deceive buyers. Contemporary illustrations of this practice have included the sale of grand pianos and expensive women's apparel as new when they have actually been used. In the case of Scenario 1 heading this chapter, it is important to judge what the intent of Curry Management was when they selected the brand name HATSUI.

It must also be noted here that a legal interpretation of intent includes *foreseeability*. Irrespective of the *purpose* of a decision, if a prudent decision maker can predict a substantial portion of the target market may be misled, intent is established. This broadened definition of intent carries with it an obligation to actually assess how consumers will interpret a claim, implied or expressed, whenever such a claim might reasonably be considered as questionable on grounds of fact.

Next, the *means* or method used to implement a particular marketing program must also be ethically analyzed. For example, FDA regulations require food product labels to disclose the addition of the popular flavor enhancer monosodium glutamate (MSG) to any product because some medical studies link the substance to allergic reactions. However hydrolyzed vegetable protein (HVP), another natural flavoring, can also contain MSG in concentrations up to 40 percent and is unregulated. As a result, some food processors have circumvented a possible difficulty by using HVP as a flavoring *and* promoting their product as "containing no MSG." In such cases, the methods selected to "comply with the law" raise ethical questions. (Recall that one of the As in the ABCs is Above the Law.)

Third, *consequences* are also an important factor in judging when a product has been unethically managed. Consider the consumer shopping for rental cars to a particular destination. Most of the time, ads are a starting point for seeking out this product. The ads often promise low daily rates but, upon examination of the fine print on model availability, insurance and other costs, the final bill is much higher. Few consumers realize these additional costs until they actually engage in the purchase process. As a consequence of this tactic, the product actually available and purchased (and its price) frequently differs from that initially desired. Thus, despite meeting the technical requirement of disclosure, because of its consequences, this approach may be unethical. Scenario 2 at the beginning of this chapter presents another example. In this situation, it seems important to consider what the consequences of the wide-spread use of radar detectors would be for society.

IDEAS FOR ETHICAL MARKETING

How can marketing managers improve the level of ethical orientation of the product management process? *First, marketers should include a formal ethical analysis as part of their product development process.* Marketers have long subscribed to a specific analytical sequence as part of new product development. This usually begins with idea generation, followed by a sequence of screening activities: economic and business analysis, product development/evaluation (including engineering and manufacturing feasibility), test marketing, and, finally, rollout to the intended market. As part of this process, a specific ethical product analysis should be conducted. Among the questions to be asked would be the following:

- Is the product safe when used as intended?
- Is the product safe when misused in a way that is foreseeable?
- Have any competitors' patents or copyrights been violated?
- Is the product compatible with the physical environment? (Products that use scarce resources, pollute the environment, or are inherently hazardous should undergo special scrutiny. The CERES Principles shown earlier in Exhibit 3-5 could help this assessment.)
- Is the product environmentally compatible when disposed of? (Special consideration should be given to whether product packaging can be recycled or, at minimum, is biodegradable—though biodegradability is questionable given that conventional landfill practices inhibit or prevent degradability.)
- Will informed organizational stakeholders object to the product?

Second, product managers should provide sufficient product instructions as well as appropriate warning labels for all products they introduce and maintain in the marketplace. As noted earlier, the fundamental duties of the marketer include fully informing consumers of any risks associated with the product, how to protect themselves from such risks, and clarifying any potential misunderstandings about product performance. This affirmative approach actually benefits sellers by protecting them against some forms of product liability jeopardy. Exactly what information needs to be disclosed depends on the specific product category involved. In many cases, the average consumer may properly assume the appropriate function of the product. For example, most consumers realize power lawnmowers should not be used to trim hedges.

Nevertheless, the courts or society may hold the product's manufacturer to a higher standard. Thus, the amount of information disclosed should cover the product usage requirements of the majority of consumers, including, some would say, even the stupid and feeble minded. (As reported to the Consumer Product Safety Commission during its deliberations on lawn mower safety, at least one consumer believed using a power mower to trim hedges was proper after a few cocktails!)

Labels on packaged food products have received special attention because inflated health claims have been made about what is essentially junk food. For instance, granola cereals, which have a high sugar content and relatively low fiber, illustrate a product masquerading as a health food. The Food Labeling and Nutrition Act of 1990 included a specific listing of all major ingredients (with sugar and other sweeteners consolidated in a single section), a summary of nutritional information (specific calorie, fat, cholesterol, and sodium content), with restrictions when to specify the allowable usage of the words "light" and "natural." The FDA already had an informal policy requiring foods promoted as "light" to contain one-third fewer calories than regular product variations. Some of those recommendations were ultimately followed, and ingredient labeling is now the norm. However, whether the regulatory steps taken are sufficient to protect consumers remains a point of debate and provides room for ethical reasoning over and above simply observing the law.

Third, when problems occur with any product that endangers consumer safety, firms should be proactive in recalling the product from the market. There have been too many sad chronicles of organizations dragging their feet in product recalls when product dangers have obviously been exhibited. The defensive reaction of Firestone regarding their tires in Ford Explorers' rollover is a "classic" illustration of this phenomenon. The well-known example of the Tylenol recall in the early 80s, based on several consumer deaths that, as it turned out, were not the fault of the manufacturer, Johnson & Johnson, provides an example of outstanding care for consumers that ultimately benefited the company in terms of consumer confidence—and a dominant position in the market for analgesics.

Organizations that are serious about proactive product recalls need to develop effective mechanisms to reach dealers and consumers and provide proven "reverse channels of distribution." These guidelines should allow organizations to remove products from distribution outlets and to inform product users quickly, should the need arise. Such product removal policies will generally require contingency funds that allow the manufacturer to buy back all unused products (including promotional samples) and to subsidize distributors to help them issue warnings for potential product users when a product danger exists.

Fourth, just as organizations should have ethical standards for developing and introducing new products, there should also be specific ethical policies that apply to product elimination. Each year products disappear from the marketplace because their apparent usefulness or profitability has diminished. However, product elimination may cause hardships for some. Brand loyal consumers will miss a product withdrawn from the marketplace and, on occasion, actual medical dependency may be involved. Users reasonably expect replacement parts and repair services to be available while they own the product. Ethical considerations that should come into play in the course of product elimination are the following:

- Customers should be consulted with regard to their needs *prior* to the product elimination decision.
- Customers should be notified after the elimination decision has been made. There should be a reasonable period before the actual discontinuance of the product occurs.
- Companies should have a parts replacement policy that ensures availability for a reasonable time period. Replacement parts should be maintained by the organization for the expected usable life of products currently in the marketplace.

CONCLUDING COMMENT

In this chapter, a number of legal and ethical issues confronting product managers—product safety, obsolescence, socially controversial and environmentally damaging products—have been reviewed. (For another controversial product name issue, see Exhibit 3-8.) Realistically, there will always be some unethical marketing managers who will attempt to exploit products and customers unscrupulously to maximize financial gains, at least in the short run. But to those product managers concerned with maintaining a marketplace where competition among products is fair, we offer several ethical guidelines concerning new product development, product formation, product recall, and product elimination. As one writer has noted:

> Products are our shared human creations through which we interconnect our ideas, efforts, resources, and technologies as well as express our life concepts, lifestyles, and life-qualities. Every product is a complex of aspirations, expectations, experiences, expressions, and ethics. As such, ethics cannot be turned off and on throughout the product management process. Ethics is present always, and it always pervades. . . . Ethical product management is grounded in confronting this challenge with quality consciousness, deep commitment, and constant vigilance. Ethical product management emerges through each caring, serving, and wise product-market realization. It involves a heroic struggle masked in practical tensions.[33]

EXHIBIT 3-8   Should Sports Teams Change Their Names?

A marketing and branding issue arose in the last few years about the "moniker" that colleges and professional sports organizations had given their teams. The major force for their change was the Native American community. Some of its leaders felt that the names and mascots that teams employed demeaned the culture and background of Native Americans.

Several well-known colleges changed their names in the late 80s and early 90s (Marquette Warriors to Golden Eagles, St. John's Redmen to Red Storm, and the Eastern Michigan Hurons to Eagles—despite opposition from Michigan's Huron nation representatives). Pro teams using these names and mascots— Cleveland Indians, Atlanta Braves, and Washington Redskins—resisted the trend and their names continue today. **Do you think teams with Native American names should be changed?**

One of the most controversial debates occurred at the University of North Dakota with its "Fighting Sioux" nickname. Defenders of the name point out that the Sioux actually call themselves by that name (as opposed to a name like the Redskins). Its logo—a majestic Indian head logo—was actually designed by a Native American artist. One of the school's benefactors donated $104 million to build a new hockey arena (UND has one of the premier hockey programs in the United States). Protesters recoiled at the proposal to put several thousand Fighting Sioux inside the arena. They wanted the school to change its sports name, but the benefactor said he would pull his check if they did so. The school didn't, so the arena was built. Opponents viewed this decision as money winning out over principle. However, the excess revenue goes to the school to be spent on academic as well as other sports programs.

The professional sports area has not been totally insensitive to criticisms about names. The best known (and needed) name change occurred in 1996 when the Washington Bullets professional basketball team changed their name to the Wizards in response to the violence occurring in many cities. Although not a team, Converse, an athletic shoe maker, proposed the name for a new basketball shoe as "Run N Gun"—describing an upbeat style of play. The company was criticized because some of buyers of the shoes were young men who may think the company condones violence. The final name they selected appears equally effective: "Run N Slam."

This issue of sport teams and their names is likely to continue to generate some controversy in the future. **What is your view?**

Source: Partially adapted from Mark Yost, "A Team Named Sioux," *Wall Street Journal,* December 27, 2002, W9.

Chapter Four

Ethical Issues
in Distribution Channels
and Pricing

Scenario 1

Coca-Cola Corporation has "arguably the strongest and most pervasive marketing and distribution system in the world" according to Douglas Daft, then chairman and CEO. The Coke brand is served in over 200 nations, and over 9 million stores sell it. Overseas markets now account for two-thirds of the Atlanta-based firm's sales. Some of the relationships that Coke has built with foreign distributors caused the company's image to be tarnished because they have dealt with "relatives of dictators in the Middle East, Latin American bottlers who allegedly work with assassination squads and Marxist rebels in Colombia."

To keep posting respectable growth figures, pressure was felt by every division to keep volume increasing. One method of questionable marketing to distributors was to engage in "channel stuffing" in Japan and some other countries. Channel stuffing is the practice of overselling a channel member or distributor in order to meet a sales quota, revenue target, or to clear away old inventory. Incentives to members or coercion can allow the technique to be successfully executed in the short run. A suit against Coke contends, "Coke induced its Japanese bottlers to take $233 million worth of 'excess, unwanted and unneeded' concentrate in 1999; it compensated them with rebates and extra funds to cover marketing and the installation of thousands of new vending machines in underserved locations."

In concluding a lengthy article about Coke, *Forbes* stated: "Now if only the company could teach its overseas partners a thing or two about ethics."[1] **What should Coke's posture be about its international distributors? Also, is "channel stuffing" an ethical practice?**

Scenario 2

Carlos Barrabes operates a family owned mountain climbing gear shop in Benasque, Spain, near the Pyrenees Mountains that divide France and Spain. To take advantage of wholesale prices that are lower in Europe than in the United States and the difficulty for taxation authorities in collecting duties and sales tariffs for on online purchases, Barrabes put his shop into the dot-com world, and now generates 25 percent of his total sales through internet purchases in the United States. Other European climbing equipment outlets have followed suit and have effected a significant reduction in sales for U.S. retailers. In response, some U.S. retailers have called for a boycott of European Internet retailers, and some U.S. manufacturers have recently refused to sell to Barrabes and some of the other non-U.S.-based retailers known to sell significant volumes in the United States.[2] **What, if anything, is wrong with the Barrabes approach and the responses of U.S. companies?**

Scenario 3

For its 2003 season, the Ottawa Senators Hockey Club has instituted what is known as "variable pricing" for its tickets. Regularly, ticket prices average $40. However, for games with arch-rivals, the Toronto Maple Leafs and the Stanley Cup Champions, the Detroit Red Wings, prices jump to an average $48, a 20 percent hike. Other hockey and baseball clubs have engaged in similar tactics.[3] Although variable pricing has become common in such areas as the airlines and theater as a way to fill seats, the adoption of this policy by sports teams to earn extra dollars for high demand situations—weekends, star players, and visiting teams with extra drawing power—has created controversy among fans. **Is it fair to take advantage of people who are willing to pay extra for certain contests?**

Scenario 4

The increasing cost of pharmaceutical products has prompted lots of criticism. Several European countries, Canada, and a few U.S. states have either enacted price controls or established other programs designed to limit the prices charged for prescription drugs. Some of these regulations are targeted to purchases by low-income citizens, for example, Medicaid (state-administered medical insurance programs for low-income persons) enrollees or seniors. Some retail pharmacies in Europe and Canada have taken advantage of their lower wholesale prices by marketing aggressively to the U.S. market via the Internet. While the Pharmaceutical Manufacturers Association (Pharma) has sued to stop many such programs, several pharmaceutical producers have responded to the criticism of high drug prices by putting into place special programs that provide a flat monthly fee to low-income seniors and to persons with disabilities who are enrolled in Medicare, the federally sponsored medical insurance program that currently provides minimal prescription benefit. For example, with Pfizer's *Share Card,* eligible consumers can pay $15/month to obtain any prescribed Pfizer product from participating pharmacies.[4] **Should targeted "disadvantaged" groups be able to purchase drugs for less than people who are not included in these programs? Should pharmaceutical companies be allowed to sell their products in the United States for significantly higher prices than anywhere else in the world?**

As implied by these examples, this chapter examines a range of ethical concerns facing managers responsible for distribution and pricing. Exhibit 4-1 summarizes several legal guidelines that set the ground rules for distribution decisions in the United States. For example, certain practices, such as tying the sale of one product to the purchase of another or exclusive dealing arrangements, are explicitly covered by law. Since the law is the ethical floor (second A in ABCs of Chapter 1), some practices labeled as unethical are, in fact, also illegal. We discuss distribution, retailing, and pricing issues that meet legal guidelines, but have some questionable (ethical) aspect to them.

First, we discuss ethics in managing the channel of distribution, beginning with the supplier and moving to the final consumer. Among the areas to be analyzed are several overarching ethical concerns involving purchasing, wholesaling ethics, and ethical issues stemming from retailing and franchising. Then we turn our attention to pricing both within the business-to-business sector, as well as in the channel of distribution to the end consumer. The areas of ethical analysis receiving particular focus here are price setting, discounting, and price advertising. Finally, we conclude with several ideas for ethical marketing in these areas.

CHANNEL OF DISTRIBUTION ISSUES

A distribution channel often refers to the route taken by finished goods as they move from manufacturer to end consumer. Our conception of a distribution channel is a bit broader in that we see channels as beginning with the

Exhibit 4-1   Legal Issues Affecting Distribution Decisions

Mergers.   Vertical and horizontal integration is particularly significant in channel management. A merger is one means of achieving such integration. Mergers are not illegal *per se;* they are subject to the 1914 Clayton Act (sections 3 and 7). Section 7 prohibits mergers or acquisitions in which the effect "may be substantially to lessen competition, or tend to create a monopoly" in "any line of commerce in any section of the country."

Dealer Selection.   In general, manufacturers have the right to select the middlemen with whom they will deal. This right was formalized in section 2(a) of the 1936 Robinson-Patman Act which amended the Clayton Act.

Exclusive Dealing.   Agreements by middlemen that they will not handle the products of a manufacturer's competitor are not illegal *per se.* They are, however, subject to the provisions of the Clayton Act (section 3) and the 1914 Federal Trade Commission Act (section 5), that is, the arrangement must not substantially lessen competition or tend to create a monopoly, and both parties must enter voluntarily into the agreement.

Exclusive Territories.   Agreements between manufacturers and middlemen giving a middleman the exclusive right to sell the manufacturer's product within a defined territory are not illegal *per se.* The key to legality appears to be a vertical agreement between the manufacturer and each individual middleman.

Tying Arrangements.   A tying arrangement forces middlemen to buy one product only if they buy others. This activity is illegal under section 3 of the Clayton Act, which prohibits activities such as tie-in sales, exclusive dealing arrangements, and requirements contracts in which the effect of such arrangements "may be to substantially lessen competition or tend to create a monopoly."

Source: Partially adapted from Lynda J. Oswald, *The Law of Marketing* (Cincinnati, OH: West, 2002), 101–3.

supplier of materials and ending with the customer. Thus, a typical channel is depicted as follows:

Supplier → Manufacturer → Wholesaler → Retailer/Dealer → Customer

In order to meet customer needs, the varying organizational goals of the channel members must be compatible. Each of these channel linkages (e.g., manufacturer with wholesaler) can present ethical problems for either party. For instance, dealers or retailers want to offer a variety of products to satisfy their customers, while wholesalers may want to push primarily one manufacturer's brand in order to gain the largest quantity discount. Large retailing companies, especially when experiencing competitive price pressures, may seek to gain special pricing advantages from their suppliers while suppliers may favor certain retailers in order to gain extraordinary exposure to consumers. Thus, conflicts in channels, particularly where market power is uneven, are a major factor contributing to potential ethical problems.

Overarching Ethical Concerns

Before examining ethical concerns *within* the channel of distribution, we address several issues that pervade the entire channel. The first relates to the issues of *power and responsibility*. Simply put, the organization within the channel with the greatest power is the channel leader (sometimes called the "channel or category captain"). With this leadership comes the potential for ethical abuse. Reports of large manufacturers or retailers taking advantage of small, dependent suppliers are legion. Whether this power leads to coercion within the channel can be viewed as an ethical issue. Firms such as Wal-Mart, General Motors, McDonald's, and IBM appear to have inherent ethical responsibilities to other members in the channel based purely on their size and market power. In other words, they have special ethical obligations precisely because they *are* powerful.

Exhibit 4-2 summarizes the *power-responsibility equilibrium*. An understanding of this conceptualization leads to a duty-based ethic that can be applied to channel conduct. Basically, this perspective holds that power and responsibility must be approximately equal for any business institution to be effective in society. A corollary statement defines the "iron law of responsibility," which stipulates that, in the long run, those who do not use power in a way that society considers responsible will lose it. In a channels context, this implies that economically strong organizations, whether manufacturers or retailers, must use their power beneficially and prudentially, or they may lose it through government regulation, societal sanctions such as consumer boycotts, or countervailing efforts by organizations (or groups) disadvantaged when power is not used in ways that benefit them.

In recent times, the growth of high-volume chain retailers in discount stores (e.g., Target and Costco), supermarkets (e.g., Kroger, Safeway, Albertsons, Winn Dixie), drugstores (e.g., CVS, Walgreen, Eckerd, Thrifty), and electronics stores (e.g., Best Buy, Circuit City, Virgin Megastore) shifted the historical power balance favoring manufacturers over retailers. With this power shift, new ethical issues have emerged, including slotting allowances (see discussion later in this chapter). Both suppliers and smaller retailers acknowledge that some abuses of power exist. The common sentiment is that retailers exercise great control over the market for products on their shelves.

Exhibit 4-2 The Power-Responsibility Equilibrium

Power-Responsibility Balance	Direction of Change
$\dfrac{\text{Power}}{\text{Responsibility}} > 1$	1. Lose power 2. Increase responsible behavior 3. Combination thereof
$\dfrac{\text{Power}}{\text{Responsibility}} < 1$	1. Lose power 2. Increase responsible behavior 3. Combination thereof

The power-responsibility-equilibrium states that whenever power and responsibility are substantially out of balance with each other, long-term forces will be generated to bring them closer into balance. If power is greater than responsibility as in the top of the diagram, the organization may lose power or increase its responsibility or a combination of both. If responsibility is greater than power, the firm is likely to seek power or lose some responsibility or both.

Source: K. Davis, W. C. Frederick, and R. L. Blomstrom, *Business and Society,* 2d ed. (New York: McGraw-Hill, 1980), 33–34.

Thus, retailers must now shoulder more of the ethical responsibility for what happens in the channel. Of course, this concern is only new in the sense that the ethical burden has now shifted to major retailers: similar concerns exist where manufacturers or wholesalers had—and in some cases still have—more power than retailers (e.g., the auto industry).

A second overarching concern within channel relationships is *gift-giving/bribery.* A long-standing business custom is to entertain clients or give gifts to business associates. The major ethical question is: When does a gift end and a bribe begin? Some retail buyers and purchasing agents are offered expensive gifts or vacation trips as inducements to do business with a certain supplier. The reverse is also sometimes the case as buyers may demand special considerations as a condition of purchase, a practice that may be considered *extortion.* It is a responsibility of channel members to get out clear guidelines to deal with such practices. (For a more complete discussion, see the Gifts and Entertainment section of Chapter 6.)

A third issue is *price setting.* Channel members, whether manufacturers, retailers, or wholesalers, must make a determination about prices. The setting of prices at artificially high levels may be legal, but may not be ethical. A more common practice today is sometimes artificially low prices. Various channel members may be "squeezed" by other more powerful members to give price concessions. For instance, one technique involves taking unauthorized invoice deductions, such as a 2 percent discount for early payment, even when the deadline is passed. Exhibit 4-3 discusses Wal-Mart's unparalleled pricing and channel power.

A fourth issue, the *advertising of prices*, has long been of concern to consumers and social critics. Of course, laws exist to curb "bait-and-switch" tactics and other forms of blatant deceptive pricing. For example, the Federal Trade Commission (FTC) has rules governing availability of advertised specials. As discussed later in this chapter, the use of small-print qualifiers in advertisements for financial institutions, airlines, and rental cars has been much criticized, as has the difficulty to prove the retail pricing claim of "guaranteed lowest price."

A final area of concern is *competition*. The intensity of competition within the channel of distribution is now particularly acute. Competition both at the same level within the channel (wholesaler vs. wholesaler) and at different levels (manufacturers who bypass intermediaries vs. retailers or wholesalers) raises ethical issues. Why? The markets for many products in the developed world are mature, and, thus, most gains come at the expense of competitors rather than from growing markets. Although consolidation has occurred at the retail level and some of the largest consumer packaged goods firms have merged (e.g., Philip Morris [now Altria] bought General Foods and then acquired Kraft), most observers view the competitive situation as more cutthroat.   **Think of your favorite brand—do you know who the parent company is?** Some managers use competitive pressures as a rationalization for unethical conduct. For example, if one competitor engages in lavish entertaining to woo clients, then others do too. The trend toward more intense and global competition shows no sign of abating, and ethical concerns continue to be an outgrowth of this situation. To be more competitive, most chains in the United States and elsewhere have expanded trading hours in the last decade. The lone American exceptions are Chick-fil-A and Hobby Lobby, which are both closed on Sundays.

Ethics in Purchasing/Supply Management/Procurement

Manufacturers, nonprofit organizations like hospitals, and services firms all deal with suppliers. The point of contact for suppliers is usually the purchasing function. Most large organizations have a separate procurement unit staffed by professional buyers. Ethical issues sometimes arise when the individuals in the purchasing department view their personal goals as more important than the organizational ones. On the other hand, ethical questions

Exhibit 4-3   Is Wal-Mart Too Powerful?[1]

The undisputed low price retailer and now the world's largest is Wal-Mart. In fact, it is now so large that Wal-Mart does more business than Target, Sears, Kmart, J. C. Penney, Safeway, and Kroger combined. The company sold about $250 billion of products in 2002. The formula for this success is simple: give the consumer what he or she wants at the lowest price.

Initially, Wal-Mart positioned itself as a "Buy American" store, but as its phenomenal growth has continued, the firm has backed away from the patriotic appeal. Now, most of what the firm sells under its private label is made outside the United States. In fact, Wal-Mart alone accounts for 10 percent of all China's imports to the United States.

Much of Wal-Mart's current and future growth is expected to come from the supercenter, patterned after Europe's hypermarche. Today, Wal-Mart operates over 1,300 supercenters and is the nation's largest grocer, with 19 percent market share, and the third largest pharmacy, with 16 percent. The company plans to open 1,000 more supercenters in the United States alone in the next five years.

This size and growth has led to several ethical questions (sex discrimination suits, failure to pay overtime, and suppliers' hiring illegal workers) and concerns being raised about Wal-Mart besides the traditional criticism that small town retailers have been driven out of business by this low-price competitor. The selections below examine issues directly related to this chapter.

Downside of Power

Wal-Mart might well be both America's most admired and most hated company. But the more size and power that "the Beast of Bentonville" amasses, the greater the backlash it is stirring among competing retailers, vendors, organized labor, community activists, and cultural and political progressives. America has a long history of controversial retailers, notes James E. Hoopes, a history professor at Babson College. "What's new about Wal-Mart is the flak it's drawn from outside the world of its competition," he says. "It's become a social phenomenon that people resent and fear."[2]

Policy toward Suppliers

Wal-Mart wields its power for just one purpose: to bring the lowest possible prices to its customers. At Wal-Mart, that goal is never reached. The retailer has a clear policy for suppliers: On basic products that don't change, the price Wal-Mart will pay, and will charge shoppers, must drop year after year. But what almost no one outside the world of Wal-Mart and its 21,000 suppliers knows is the high cost of those low prices. Wal-Mart has the power to squeeze profit-killing concessions from vendors. To survive in the face of its pricing demands, makers of everything from bras to bicycles to blue jeans have had to lay off employees and close U.S. plants in favor of outsourcing products from overseas.[3]

(continued)

Difference between Price and Cost

Wal-Mart has also lulled shoppers into ignoring the difference between the price of something and the cost. Its unending focus on price underscores something that Americans are only starting to realize about globalization: Ever-cheaper prices have consequences. Says Steve Dobbins, president of thread maker Carolina Mills [whose company was adversely affected by Wal-Mart's decisions—authors' note]: "We want clean air, clear water, good living conditions, the best health care in the world—yet we aren't will to pay for anything manufactured under those restrictions."[4]

Integrity Emphasis

To a person, all those interviewed credit Wal-Mart with a fundamental integrity in its dealings that's unusual in the world of consumer goods, retailing, and groceries. Wal-Mart does not cheat suppliers, it keeps its word, it pays its bills briskly. "They are tough people but very honest; they treat you honestly," says Peter Campanella, who ran the business that sold Corning kitchenware products, both at Corning and then at World Kitchen. "It was a joke to do business with most of their competitors. A fiasco."[5]

"Morality"-Based Decisions

Wal-Mart cites customer preferences as the reason it does not stock CDs or DVDs with parental warning stickers and why it occasionally yanks items from its shelves. In May, 2003, it removed the racy men's magazines *Maxim, Stuff,* and *FHM.* A month later, it began obscuring the covers of *Glamour, Redbook, Marie Claire,* and *Cosmopolitan* with binders. Why did Wal-Mart censor these publications and not *Rolling Stone,* which has featured a nearly naked Britney Spears and Christina Aguilera on two of its recent covers? "There's a lot of subjectivity," concedes Gary Severson, a Wal-Mart general merchandise manager. "There's a line between provocative and pornographic. I don't know exactly where it is."[6]

What are your views on Wal-Mart? Which of these five areas do you see as the most ethically charged? Can a company be ethical and socially irresponsible at the same time? Do consumers bear some responsibility?

---

[1]This exhibit is based on the articles cited below.
[2]Diane Brady et al., "Is Wal-Mart Too Powerful?" *Business Week,* October 6, 2003, 102.
[3]Charles Fishman, "The Wal-Mart You Don't Know: Why Low Prices Have a High Cost," *Fast Company* (December 2003), 7D.
[4]Ibid., 80.
[5]Ibid., 73.
[6]Brady, "Is Wal-Mart Too Powerful?" 104.

in purchasing can also occur when the department is forced to implement corporate policies that may lead to discriminatory practices (e.g., reciprocity with suppliers or preferences for friends or relatives of key executives). In a study of United Kingdom purchasing executives, gifts were the most frequently identified ethical concern.[5] Policies that discriminate either against or in favor of minority suppliers also may present ethical dilemmas. In addition, ethical issues arise when power imbalances in the buyer-seller relationship are abused to advance organizational goals. To guard against problems occurring in the purchaser-supplier interface, three possible avenues exist. Companies can (a) develop appropriate corporate policies, (b) stress moral values, or (c) promulgate professional standards.

Purchasing Policies

While 90 percent of large companies have formal written ethics policies, only about half of what may be termed major firms in the United States and Canada have written policies explicitly designed for the purchasing department.[6] Such policies have been found to reduce the acceptance of gratuities. For example, we believe accepting tickets to one sporting event would be an acceptable practice in many of these companies. However, purchasing agents who repeatedly accept tickets, lavish trips, or other major perks may be acting in an unethical manner, even if there is no written prohibition of the practice. In this respect, it may be important to distinguish between gifts that constitute "appreciation" for an ongoing business relationship versus an "incentive" to buy or increase purchases. A thornier issue is the fact that purchasing agents are (sometimes or often) prohibited from accepting such gifts while senior managers act as if ethical codes do not apply to them! Despite substantial progress in recent years, calls for improving ethical standards in purchasing and throughout the organization continue.[7]

A 1998 study by the Center for Advanced Purchasing Studies suggested that unethical behavior can take many forms, but a useful framework is to classify according to two broad categories:

- *Deceitful practices*—involving deception of the supplier such as lying, obscure contract terms, disclosing proprietary competitive information
- *Subtle practices*—which might include requesting reciprocal gift giving, manipulating the bid process, or selecting vendors based on top management suggestions[8]

Some interesting findings in this study reveal the key perceptions that both parties place on ethics in the buyer-seller relationships. First, buyers and suppliers both feel that these broad categories are appropriate in classifying the other's behavior. Second, the mere *appearance* of an unethical action by one party can drastically affect the other's perception of how ethical the action truly is. Third, if a buyer perceives that a supplier is using unethical tactics, the buyer is likely to perceive the supplier as an underperformer, perhaps trying to hide problems with the product or its manufacturer. Finally, the most experienced buyers feel that gains in the short-term due to unethical practices create bigger problems in the long run, as suppliers react by increasing prices or refuse to accept reasonable terms.

Electronic Procurement[9]

As technology has taken a central role in facilitating purchasing relationships in recent years, many organizations have been challenged by the implications that this has on ethical behavior. Why should electronic procurement be any different from traditional procurement? According to Julie Roberts, "One cause might be summed up as 'faceless transactions.' When conducting business while staring at a computer screen that doesn't respond or give any indication of emotion, it is easy to become disengaged and forget that a person is actually the recipient of the other's ethical decisions."[10] While the lack of traditional personal interaction might induce certain inappropriate behaviors, some believe that the electronic audit trails produced by software packages actually provide more protection against problems, since the purchasing process is fully transparent. For some, the electronic tools are simply too unfamiliar, which breeds a certain degree of mistrust, particularly when there are new people participating in the process.

New models of buyer-supplier interaction facilitated through technology present special problems not previously encountered. For example, private electronic marketplaces permit selected vendors to interact with a buyer in a closed environment. This situation invites exclusive dealings with a selected group that may not consistently represent the best possible set of suppliers consistent with an organization's mission. Another issue that arises in public electronic marketplaces is when vendors submit bids. What information should be publicly viewable? Should a buying firm be required to reveal its identity publicly in such a forum, possibly revealing sensitive information to competitors? Should competing vendors be required to reveal their identities, for that matter? Questions such as these recently caused about one in five purchasing organizations to revisit their ethics policies.[11]

Moral Principles and Purchasing

A second approach to enhancing ethics in purchasing/procurement calls for a return to moral principles (such as those discussed in Chapter 1), which can be an alternative to increasingly complex corporate policies or costly government regulation. Typically, legalistic approaches lead to a "letter of the law" mentality rather than relying on the spirit of fair and honest business practices. Emphasizing the value of an ongoing partnership between purchaser and supplier often proves effective. This situation can be contrasted with the federal government's procurement process, which stresses an arm's length relationship between supplier and purchaser. An example of one type of thinking that is not mechanically rule bound relates to the obligation of a purchaser to adhere to proposal deadlines, that is, refuse to consider any proposals received after that deadline. Of course, one might question the ethics of setting a deadline for proposals, if a buyer has no intention of observing it. A related issue is whether the late bidder has improperly obtained information about earlier, competing bids, permitting it to formulate a winning proposal.

Professional Standards

A third possibility, advocated by the Institute for Supply Management (ISM—formerly the National Association of Purchasing Management), is to increase the professionalism of both buyers and suppliers. ISM views enhanced professional conduct as a major safeguard against unethical behavior. According to the ISM, the connection between professionalization and ethical behavior has been established.[12] Part of the ISM effort involves revising the ethical standards of their profession. The preamble to their code incorporates some of the basic moral principles noted earlier. The code begins:

LOYALTY TO YOUR COMPANY
JUSTICE TO THOSE WITH WHOM YOU DEAL
FAITH IN YOUR PROFESSION

From these principles, the ISM has developed its "Principles and Standards of Ethical Supply Management Conduct." (See Exhibit 4-4 for the association's statement approved in 2002.)

Ethics in Channel Management

In the distribution of consumer goods, especially packaged products, several developments have altered the balance of power between manufacturers and retailers. With the widespread implementation of scanner systems pioneered in supermarkets, but now used by virtually all retailers catering to consumers, retailers now have the data to know exactly which manufacturer's brands are contributing most to the retailer's profit margins. Two of the most interesting retail buying practices that have ethical implications are forward buying and slotting allowances.

EXHIBIT 4-4   Institute for Supply Management Principles
and Standards of Ethical Supply Management
Conduct

LOYALTY TO YOUR ORGANIZATION
JUSTICE TO THOSE WITH WHOM YOU DEAL
FAITH IN YOUR PROFESSION

From these principles are derived the ISM standards of supply management conduct. (Global)

1. Avoid the intent and appearance of unethical or compromising practice in relationships, actions, and communications.
2. Demonstrate loyalty to the employer by diligently following the lawful instructions of the employer, using reasonable care and granted authority.
3. Avoid any personal business or professional activity that would create a conflict between personal interests and the interests of the employer.
4. Avoid soliciting or accepting money, loans, credits, or preferential discounts, and the acceptance of gifts, entertainment, favors, or services from present or potential suppliers that might influence, or appear to influence, supply management decisions.
5. Handle confidential or proprietary information with due care and proper consideration of ethical and legal ramifications and governmental regulations.
6. Promote positive supplier relationships through courtesy and impartiality.
7. Avoid improper reciprocal agreements.
8. Know and obey the letter and spirit of laws applicable to supply management.
9. Encourage support for small, disadvantaged, and minority-owned businesses.
10. Acquire and maintain professional competence.
11. Conduct supply management activities in accordance with national and international laws, customs, and practices, your organization's policies, and these ethical principles and standards of conduct.
12. Enhance the stature of the supply management profession.

Approved January 2002.

Source: http://www.ism.ws/ISMMembership/PrincipleStandards.cfm.

Forward Buying

This practice pertains to purchasing products "on deal" for future needs during the end of a deal period while the prices are still low. Forward buying necessitates adequate warehousing facilities on the retailer's part. The savings can be passed on to the customer, taken as profits or used to subsidize other costs. An ethical question occurs because some proportion of deal dollars are considered as profits. In other words, only a small percentage actually ends up as savings to the final consumer. Many retailers would maintain that retaining such savings as profits is not an ethical issue. Rather, they are simply engaging in a "good business practice" which may change depending on competitive pressures. However, some suppliers and consumers may have a different opinion.

(This is but one of many situations where special savings are provided to retailers that may not be passed on to consumers; others include promotional allowances and quantity discounts. With respect to promotional allowances, the question may be even more challenging in that the allowance is meant to underwrite advertising, special displays, etc., but retailers may simply take the allowance as an extra discount.)

Slotting Allowances

One of the most pervasive channel activities in recent years is the imposition of slotting allowances on consumer packaged goods manufacturers. This practice involves distributors or retailers requiring additional compensation (in the form of money or free goods) to take on a new item in their warehouse or store. The tactic originated in Europe and Canada, then moved into the Northeast in the early 1980s. Slotting fees now have become a major expenditure for companies trying to place their products on retail shelves. One estimate holds that 55 percent of all promotional expenditures (consumer and trade) go for this purpose, and 70 percent of all slotting fees contribute directly to the retailer's bottom line and not to lowering the cost of goods sold.[13] A Nielsen Survey "indicated that 85% of retailers reported charging slotting fees, while 42% of manufacturers reported that they were charged increased slotting allowances and 28% of retailers reported having increased their slotting fees."[14]

The justification for slotting fees is that new products have proliferated—over 10,000 items are introduced annually with a doubling of new products in supermarkets during the last decade—to the point where the retailer must be compensated for storing, handling, shelving, and eventually removing these products. Most retailers now require manufacturers to cover these major expenses. (Wal-Mart is an exception; it does not charge slotting fees.) About 100,000 items are available, but only about 30,000 can fit in the typical supermarket. Some retailers are even charging a $2,000 "failure fee" for products they must pull from the shelves. The analogy often used in discussing slotting fees is that supermarket shelves are valuable "real estate" and retailer should be able to make money "renting" shelf space to manufacturers. Examples of slotting fees paid are Frito Lay paying $100,000 to chains to carry new products. Truzzolino Pizza Roll was charged $25,000 by one chain to carry its products, and Lee's Ice Cream, a Baltimore company, was asked to pay $25,000 for each flavor it wanted stores to carry.[15]

Although retailers consider these slotting fees as "forms of insurance or incentives," they have received much criticism. Some more outspoken critics call them "ransom," "extortion allowances," or even "institutional bribery." From a legal standpoint, the fees are of concern because they are usually charged to less well-known brands and may represent a type of price discrimination. The FTC has investigated the antitrust implications of these fees,[16] and several court cases have now been decided. At this writing, the general impression from a legal standpoint is that slotting allowances and similar practices in which large distributors—retailers and wholesalers—who "induce discriminatory allowances" may be subject to antitrust enforcement on the grounds that they unfairly harm smaller competitors at the same (typically retail) level of distribution. The argument that these fees may preclude smaller suppliers from having significant access to consumers is apparently not legally compelling at this time. However, the debate over slotting allowances continues, both in and outside the United States.[17]

Several ethical concerns about fees have surfaced. First, the slotting fees commonly are negotiated privately and orally. This approach makes one suspect that the retailer has something to hide and may be treating various manufacturers quite differently. Second, slotting allowances may be stifling innovation. Often, smaller manufacturers are first to introduce new product categories. And some supermarket buyers reportedly charge hundreds of dollars as presentation fees for a new item. Exhibit 4-5 discusses the problem Honest Tea (recall Exhibit 3-7, p. 108) has encountered with slotting. Are innovative products being kept from the market by major supermarket chains? Do slotting fees effectively limit consumer access to information? Slotting fees effectively add a significant number to a manufacturer's marketing expense. Is this fair to smaller manufacturers whose sales volume may not support this expense, that is, do not meet the volume/profit standards of mass merchandisers? Does it drive out other forms of promotion that would otherwise be available to build brands? Is it fair to consumers who might otherwise be attracted to the brands/products thus precluded from store shelves? Slotting fees continue to remain an issue because some supermarkets are demanding fees for every stage of a product's life (e.g., annual renewal fees), and because the practice, originally confined to the grocery trade, has now spread to other retail settings such as drug chains, computer stores, and bookstores.

Exhibit 4-5   Honest Tea and Slotting Fees

Slotting fees narrow the variety on store shelves, because they favor the biggest manufacturers, which can pay the most in fees every time they have a new flavor, brand, or type of package. According to the FTC, a nationwide product rollout might cost $2 million in slotting fees alone. The little guys just can't compete—which is why the Senate Committee on Small Business and Entrepreneurship asked the FTC to look into slotting fees in the first place, back in 2000.

"There's no question that we've had opportunities that we've just had to forgo around the country because either we have not been able to, or not been willing to, pay what it takes to get there," said Seth Goldman, founder and president of Honest Tea, a Bethesda-based maker of bottled organic iced tea.

Goldman said some stores have stocked Honest Tea for 11 months and then discontinued it, only to ask to have the product back a month later, along with another slotting fee. One major grocery chain demanded that Honest Tea buy coolers to display its iced tea, but when the company ponied up, the chain came back and demanded $1,000 per cooler to pay for the space they occupied in the store.

"We couldn't do it. We pulled out," Goldman said.

In part because the industry is eager to get organic products, Honest Tea has been able to grow and get more negotiating leverage. But coming up with cash is still a problem, so in lieu of a slotting fee, Honest Tea might throw in a free case of tea for every flavor that each store in a chain picks up. With a wholesale price of around $10 a case, "it can add up to tens of thousands of dollars," Goldman said.

Source: Margaret Webb Pressler, "Shelf Game: When Stores Force Makers to Pay Them Fees, You Lose," *Washington Post,* January 18, 2004, F5.

To help resolve this issue, a virtue ethics position might state that manufacturers and retailers should be open and forthright in their dealings and should share the burden of new product introductions. Then, only justifiable costs could be passed along via slotting fees. A utilitarian (cost-benefit) approach might argue that the retailer appropriately gains from slotting fees because these charges are justifiable in terms of costs. To the extent that the monies from slotting lead to higher profitability, retailers have a greater flexibility to provide innovative services to their customers.

Ethics in Wholesaling

Wholesalers are relatively invisible institutions in the channel of distribution. Their lack of consumer contact, location in generally out of the way places, and various specialized functions (e.g., drop shippers or rack jobbers) all make wholesaling activities somewhat mysterious. Just as manufacturers have recently been squeezed by retailers, wholesalers have long had to cope with pressures from both manufacturers and retailers. One ethical question does arise in parallel channels where manufacturers use wholesalers (and independent representatives) for the low-volume/high-risk segments of the market and compete with them for the choicer parts of the business. Other ethical issues pervading wholesaling are generally similar to those discussed earlier and elsewhere. For instance, ethical questions pertaining to purchasing, personal selling, gift giving, and entertainment (see also Chapter 6) are among the most central.

Wholesaling is usually regarded as a declining industry in most lines of trade. However, the growth of mass merchandising in retail lines where independents and small chains persist, combined with consolidations and mergers that extend wholesaler customer bases to whole regions, has put some wholesalers in a position comparable to that of the largest retailers. For example, W. W. Grainger, a $5 billion industrial wholesaler headquartered in Chicago, is the largest company of its type and conducts more than 100,000 transactions daily.[18] Thus, it is subject to the same power/responsibility concerns as dominant retailers.

Ethics in Franchising

The growth of franchises is one of the major contemporary developments within the United States and international distribution system. About one-third of all retail sales in the United States now flows through franchise systems. Examples include Nissan dealerships, bp (British Petroleum) stations, Pepsi and Miller distributorships, Curves fitness centers, Holiday Inn motels, Budget Rent-a-Car agencies, and Pizza Hut restaurants. Franchising has come to dominate the marketing of many consumer products and services. Franchises are essentially legal agreements between a franchisor and franchisees regarding the use of brand names, product lines, suppliers, locations of outlets, operating policies, and advertising strategies. Many of the serious potential problems that might occur between these contracting parties are covered in law by the franchise agreement. Still, ethical issues do arise to the extent that (a) areas of mutual interest and potential conflict are not included in the contract, (b) contractual terms are open to differing interpretations, and (c) compliance with contractual terms is either not enforced or indeterminable through normal reporting or other control mechanisms.[19]

One inherent ethical concern relates to the power-responsibility issue introduced earlier in the chapter. The franchisor is usually a large national or international organization, and the franchisee is commonly an individual or small group of people. The power-responsibility equilibrium (see Exhibit 4-2) applies to this relationship. It appears that since franchisors have most of the power, they must also shoulder more responsibility. Franchisees are employing a variety of techniques to shift the balance of power more in their favor. We now turn to recent examples that illustrate the ethical issues that may surface in the franchisor-franchisee relationship.

The automobile manufacturer-dealer franchise relationship is under particular scrutiny. Ford and other car manufacturers have found it necessary to warn its dealers about tinkering with the company's consumer satisfaction instrument. Some dealers tried to inflate their "satisfaction scores" and circumvent the evaluation process. This happened when some dealers tampered with the forms; others completed the surveys on the customer's behalf and mailed them to Ford. Additional tactics used were giving gifts to customers who sent the survey to the dealership instead of the company, giving rewards to customers who rated the dealer favorably, coaching customers on how to fill out the survey, and even tossing out negative ones. While one might ask whether the manufacturer placed too much emphasis on this one instrument, if it caused dealers to adopt such extreme measures, does that excuse unethical behavior by the dealers? Nonetheless, a concern for "ethical systems" would lead to some combination of monitoring and a scheme that offered less temptation or incentive for tampering.

Fast-food franchises in predominantly black neighborhoods were found to have higher prices than similarly situated outlets owned by the franchisor. The differences could not be explained by differences in either costs or competition. Franchisees apparently take advantage of the pricing autonomy provided under their franchise agreement. The effect may arguably be judged unfair and—if the practice were widely known—would also be a public relations disaster for all concerned.[20]

Another ethical criticism of franchise agreements is that the documentation is often written in legal jargon that is almost impossible for the average franchisee to understand. Often franchisees argue about clauses in their contract they did not know existed, but in fact they do; the language is not transparent. Interpretation of contractual terms can also be debated heavily. Moreover, the potential resolution to conflicts that might arise is likely not specifically addressed in the contract. Ideally, all contracts would be completely transparent so the franchisee is fully educated about the investment they are making so conflicts can be avoided before they have the potential to develop.[21]

Positive developments in the franchising arena include the growth in prominence of two industry trade associations. First, the International Franchise Association (IFA) is a membership organization that connects franchisors, franchisees, and suppliers. The code of ethics developed by the IFA (www.franchise.org/welcome_about/code.asp) is designed to encourage best practices among its members. The main categories of the code include trust, truth, and honesty; mutual respect and reward; and open and frequent communication. The IFA does not intend to prevent all legal disputes between franchisors and franchisees, but it does expect its members to conduct themselves in accordance with the organization's core values, especially when legal issues arise.

Second, the American Association of Franchisees and Dealers (AAFD) is a national nonprofit trade association with the interests of franchisees in mind. Its mission is to bring fairness to franchising. Specifically, the organization acknowledges those businesses that engage in "Total Quality Franchising" and lists a "Franchise Bill of Rights" on its Web site (www.aafd.org). Participating franchisors recognize their franchisees' right to have an independent association, and are willing to work together to make the system successful. They understand that by achieving a level of balance, success is imminent. Best Inns and Suites, Great Harvest Bread Company, and Meineke Discount Muffler Shops are a few of the AAFD-accredited franchises.

Ethics in Retailing

Many potentially troublesome issues arise in the retail sector. The retailer not only interacts with consumers on a daily basis, but also interfaces with manufacturers and other channel members. We find ethical problems arising in retail buying, the product assortment, retail pricing, sales personnel, and retail advertising.

Retail Buying

Retailers often employ professional buyers to secure their merchandise. Buyer activities are similar to those of purchasing agents, and the issues related to ethics in purchasing apply as well to retail buying. The extensive amount of travel involved in selecting products means retail buyers often do much of their work off-site. Use of expense accounts, their negotiation practices, and ongoing relationships with key suppliers can sometimes lead to ethical problems.

One particular issue that has arisen in recent years is the bribery of retail buyers. Two reasons can be given for the growth of this practice. First, the absolute size of many retail accounts has grown due to organizational mergers. One buyer can account for millions of dollars of sales. Therefore, the patronage of this person can be vital to the existence of the selling firm. Second, based on U.S. Department of Commerce statistics, imported merchandise amounts to about 30 percent of retail sales, more in such key categories as electronics, shoes, and clothing. It is common knowledge that bribes are customary in some foreign countries and certain manufacturers continue to use these practices to entice buyers from U.S.-based companies (see Bribery and Facilitation section of Chapter 6).

Explanations of why retail buyers are susceptible to bribes may be as simple as having employees who are disgruntled or just plain greedy. The problem for retailers is that the dishonest buyer often does not negotiate favorable discounts (such as advertising allowances) provided to more scrupulous and honest buyers. This is not to suggest that unethical practices are rampant. We know that many retail buyers walk away from bribes that are offered. A mechanism to deal with the problem is for the employer to place limits on the amount of gifts buyers may receive. For example, Wal-Mart doesn't even allow its buyers to accept a free lunch. Certified Grocers-Midwest sends letters to vendors each year stating that any Christmas fruit basket, flowers, or similar holiday gift worth more than twenty-five dollars will be returned. It suggests vendors make contributions to their favorite charities instead.

Product Assortment

An ethical issue can arise from the products retailers choose to carry. The quality of the products sold represents one potential problem. For example, sometimes retailers acquire lower quality merchandise to be utilized for so-called clearance sales. One retailer cunningly brought in truckloads of special merchandise for a going-out-of-business sale that lasted for at least six weeks. Consistency of merchandise quality is essential for any retailer's success. The use of price lines (e.g., Sears's good, better, and best lines of paint) should represent meaningful differences in product quality (not necessarily in cost) and not be intended to confuse the consumer. Adherence to this policy means the retailer subscribes to the principle of meaningful consumer choice. Customer service, return policies, and merchandise value are also areas where the "total product" offered by a retailer has ethical implications. For example, Target (formerly Dayton Hudson Corporation) clearly states its position on these matters in its vendor compliance statement (see www.targetcorp.com—About Us section).

Retailers also have a responsibility to monitor the safety of products they sell. They have a duty to warn consumers whenever they know of a dangerous product and to cooperate in product recalls. Retailers of products such as firearms, alcoholic beverages, farm pesticides, and prescription drugs must be especially aware of these products' safety implications. (See Chapter 3 for more details on these issues.) Mindful of these implications, some retailers refuse to sell 40-ounce beers, cheap wine, and tobacco products, and some cinemas restrict themselves to family movies.

Retail Pricing

Dubious retail pricing practices such as bait-and-switch, lowballing, and resale price maintenance are all covered by legal statutes or regulations. We examine the general topic of ethics in pricing later in this chapter. One concern that is relevant here, however, is the overall pricing strategy taken by retailers. Some retailers "mark up" goods so they can then put them on sale and maintain their profit margins. Continuous specials and price promotions, even during peak selling seasons like Christmas, may jade and confuse consumers. The word "sale" has arguably lost its meaning, and many consumers are fed up with constantly changing sale prices that make it difficult to recognize a "fair deal." The operable "virtues" in this regard are transparency and fairness; competitive jockeying and deception, particularly insofar as they put less sophisticated consumers at a serious disadvantage, are obviously deficient.

In reaction, many retailers have moved toward a concept called "everyday low prices." Here prices are marked lower than the regular price, but a bit higher than during sale periods. (In a few instances, retailers may only have sales on rare occasions such as to close out merchandise at the end of a season.) Some retailers may use the "everyday" tactic in questionable ways. Another pricing strategy is to charge less for large sizes. However, Wal-Mart stores sometimes charge more per unit of measure (weight or volume) for products in larger "economy" containers or in so-called "value packs," for example, two packages taped together. For example, in its Mesa, Arizona, store, in August 2002, Minute Maid orange juice sold for 8.2¢/ounce when purchased in an 8-ounce can and 12.4¢/ounce when purchased in a 12-ounce can. Similar examples were cited for Country Time lemonade, Jif peanut butter, 'Cool Whip,' and Pringles potato chips.[22] **Do such practices amount to deception?**

It can be argued that the use of price promotions to build store traffic, clear out discontinued items, or introduce new products provides real value to consumers and suppliers. While the *intent* to deceive is unethical, one should be careful about ascribing ethical merit or concern based on the mere fact of having or not having price specials. Some other retail pricing practices that may have ethical implications are raising prices to take advantage of special opportunities such as welfare check day in low-income neighborhoods or weather emergencies. Finally, the previous discussion of slotting allowances is also pertinent here.

Retail Selling

Selling in a retail environment raises a number of potential ethically charged issues. (For a more complete discussion of ethics in selling, see

Chapter 6.) First, retail salespeople often face ethical dilemmas where they are torn between short-term pressures from management, such as achieving an ambitious sales quota, and long-term goals of achieving customer trust. For example, should retail sales clerks inform one of their best customers who is planning to make a purchase today that the item is going on sale next week? Second, the variety of tasks retail salespeople perform (e.g., from entering the sale to handling customer complaints) can cause a number of ethical problems (e.g., under what conditions should a salesperson refuse to exchange a customer's merchandise?). Third, retail salespeople generally receive little sales training on how to handle ethical issues. Few retailers provide the necessary guidance to deal with these three areas.

Several retail selling situations pose ethical problems. These range from deliberately overcharging a customer to undercutting other salespeople. In order to give the proper guidance to retail salespeople, management was advised to take several actions, including (a) establishing policies that are both specific, yet flexible; (b) holding periodic sessions where salespeople and management can openly discuss ethically troublesome issues; and (c) maintaining a high ethical posture (i.e., lead by example). Although aggressive retail salespeople were originally included in these points, we believe that not every activity found distasteful is a breach of ethics. Thus, pushy, but not dishonest, selling is generally ethical. However, one might reasonably argue that aggressive sales tactics with psychologically vulnerable people is unethical. Telemarketing aimed at the elderly seems to merit special attention in this regard.

Another ethical issue regarding retail salespeople is the use of *push money* (also known as PMs or spiffs) as an incentive to promote a particular product. Spiffs can take the form of a shoe company offering a free pair of shoes to a store salesperson with the highest monthly sales or a beer distributor offering local restaurant servers a 50 cent inducement for every bottle sold. Push money is usually a legitimate and potentially worthwhile sales promotion, because it gives the product an extra push at the point of sale. However, it can be misused if the vendor provides the incentive without the approval of store management. The same incentive ideally should be offered to all salespeople, and it should not involve "unfair" or "predatory" behavior. Also, of some concern is the prospect that spiffs distort sales efforts relative to customer needs. For example, travel agents may not offer otherwise desirable travel options to their clients unless a spiff is offered.

Retail Advertising

Few topics generate as much immediate reaction from the public as advertising by retailers. Almost everyone has had the experience of seeing a retailer's ad that promises an extraordinary low price or a hard to find item, only to learn the advertised product is not available or comes at a much higher cost. In fact, the Better Business Bureau has developed an extensive self-regulatory Code of Advertising outlining their position on 20 practices, such as advertising by factory outlets and the use of the word "sale" (see www.bbb.org/membership/codeofad.asp).

Responsibility to Stakeholders

Since retailers are such visible institutions in society, their responsibilities to employees, customers, suppliers, shareholders, and the local community are closely scrutinized. The wave of mergers and consolidations within the retailing community in the 1990s shifted some of these responsibilities from local to national, or sometimes international ownership (e.g., British American Tobacco [BAT] and Dutch food marketer Ahold have purchased several U.S.-based retailers). We believe that retailers concerned about their ethical posture should continue to evaluate their performance with various stakeholders (recall our discussion of stakeholders in Chapter 1). One retailer that has an exemplary record in dealing with its stakeholders is Target, which historically has contributed 5 percent of its taxable income to community giving and has major initiatives on diversity and the physical environment (see Web site noted earlier).

Status of Ethics in Retailing

An inherent perceptual problem exists between the retailer's view of its ethical position and the consumer's view. Other than retailers generally regarded as most ethical (e.g., Nordstrom or Penney's), few stores would likely perceive their ethical responsibility to include calling a consumer who received a rain check for an inexpensive item. Consumers, on the other hand, hold retailers to very high ethical standards. They often expect complete disclosure of information about prices and merchandise availability, including notification of when a rain check item is available. Retailers need to be aware of this implicit "ethics gap" (first coined by Professor Clarence Walton) and fully inform consumers of their policies, so that misunderstandings and disappointments are kept to a minimum. In that sense, good ethics is simply good business practice; even retailers that do not promote themselves on the basis of ethical conduct must observe high ethical standards in order to maintain their position with key stakeholders.[23]

The overriding problem is that *caveat emptor* (let the buyer beware) often shortchanges ethics in retail settings. Abuses may occur with the products themselves, pricing, selling, and information sharing. Many consumers are ill-equipped or indisposed to engage in presale tests of truth, usefulness, and fair pricing. Postpurchase remedies and legal sanctions may not be accessible or sufficient to prevent abuses in many cases. Therefore, retailers must continue to strive toward closing this ethics gap in all marketing activities.

Ethics in Logistics Management

An important aspect of distribution is the management of the logistics function—activities having to do with transportation, inventory controls and storage, and order processing. Except for the goal of efficiency, logistics is commonly viewed as mechanical and without ethical content. However, some ethical issues are embedded in this function.

One of these is the degree of fairness in responding to orders when deadlines compete for resources—labor and product availability. It is common to give preference to "key" (usually large) accounts in this circumstance, delaying service to other customers who expect a "first come, first served" response. While congestion in order processing may require putting some customers ahead of others, either the first-come, first-served approach should be used, or those customers who are disadvantaged by this should be informed and given the opportunity to take their business to another vendor. Another issue relates to the environmental impact of alternative transportation methods. The trade-off between speed and cost of alternative modes of transportation is well known. The current preference for trucking as the best balance of this trade-off, however, comes at some environmental cost in traffic congestion, air pollution, and energy consumption that is seldom calculated in the transportation decision.

Pricing Issues

One of the most difficult marketing topics to examine from an ethical viewpoint is price. Contributing to this difficulty is that pricing decisions are still regarded as more art than science. Thus, price setting is not the deterministic process with accepted procedures that theoretical economics would indicate. The major limitations for pricing are set by cost considerations, competitive conditions, corporate objectives, and existing law (see Exhibit 4-6). For example, attempting to discriminate on price among similar classes of buyers or to collude with competitors to fix prices are explicitly covered by these laws. Still, pricing remains a difficult issue from an ethical perspective because of the sensitivity and concern for monetary matters by corporations and consumers alike. Perhaps no other area of managerial activity is more difficult to depict accurately, assess fairly, and prescribe realistically in terms of *morality* than the domain of price.

Apart from actions that are unlawful, several situations illustrate the troublesome nature of ethics and pricing. Among the most frequently

Exhibit 4-6 Legal Issues Affecting Pricing Decisions

Predatory Pricing. In times past, a firm might sell its products for less than their cost for a period of time, in hopes of driving a competitor out of business. Such practices are regulated at the national level by antitrust legislation (Sherman and Clayton Acts).

Horizontal Price Fixing (Collusion). Agreements among direct competitors to charge an identical price are generally held to be illegal *per se* under the Sherman and Clayton Acts. Collusion on prices is difficult to prove because identical or very similar prices may also result from legal tactics such as (a) extremely competitive markets where prices are generally equalized (e.g., gasoline and beer), or (b) the industry following a price leader and engaging in parallel pricing.

Price Discrimination. Selling a product of like grade and quality to different consumers for different prices is illegal under the Robinson-Patman Act (RPA) "where the effect of such discrimination may be to substantially lessen competition or may tend to create a monopoly in any line of commerce." The RPA provides for *bona fide* efforts to meet competition and cost differences (e.g., quantity discounts), and it covers promotional allowances. As a practical matter, the FTC and Department of Justice seldom take enforcement actions under the RPA today.

Price Deception. Posted prices for some products, particularly consumer goods, sometimes bear little relationship to the actual price of the product. Bait-and-switch tactics (advertising a product for a low price to get consumers into the store and then pressuring them to buy a higher priced model), "buy one, get one free" promises, and "going out of business sales" are examples. Laws, such as the Automobile Information Disclosure Act, Truth in Lending Act, and unit pricing statutes have been enacted to combat deceptive advertising. The Federal Trade Commission also has issued "Guides against Deceptive Pricing."

Markup Pricing. There are state laws that set the minimum amount that any product must be marked up. For example, some grocery products must carry a 6 percent markup. Therefore, supermarket chains may not sell these products for less than 6 percent above their cost. These statutes are sometimes controversial because retailers do not always follow them, and they tend to take away efficiency advantages of chain stores and other mass merchandisers.

Vertical Price Fixing (Resale Price Maintenance). "Fair-trade laws" used to allow the manufacturer to control prices at all levels in the channel of distribution. The Consumer Goods Pricing Act of 1975 repealed earlier statutes in this area. Despite the absence of these laws, some manufacturers exert substantial control over pricing their products. They argue that this is justified to maintain a quality image.

Source: Partially adapted from Lynda J. Oswald, *The Law of Marketing* (Cincinnati, OH: West, 2002), 120–22.

occurring circumstances (left column) and their related ethical problems (right column) are the following:

Pricing Situation	Ethical Concern
(1) The market is at overcapacity.	Firms may dump products on the market at cost or below, undermining competitors and, for environmentally sensitive products, encouraging wasteful consumption.
(2) The market is characterized as an oligopoly.	"Leader" firms may price high to signal other competitors that a given price will be the norm for some time.
(3) Products are undifferentiated.	Quality firms prefer to compete on nonprice dimensions, and this may lead to higher prices and illusory differentiation.
(4) Pricing is on an individual job basis.	Different customers may be charged differing prices for similar work.
(5) Profit is the sole evaluative criteria for company performance.	Firms may ignore social costs such as pollution.
(6) Top management is perceived not to be concerned about pricing ethics.	Firms may place pressure on middle managers and sales reps to price gouge or otherwise exploit "market opportunities" such as shortage conditions.
(7) Employees have regular and frequent opportunities to meet with competitors.	Firms may be tempted to engage in informal price fixing.
(8) Ethical rules and compliance procedures are lax or do not exist.	Firms and their employees may "short" the buyer or discriminate against vulnerable customers.

The notion of price is also closely tied to utilitarian ethical thinking. Consumers enter into an exchange with the seller when they perceive the benefits from the product to exceed the costs (defined here as price). Marketers, of course, are interested in making a profit from this exchange. In fact, price is the *only* revenue generator of the marketing mix variables. A reasonable profit enables a firm to continue to market products for the benefit of society. Thus, the good of society is being satisfied by a firm achieving a reasonable profit. However, the logical extension of this argument is often what gets business firms in trouble. In theory, price setting generates a Pareto optimum, that is, it meets the utilitarian criterion for the transacting parties, only under conditions of perfect competition—available alternatives, perfect information, and resource mobility. This interpretation also ignores externalities or third party interests. Much can be justified in the name of profit. However, such ills as deceptive advertising, environmental damage, product defects, and ignoring the poor and minorities sometimes result from the overemphasis on the profit motive and its utilitarian rationale, because the market conditions that would justify it as the sole criterion for determining price (or making any other business decision) are absent.

We advocate considering two other philosophical views toward price. One is the concept of *proportionate reason*. Here the price set by a firm should be either equal to or proportional to the benefit received. Greater benefits, for example in terms of the lifesaving services of some surgeons, then would dictate higher prices. Ethical questions arising from this approach are:

- Does the perceived benefit of a product morally justify charging a higher price, especially when the action also has some negative side effects (e.g., charging very high prices for electronic games and athletic shoes aimed at youngsters who experience peer pressure to buy these games even though they [or their parents] often have limited means)?
- Is it wrong to charge a price that yields an extraordinary profit margin merely because customers are willing to pay the price (e.g., women's perfume or designer watches)?

The second philosophical perspective for dealing with price is the *principle of fairness*. This perspective implies that manufacturers should be fair in their pricing to channel intermediaries and customers, wholesalers should be fair to retailers, and retailers should be fair to end consumers. Pricing fairness may also be a buyer issue when large retailers squeeze suppliers who have no choice but to go along by making late payments, taking unearned discounts, utilizing variable pricing (as in Scenario 3 at the beginning of the chapter), or insisting on extraordinary services. This commonsense approach is intuitively appealing, but may be difficult to apply in practice. In theory, competitive conditions, risk, the amount and cost of capital, and predictable volume of sales would all go into calculating a "fair price." Returns to other channel members are also an issue in this calculation.[24] In practice, it is often hard to define fairness in a highly competitive environment. An historical discussion of "fair" prices is shown in Exhibit 4-7.

Ethics in Price Setting

Setting a price for a product is often a difficult decision to make. Marketers rely on several bases from which to set prices: costs, competitors, customers, and, sometimes, the government. One typical ethical abuse is price gouging (i.e., taking advantage of those who must have your product and are willing to pay an inordinately high price for it). Price gouging is commonly viewed as unethical. However, what constitutes price gouging is less

---

EXHIBIT 4-7   Just Price

- One researcher found that in states where the state monopolized the liquor trade, the prices of advertised liquor brands tended to be lower than advertised prices in states where liquor retailing was in private hands. How could this be? The researcher conjectured that

  > Monopoly states . . . apparently set the prices (or margins) largely with reference to other monopoly states. As a group, they apparently believe (judging by the trade literature) that their present revenues are "fair" and "what is necessary."

- The department of Water, Sewage, and Gas in Palo Alto, California, has a lifeline rate for water. It is a low rate to ensure that no family is denied water.

These are examples of *just price,* an ethical concept of pricing that arose during the Middle Ages. Medieval theorists were less concerned with what does happen than with what should happen, a charge that is sometimes laid in modern times to economists. Thomas Aquinas saw the just price as being equal to the sellers' cost, where cost could include, for example, the loss one suffers in parting with a cherished item and the cost of moving and storing goods. Other theologians considered that the market price, the price set by common estimation, was the just price. The merchant was exhorted to avoid the sin of greed, meaning that he should not buy merchandise to sell it unchanged at a higher price or charge more than he needed to maintain himself and his family in a style suitable to his station; to charge more to someone in dire need was to commit the sin of avarice.

It has been argued by some that businesses engage in a modern form of the just price when they base their prices on full cost. A full-cost price does not go up during periods of high demand, periods of shortages, and it does not go down when demand weakens. By not raising prices in times of high demand, the argument goes, businesses act responsibly by not exploiting the consumer when they might. (But when demand falls . . .)

Ethical concepts like just price assume particular importance in nonprofit organizations, most particularly in organizations that receive a major portion of their funds other than from their fees and prices, that is, other than from things they sell, and in which professionals are involved in administrative decisions.

Source: David L. Rados, *Marketing for Nonprofit Organizations,* 2nd ed. (Westport, CT: Auburn House, 1996), 274–75.

---

clear. Most observers believe prestige pricing (sometimes disparagingly called "snob appeal" pricing), like that used for Cross pens and BMW or Lexus automobiles, is acceptable. Other observers look at it from the perspective of lower income consumers: "charging higher than necessary prices for the essentials of life is morally offensive compared with charging high prices for luxuries."[25]

Web-based pricing tools have allowed firms to set (and rise or lower) prices. After entering in large amounts of dates from the previous few years, retailers and manufacturers can adopt "perfect pricing." However, ethical issues can rise from these sophisticated tactics.

> Still, perfect pricing, if botched, could spark a consumer backlash. Amazon.com already has had a taste: Shoppers complained to the online retailer two years ago when they realized it was testing different prices for the same items in different markets. Amazon abandoned the test after just five days and went back to uniform pricing. In another case, former Coca-Cola CEO M. Douglas Ivester unleashed a storm of protest by simply musing to a journalist about someday being able to raise prices automatically at vending machines during hot weather, when demand would be higher.[26]

Industrial Products

The ethical issues associated with the pricing of industrial goods often revolve around the competitive nature of the market and the type of buying relationship. Areas where industrial firms have run afoul of the law are in *price fixing* and *competitive bidding*. Legal restrictions now exist to help ensure that price fixing does not occur and that bidding is fair. However, in industries such as defense contracting and construction, bid rigging, corporate pricing espionage, and other price-related scandals still seem to occur. It appears that an intense competitive environment may cause industrial firms to lower their ethical standards in order to get profitable business.

In business-to-business pricing of products, the ethical responsibility of each party increases as firms move more toward a long-term relationship. Cooperation, not conflict, with suppliers seems to be the watchword during this era of growing emphasis on quality and cost control. Traditional negotiating practices associated with pricing industrial products—in which much relevant information is hidden and bluffing is common—is now giving way to a more forthright system where information on costs is shared along with design and engineering responsibilities. For example, A. O. Smith, the Milwaukee-based manufacturer of automobile frames, set up a research and development office in Detroit to work more closely with the car makers. Thus, interorganizational linkages are strengthening such that ethical problems in industrial sector pricing may be diminishing.

Consumer Goods

On the surface, ethical issues seem more predominant in the pricing of consumer goods. Because prices are not the subject of much everyday discussion, consumers may be less well informed than the professional buyers employed by business and government and, because individual consumers are less able to influence the price they pay for most goods and services, they are the least powerful member of the marketing channel. Words like "deceptive," "unfair," and "misleading" are sometimes associated with prices for consumer products. Much advertising, especially by retailers, features price. Therefore, the sheer magnitude of price information causes ethical concerns to surface. To combat this problem, Ethan Allen—furniture maker and retailer—has adopted a one price policy (e.g., a particular item is priced the same in all U.S. stores) that includes free delivery.

Services

The service sector of the economy represents one of the major growth areas of the future. Since services are often labor intensive, they are more variable and perishable than most tangible products. Thus, pricing becomes more difficult as costs are harder to estimate accurately. Relatively high gross margins permit a great deal of room for negotiation. Comparisons between alternative providers are difficult and frequently unthinkable due to the personal dependency factor that characterizes many services. For example, most consumers would not "shop" heart surgeons based on their fee. Furthermore, project-based services tend to produce individualized pricing. Capacity limitations prompt higher prices at peak times and lower prices during slack periods. Services are frequently bundled together in pricing, making cost estimates for individual elements difficult and, in many cases, irrelevant. Long-term relationships permit—and may require—a mix of both high- and low-profit transactions. Thus, a general lack of transparency and the problem of meeting different, but often unknown, customer expectations necessarily complicates pricing in the service sector. From the consumer's perspective, the risk in securing services is typically viewed as higher.

One specific ethically questionable area deals with pricing practices in the financial services industry. In promoting various services, minimum balance requirements and service charges are often not spelled out or are buried in fine print or arcane language. Only the most favorable interest rate is promoted. Many consumers do not know what "daily interest" means, or how often interest is compounded, or what service charges are associated with what specific balance amounts.

Services aimed at business-to-business customers also can lead to ethical issues. Despite the fact that these buyers are supposed to be more knowledgeable and have more avenues of recourse, abuses do occur. Probably one of the most egregious examples was recounted in Barbara Toffler's exposé on the former accounting firm, Arthur Andersen, and its ethical compliance consulting practice that she headed:

> Our job was to help the newly appointed business practices officer get going. Since she was new, the project looked like a blank slate—which meant, I quickly

learned, a blank check. The client wanted some basic education on what an ethics and business practices office did, and some guidance in establishing the components that did not already exist, as the development of some training materials.

It should have been a $50,000 to $75,000 engagement. It wasn't. We took advantage of our neophyte and steadily built a dependency on our team by such things as giving her weekly "homework" assignments to help her learn about her new position, and devising a monthly step-by-step plan that basically said to her that she wouldn't be able to sustain her responsibilities without us being present. Before she knew what hit her, she had an action plan priced at around $250,000 a month. We had seen a key vulnerability—that the client didn't really have an official budget and that the contact was new in her position—and pounced. After about a month and a half of this, the CEO, whom I knew well, finally put a stop to it. I had worked with this company before, and I knew they trusted me. But I was struggling to make it in this culture, and Billing Our Brains Out was the only way I saw to do so.[27]

Ethics of Nonprice Price Increases

One practice—called downsizing—often associated with pricing ethics is reducing the quality or quantity of a product without reducing the price. The confectionery industry is one of the best-known practitioners of this "nonprice price increase" by shrinking the candy bar but not the price. Similarly, certain paper products manufacturers regularly reduce the number of units (diapers, tissues, napkins) per package, but keep the price the same. Marketers of baseball cards have sometimes reduced the number of cards per package or eliminated the bubble gum while keeping the price the same. Comparable to downsizing is the practice of supersizing items—with a negligible production cost increase—at a price that is higher, but not quite proportionally so. This practice is employed by marketers in many countries. Both sides of this controversial practice are explained using a Brazilian example.

> The local unit of France's Danone Group says it shaved nearly one ounce off the package size for two types of cookies and crackers when it relaunched them under a new brand name. In a statement, the company says its cookies and crackers, or biscuits, "are new and have a revolutionary concept, different from other biscuits that currently exist in the Brazilian biscuit market."

Consumer-protection groups brush off such explanations.

> "If the companies weren't trying to fool buyers, they would have informed them of the change in a clear manner," says Maria Ines Fornazaro, executive director of Sao Paulo state's consumer-protection agency, Procon. "The vast majority of consumers hadn't noticed the amount changed because the size of the packaging remained the same."[28]

Manufacturers defend these practices for several reasons. First, nonprice price increases are often a convenient way to respond to cost increases when price structures are not flexible, for example, products sold in vending machines. Second, the practice sometimes brings the product packaging and content amount more in line with competition. (This rationale was probably also used by Dannon in the United States when it decreased the size of yogurt packages from 8 to 6 ounces and kept the price the same, probably because Yoplait had moved to 6-ounce containers several years earlier.) Third, modern technology allows companies to reduce the weight of the package or contents while maintaining its yield of finished product.

Critics counter these arguments with comments that it doesn't change the fact that the consumer is getting less product, and it is a way to increase margins at the expense of the consumer. Even less defensible is the practice of pricing products in larger, "economy-size" packages at a higher unit cost, relying on the consumer's assumption that such packages almost always deliver product at a lower unit cost (discussed earlier). This issue has received more attention recently with several state attorneys general claiming these practices are deceptive. One remedy that has been considered is requiring a notice on the "principal display panel" of a downsized product for six months. **What are your views—are these tactics unethical?**

Ethics in Price Discounting

Since the inflationary early eighties, rebates have been offered by manufacturers on almost any product imaginable, from socks to toasters to automobiles. The retail sector saw the growth of warehouse food stores, discount shopping malls, and superstores that offered name-brand appliances at substantial price savings. From such developments, an ethical problem in the retail sector has arisen. Some discount stores have billed themselves as *outlet stores* (where they offer only one manufacturer's product at presumably lower than retail prices). Consumers sometimes find that these stores do *not* really offer significant price breaks.

In general, the trend toward price discounting has made consumers not only more price conscious, but also more susceptible to discount price appeals. Scenario 4 heading this chapter presents a current price discounting scheme. Do you think it undermines the accepted notion of a "customary price" level, or misleads consumers and does not properly discharge the marketer's duties to stakeholders (i.e., customers, competitors, and the general public)?

Rebates are a popular form of price discounting. They have been used extensively for virtually all products in this price conscious era. Rebates are offered for several reasons. They draw customers into stores, spur sales of nonrebate items, allow manufacturers to differentiate themselves from their competitors, and help stores move aging products. There are a few ethical problems that have surfaced with rebates. Sometimes, manufacturers make it very difficult for consumers to "cash in" the rebate (e.g., original sales receipt, UPC code, and manufacturer rebate form). An interesting tactic has been taken by the auto manufacturers, who often use rebates to stimulate sales. With a $500 rebate, one car maker increased the sticker price of the SUV by $435 and added $25 to the standard delivery fee. *The Wall Street Journal* labeled such practices "stealth price increases" and went on to say, "Overall vehicle prices, adjusted for additional features added to new models, have actually been declining about 1% a year since the mid-1990s. With competition only getting more intense, most in the industry expect the discounting to continue. But the little sticker-price increases and elimination of options may make it harder for consumers to identify the bargains."[29]

Rebates are now being used on other relatively high-ticket items such as computers and televisions. Although the low price prompts the purchase, approximately 60 percent of purchasers never get a rebate. That includes customers who never file, as well as those whose applications are rejected because they have not complied with an offer's conditions.[30] Stakeholder analysis would include discussion of primary parties—the company and its current customers. Secondary stakeholders, such as the media and future customers, would take great interest in knowing the questionable practices of a company and may use this information in future purchases.[31] A utilitarian assessment would have to consider the impacts of rebates on all affected parties. A duty-based analysis would ask the question of whether it is the firm's intention to deceive consumers. A final question to ask is "do the ends justify the means?"   **What is your view concerning the ethics of rebates?**

Price Advertising

Some advertising relies heavily on price appeals. For instance, most retail newspaper advertising—classified ads (e.g., automotive), food ads, and ads for many services (e.g., lawn care)—use primarily price-oriented messages. As mentioned earlier, price advertising for services often utilizes large and bold print to indicate a low price. Typical are the ads for airlines, auto rentals, and many financial services. However, the small print at the bottom of the ad usually places many restrictions on the advertised price. Much of this type of advertising can be misleading (if not outright deceptive) and raises significant ethical questions. For example, airlines commonly list the one-way fares in their ads and indicate in the small print that the price is only good for a round trip.

One outgrowth of the price discounting trend is the extensive advertising of "lowest-price" claims. Retailers more frequently contend that they will not be undersold and "guarantee" that they will offer the consumer the lowest price. These assertions signify that the retailer monitors all of its competitors' prices, or imply the consumer is to be a full-time price-comparison investigator. Neither of these implied actions is very realistic. The pervasiveness of the "we-won't-be-undersold philosophy" is illustrated by the fact that some of the nation's top retailers have been reprimanded by the Better Business Bureau or by state or local consumer protection offices for using such practices.

To counteract this trend, which has led to negative publicity of retail pricing in general, the aforementioned Council of Better Business Bureaus code for advertising specifically addresses price promotions. The first seven points (out of 20) in the code outline specific acceptable practices in a range of price advertising areas such as credit terms and use of the word "free" and "bait" in advertising and selling (see http://www.bbb.org/advertising/adcode.asp).

IDEAS FOR ETHICAL MARKETING

We propose several ideas that both distribution and pricing managers might utilize in their firm to encourage ethical behavior in the areas of distribution and pricing:

First, firms should develop explicit guidelines to cover the purchasing function within the organization. Rather than rely only on codes and guidance provided by trade and professional organizations, such as the Institute for Supply Management (recall Exhibit 4-4), we advocate companies (even small ones) considering the development of explicit guidelines geared toward their industry. Exhibit 4-8 depicts an excellent 12-point process a company can use for this purpose. Committing the organization's policies to writing and setting specific value limits on gifts seem to be good ways for a company to implement such procedures. Furthermore, setting penalties for violations is an essential part of this policy-setting process; if enforcement does not happen, the guidelines can quickly be viewed as mere platitudes, never to be taken seriously. And senior managers should abide by the same rules as purchasing agents.

Second, retailers should set up mechanisms for discussing ethical issues within their companies that are most relevant to their business. Retailers interested in a more concerted effort toward integrating ethics into their organizations need to decide how to best evoke ethical questions. Some use short phrases that convey to employees the company philosophy. For example, Olive Garden, the restaurant chain, places four words on the revolving door to the kitchen that serve as a constant reminder for the waiters and waitresses. They are *honesty* (noteworthy because it appears first on the list), *action, detail,* and *urgency.*

This is a good beginning, but retailers can go further. For example, Ralph's, the California-based supermarket chain now part of Kroger's, requires its managers to sign the company code of ethics every year. The company also holds an annual seminar for its marketing staff to teach them about ethics and remind them of pertinent and emerging legal requirements. The discussion of ethics is clearly facilitated using this approach. Other

Exhibit 4-8   An Ethics Proposal for Purchasing Managers

A prominent marketing executive and past president of the Council of Sales Promotion Agencies suggested the following points should be followed in purchasing situations. He indicated these steps should occur.

1. Establish a definitive policy that prevents greed from overpowering common sense.
2. Commit the policy to writing and make it part of your company's standard operating procedure.
3. Set monetary maximums for gifts accepted by employees and for gifts given to clients/vendors.
4. Set value limits for major entertainment occasions (e.g., holiday parties for clients).
5. Limit the number of people in your organization who have purchasing authority.
6. Get to know your employees with purchasing authority. If you identify lifestyle characteristics that are not commensurate with salary, check into it.
7. Establish a system of checks and balances. For example, require purchase orders involving large amounts of money to be countersigned by someone else of authority in the organization.
8. Hold meetings with major vendors once a year under the guise of working toward a better relationship.
9. Check purchase orders periodically to identify patterns that may signal a conflict of interest.
10. Make it firmly understood that your organization will not do business with anyone who expects a kickback or who offers something more than excellent work.
11. Enforce penalties for violations of the policies you establish when the need arises.
12. Set an example for acceptable conduct at the very top of your organization.

Source: Interview with Vincent Sottosanti, former president and chairman of Comart Associates, July 31, 1991.

possibilities include ethical discussions at sales and management meetings. The format of such gatherings is discussed in Chapter 6. (To view Kroger's mission statement, which contains several important ethical principles, see http://www.ralphs.com/corpnewsinfo_mission.htm.)

Third, companies should consider developing a pricing "Bill of Rights" for their consumers and suppliers. Since pricing is a difficult area and one about

EXHIBIT 4-9   A Consumer's Bill of Rights for Pricing

A consumer is entitled to receive fair value for the money spent to purchase a product or service. He or she has the right to expect that the price was realistically and analytically arrived at by the firm and was calculated to give the firm a reasonable profit. The price should be fully disclosed by being stated in advertisement for the product or service, posted at the point of sale, and placed on the product (although the use of UPCs confounds this requirement). The price on the product should be the price at which the seller is willing to enter into an exchange. It should not be artificially high, so that it causes the buyer to believe he or she has received a bargain when the price is lowered in negotiations to its intended level. When the product is changed in quality or quantity, the customer is entitled to receive a proportional change in price. Price changes should be promptly announced and completely implemented. Questions concerning price should be honestly answered. Customers are always entitled to fair and equal pricing treatment in the marketplace.

Source: William J. Kehoe, "Ethics, Price Fixing, and the Management of Price Strategy," in *Marketing Ethics,* ed. G. R. Laczniak and P. E. Murphy, 81 (Lexington, MA: Lexington Books, 1985).

which customers are cynical, firms may want to consider authoring such a document. One such declaration is shown in Exhibit 4-9. It represents the thinking needed by firms that want to be more forthcoming regarding their pricing decisions. We advocate such a statement for both consumer and channel pricing decisions. If all marketing personnel agreed with this philosophical statement, we would anticipate that many ethical problems in pricing could be solved. The often used "satisfaction guaranteed or your money back" is a thumbnail version of the approach we envision. However, the firm should consider going further and being more explicit. For example, a common "lowest price" policy allows consumers who find a lower price within 30 days of purchase to have the difference rebated.

CONCLUDING COMMENT

Distribution, merchandising, and pricing decisions made by manufacturers, franchisors, and various marketing intermediaries encompass many ethically charged issues. Relationships between suppliers and purchasers, manufacturers and distributors, wholesalers and retailers, franchisors and franchisees, and retailers and consumers are inherently characterized by conflicts that generate ethical questions. Similarly, the pricing strategies employed by all these firms raise the specter of potential ethical abuse. In this chapter, we identified many of these issues and suggested directions for firms seeking to better handle these ethical questions. Regardless of the theoretical approach taken toward ethics in distribution and pricing, a key theme throughout this discussion is the responsibility associated with market power over dependent, less informed, and, therefore, more vulnerable market partners. This responsibility implies fairness and transparency in all dealings and specific efforts to avoid taking advantage of consumers, franchisees, and suppliers who, in market terms, are disadvantaged.

Chapter Five

Ethics in Advertising and on the Internet

Scenario 1

The "decommunization" of Eastern Europe since 1990 has brought the kinds of aggressive, sometimes misleading advertising and personal selling tactics not seen in North America since the 1930s, when state, provincial, and federal laws were passed restricting the types of messages used to promote consumer products. "Sure cure" medicines, "get rich quick" investment schemes, and products of dubious performance and durability are widely hawked on the streets, in flyers, and on radio and television to consumers hungry for consumption and investment opportunities. Advertising regulation is unusual in economies where most businesses are operated by the government. The transition from state-managed to market economies, therefore, is occurring at the same time as these societies struggle to establish the legal system, dispute resolution mechanisms, and institutional framework taken for granted in well-established market economies. In this void, many companies have joined indigenous entrepreneurs in taking advantage of eager and often unsophisticated consumers and the lack of effective rules. **What is the responsibility of ethical marketers, especially multinationals from developed economies, in "free for all" competitive circumstances? Should American, Canadian, Japanese, and Western European firms lobby Eastern European governments for legislation that would protect consumers from such promotional tactics?**

Scenario 2

As the number of businesses and individuals using the Internet has grown, marketers have jumped on this new medium as an opportunity to reach potential buyers of their products and services. Credit card operators "spam" millions of consumers each week with invitations to apply and receive low, even 0% interest rates; they do not disclose that these promotional rates only apply for the first few months. By way of scanning "cookies," electronic storage files housed within individual computers, booksellers learn computer owners' interests and buying habits based on their Internet activities and send targeted e-mail messages promoting specific books owners might be interested in buying. These consumers almost always have *not* asked to be put on the e-mail list. **Are these practices ethical? Should the federal government enact legislation to prevent them?**

The above scenarios offer only a glimpse of how promoting sales via advertising, direct and Internet marketing is a value-laden issue for companies, individuals engaged in promotion activities, and societies interested in maintaining fair, efficient, and sustainable markets. Business executives defend these activities as playing a central role in furthering their marketing mission, as well as being a form of free speech. Critics, on the other hand, contend some forms of promotion often take advantage of uninformed buyers, manipulate consumers, can be an obstacle to new and small competitors, and even create frivolous needs. Staunch supporters of promotion's role see it as the fuel powering the engine of a market economy. They use this economic defense to justify almost any message or medium despite such abuses as sex role stereotyping of women, exaggerated hype, unduly persuasive messages aimed at children, and intrusive telemarketing and e-mail. Critics are often equally strident in calling for strictly informative advertising such as classified ads in newspapers and an end to unsolicited direct mail, telemarketing, and e-mail. Probably policies regulating promotion should be formulated and evaluated from a perspective falling between these extreme positions. We begin by identifying the key ethical issues in advertising. We bring relevant ethical principles to bear on each to help those engaged in promotional activities solve the numerous ethical dilemmas in their work.

THE POWER AND COMPLEXITY OF ADVERTISING

Advertising is a significant economic force. Nearly $260 billion was spent on measured advertising in the United States alone in 2004, and global advertising spending is projected to be over $400 billion in 2006.[1] "Advertising consists of all activities involved in presenting to an audience a nonpersonal, sponsor-identified, paid-for message about a product or organization."[2]

Given these properties, it tends to be biased and advocative, often intrusive, and, for those who are outside the target audience, irrelevant and sometimes offensive. These characteristics lead some to feel advertising swirls about the eye of an ethical storm; it is no surprise that it comes under great public scrutiny. For example, the visibility and effect of advertising is so great that many consumers think of it as synonymous with marketing.

The subject of advertising ethics is particularly complex because three major stakeholders are involved in most advertising decisions. First, the *agency*, including its copywriters, account executives, and management, develops the creative campaign for any product and generally selects the media in which the ads are to appear. Second, *company* marketing executives, such as the brand management team and high-level marketing personnel, work with the agency in devising the campaign and, ultimately, must approve it. Third, *media*—their sales representatives, standards departments, managers, and top executives—all make decisions whether to carry the ad, based on the appropriateness of its message and likely audience. With all of the individuals and institutions involved, one might think the state of advertising ethics would be rather high. However, the complexity of these relationships and the shared responsibility they represent may work against any concerted ethical evaluation. In fact, one of your authors has dubbed these three stakeholders as the "unholy trinity" of advertising ethics since they seem to "pass the buck" to one another regarding moral standards.[3]

We believe management, whether from the agency, the client or sponsor, or the media, has the responsibility to adhere to ethical principles in ad campaigns. Ethical concerns range from the spokesperson used (e.g., well-known actors plug seemingly low-cost life insurance aimed at the elderly), to the message itself (e.g., the use of large print price appeal headlines with small print disclaimers by car rental companies and airlines), the media utilized (e.g., visual pollution caused by billboards), and the suitability of a particular ad for its intended audience (e.g., when children are audience members).

In the following pages, we address five major topics: (1) the role of advertising in society, including the positions of its various critics and supporters, and efforts to regulate advertising, both within the industry itself and by government; (2) several important ethical issues facing advertising managers; (3) a discussion of ethical concerns in Internet and online marketing; (4) recent positive developments and future challenges relating to ethical standards in advertising; and (5) specific ideas for ethical marketing that might help upgrade ethical sensitivity in advertising.

ADVERTISING AND SOCIETY

Advertising's role in society is controversial. The positions of both critics and supporters of advertising, a long-running debate, were characterized some years ago as "a dialogue that never happens." In this section we discuss perspectives that articulate both ends of this spectrum. We also examine the regulation of advertising by industry and government in the context of societal concerns.

Criticisms of Advertising[4]

The ethical criticisms of advertising can be categorized as *macro* or *micro*. Macrocriticisms of advertising generally deal with the negative social impact of advertising. For example, could the vast monies spent on advertising every year be more usefully allocated to achieve other (more socially relevant) goals? Does advertising help foster a materialistic or sexist culture? Microcriticisms focus on the propriety of specific advertising practices. For example, should cartoon characters be allowed to pitch products on programs targeted for children?[5] Should ads for contraceptives be shown on network TV?

The macrodebate about advertising ethics has a long tradition. For instance in 1907, one critic of advertising wrote, "On the moral side, it [advertising] is thoroughly false and harmful. It breeds vulgarity, hypnotizes the imagination and the will, fosters covetousness, envy, hatred, and underhand competition."[6] This argument that advertising appeals to base motives has been augmented over the years. Though advertising is very influential, some argue it exhibits no social responsibility: Advertising distorts values, especially of children; it creates insatiable desires for goods; it has degraded language, manners, dress, and tastes; and it has disrupted family authority and redefined achievement as buying and owning as the real marks of a successful life.[7]

From an ethical perspective, these criticisms can be summarized along the following lines. The first is a contention that advertising violates people's inherent rights. The argument here is that so much advertising is persuasively one-sided that it violates the principle of fairness by depriving consumers of unbiased input with which to make an informed buying decision, in effect, limiting their ability to make rational decisions on their own behalf. A second charge is that advertising encourages certain human addictions. This proposition focuses on the social appropriateness of *any* advertising campaign for such controversial products as cigarettes and other tobacco products, liquor, pornography, and firearms. The frequent use of fear appeals is a variant of this idea. Third, advertising is motivated by the desire for money, not to foster truth. Thus, a certain proportion of advertising will always be inherently misleading because, in the quest for sales, it nurtures false implications or associates product usage with a lifestyle or social image that may have little to do with the product. For example, can drinkers of Old Milwaukee beer really expect to find themselves in a situation where "it doesn't get any better than this"? Does chewing some brand of gum really lead to social acceptance or sexual attractiveness? Fourth, advertising frequently sacrifices human dignity, for example, by exploiting women as sex objects.

With regard to the micro-objections, the list of criticisms is long. A paper examining work on advertising ethics found the continued use of arguably deceptive advertising generated the highest level of ethical concern. Other issues in the "top five" involve exploitative advertising to children (see Exhibit 5-1, for an analysis of children's advertising), ads for tobacco and alcoholic beverages, the increased use of negative political ads, and stereotyping in advertising.[8] Economic considerations also figure in critiques of advertising: waste and inefficiency and the development of market power based largely on image.

Defenses for Advertising

A common response to many macrocriticisms of the advertising industry is that advertising is little more than a mirror of contemporary society. The argument goes as follows: as a "looking glass" or "mirror" reflecting the attitudes of society, one should expect that sometimes advertising is manipulative just as other forms of communication might manipulate or mislead.[9] Advertising also will sometimes be in "bad taste" just as some art or movies or political speeches are in poor taste. Defenders of advertising argue that it is an essential force in a market economy. Further, most advertising provides useful information that allows consumers to glean important facts and, thereby, enhances efficiency in product choice.[10] Therefore, despite the use of persuasion, having corporation-sponsored information about the products available in a complex, consumption-driven economy provides many more benefits than dysfunctions. This kind of pragmatic and utilitarian analysis is also commonly employed to defend advertising.

Consider the following as a "case in point" concerning the utilitarian trade-off inherent in advertising. An analysis of six decades of research dealing with perceptions of advertising concludes the typical consumer finds most advertising definitely informative and the best means for learning what is available in the market.[11] However, the study also indicates that, consistently over time, about 70 percent of consumers believe advertising is sometimes untruthful and may persuade people to buy things they do not want, but, on balance, the valuable information provided by advertising is worth the deficiencies caused by its inherent persuasiveness. Advertising's defenders are quite adamant in their view that most advertising is not only ethical, but also helpful, while granting the problematic nature of these practices. Even some philosophers have provided tightly argued analyses suggesting that the vast majority of advertising is neither manipulative nor deceptive because it generally does not violate the criteria for establishing consumer autonomy.

Advertising also is but one of many sources of information for most people. Values and attitudes are also influenced by the press, schools, and

Exhibit 5-1   Advertising and Internet Marketing to Children[1]

Advertising is ever-present in the lives of most American children. Estimates suggest that children spend an average of four hours per day watching television and are exposed to as many as 25,000 commercials in a single year.[2] Emerging media such as the Internet have further expanded advertising's reach and offer novel opportunities to target this young audience. Approximately 88 percent of children between 5–14 years of age use computers, and 53 percent have access to the Internet.[3] Concern about children's ability to comprehend and evaluate these selling messages has stimulated heated debate since the early 1970s. Embedded within this debate is the contention that advertising to children is inherently "unfair."

Children as a Target Market

In 2002, approximately $15 billion was spent in the United States on marketing communications directly targeted at children.[4] This included television and print advertising, product placements, sales promotions, packaging design, public relations, and in-school marketing. There is little doubt that television remains the most effective medium to reach children. On average, U.S. children are viewing almost five hours of television commercials per week.

Advertising's Impact on Children

At the root of the children's advertising debate is the question of children's unique vulnerabilities. Concerns about young children range from their inability to resist specific selling efforts to a fear that without benefit of well-developed critical thinking skills they may learn undesirable social values such as materialism.[5] The Center for Science in the Public Interest (CSPI) has recently issued a detailed report arguing that growing health problems such as childhood obesity and poor diets can be linked to the advertising of high-fat, high-sugar foods aimed at this young audience.[6]

The Blurring of Advertising and Entertainment

As the media landscape children face has diversified, the lines between advertising and entertainment have become increasingly blurred. This is true across media. For example, television commercials have become increasingly focused on entertainment and image creation, and are often tied to enticing Web site games and activities through brand characters. Children's magazines also often include puzzles, games, comics, or editorials that are sponsored by advertisers. Promotional tie-ins or placements in movies further muddy the distinction between advertising and entertainment designed for children. More generally, company sponsored Web sites containing games, contests, and promotions designed for children pervade the Internet. Children are ready consumers of these marketing communications: approximately 64 percent of children (5–14) who access the Internet do so to play games.[7] Engaging interactive "advergames" embed brand messages in colorful, fun, and fast-paced adventures (see, e.g., Nabiscoworld.com or Mcdonalds.com). Brands represent an integral component of the game whether as game pieces, prizes, or secret treasures. By playing the games, brand awareness is reinforced, and repeat visits are encouraged.[8] **What is your assessment of these advertising and Internet strategies aimed at children?**

---

[1]This exhibit was adapted from Elizabeth S. Moore, "Children and the Changing World of Advertising," *Journal of Business Ethics*, forthcoming.

[2]Federal Communications Commission, "Children's Television: Programming and Commercial Limits," (2003), at http://ftp.fcc.gov/commissioners/abernathy/news/childrenstiv.html. Accessed November 5, 2003.

[3]U.S. Department of Education, *Computer and Internet Use By Children and Adolescents in 2001*, National Center for Education Statistics (2003): 2004–14.

[4]Center for Science in the Public Interest (CSPI), *Pestering Parents: How Food Companies Market Obesity to Children* (2003), Washington, DC: Author.

[5]M. C. Macklin, "Children: Targets of Advertising," in *Encyclopedia of Advertising*, ed. J. McDonough and K. Egolf, 294–98 (New York: Fitzroy Dearborn, 2003).

[6]Center for Science in the Public Interest, *Pestering Parents: How Food Companies Market Obesity to Children* (2003), Washington, DC: Author.

[7]U.S. Department of Education, *Computer and Internet Use.*

[8]Professor Moore is the first author to make this observation. See her article for more detail.

---

churches, and, of course, relationships within families and among coworkers, neighbors, and friends. While influenced by advertising, it would be presumptuous to assume that these formative contexts are effectively a result of advertising. Moreover, most advertising is clearly governed by constitutional protections for freedom of speech in the belief that this is the best way to ensure the discovery of truth. Finally, inputs to buyer decisions most prominently include personal experiences with products and informal sources of product information.

REGULATING ADVERTISING PRACTICES

Consumers are protected from questionable advertising practices by both government regulation and the advertising industry's own instruments of self-regulation. Since 1924, the American Association of Advertising Agencies has promulgated a general "Standards of Practice" statement, last updated in 1990 (see www.aaaa.org/inside/standards.pdf). In the United States, more direct industry regulation is provided by a network of organizations linked to the AAAA and the Council of Better Business Bureaus (BBB): the National Advertising Review Council (which issues informal recommendations only), the National Advertising Division (NAD), and its subsidiary, the National Advertising Review Board (NARB). As mentioned in Chapter 4, the BBB has a detailed "Code of Advertising."[12] NAD, established in 1971, investigates almost 200 cases of unfairness in advertising annually. Many of the questionable ads brought to the NAD are identified by competitors, indicating that advertisers guard the honesty of each other. Most disputes brought at this level (approximately 98 percent) are resolved, but for those cases still at question, the NARB becomes a court of appeal. The NARB is staffed by members of the advertising profession, as well as informed persons from the general public. Given that this control process is an industrywide effort to maintain the integrity of advertising, endorsed and adjudicated by the industry itself, there is great pressure upon advertisers to abide by the findings of the NAD/NARB. Still, some advertising practices may require a stronger form of intervention that can only be provided by the force of government regulation. Local Better Business Bureaus also exercise some control over advertising by small firms in their geographic areas.

Comparable mechanisms have been developed in most advanced economies around the globe. However, transitional and less developed economies typically are without much in the way of either industry or governmental regulation.

In the United States, principal government oversight of advertising is provided by the Federal Trade Commission (FTC). Established in 1914, the FTC has jurisdiction over all forms of false and deceptive trade practices, including advertising. The FTC has gone through relative periods of activity and inactivity, depending on the political climate of the country. In part, the level of regulatory fervor is due to the zeal of the chairman and commissioners who control the FTC and who are political appointees. Nonetheless, at all times the FTC protects the public from the most egregious forms of deceptive advertising. One of the most recent consumer-related activities was the FTC championing the national "do not call" list to protect citizens from unwanted telemarketing calls (www.donotcall.org). The FTC is assisted in its mission by various other government agencies, notably the Food and Drug Administration (FDA), which has jurisdiction over advertising for food and drug products. For example, regulations calling for improved nutritional labeling and disclosure were the result of cooperation between the FDA and the FTC. Most states in the United States, many municipalities, and governments around the world (with exceptions noted earlier) are likely to have comparable agencies and regulations.

While many feel the combination of industry self-regulation and the Federal Trade Commission safeguards against deceptive advertising, regulatory efforts are not without their critics, some of whom believe that much unethical advertising remains. For example, University of Wisconsin Professor Ivan Preston contends advertisers, by providing only partial truth (i.e., one-sided argumentation) about their products and services, contribute to the "diminishment of the truth."[13] Why? Partial truth is a form of falsity that harms many consumers who cannot be expected to gather sufficient buying information without reliance upon advertising claims. Preston proposes a reinvention of advertising regulation via the "reliance rule," requiring that the only product claims allowed would be those that advertisers advocate as being important enough for consumers to influence buying decisions and that can be substantiated. Thus, such claims as "Pontiac sells excitement" would have no standing because it is an unprovable "puff." But a claim such as, "This model Pontiac gets 30 miles per gallon" would be permitted—assuming this fuel economy measure can be substantiated.

ETHICS AND THE ADVERTISING INDUSTRY

Other issues to be addressed relate to actors that orchestrate modern advertising: companies that *sponsor* advertising, their *advertising agencies* that create and place advertisements, and *media* that carry advertising messages. The complexity of relationships among these stakeholders seems to add to ethical conflicts. For example, media are dependent for much of their revenues on advertising that underwrites programming or helps support operations in the print media. Thus, one question often raised is the extent to which advertising is able to shape media programming, especially its influence over any news content that is critical of a sponsor. Similarly, ad agencies are most often financially rewarded based on the amount of media time they buy rather than the quality of the advertising produced. Thus, inherent pressures may prompt ad agencies to push for more advertising, rather than investing in creative content and production values that might better serve marketing objectives. (In this regard, it should be noted that ad agency fee and commission structures vary and are undergoing changes that may reduce this historical bias in favor of media space or time.)

ETHICAL ISSUES FACING ADVERTISING

A number of ethical questions have been asked about advertising. In this section, we examine several of the most frequent and ethically charged queries.

Persuasion and Advertising

One of the most persistent areas of debate about advertising is its persuasive content. One useful way of looking at this area is in terms of a continuum:

Complete truth			Total lie
Factual	Persuasive	Embellished	Deceptive
Probably ethical		*Possibly unethical*	*Illegal*

This continuum implies that as one moves from left to right the potential for ethical problems increase; strictly informative advertising is much less suspect than advertising that relies heavily on persuasion. In turn, *embellishment* (to make something appear better than it is) or *puffery* (exaggerating a claim) is even more likely to present ethical problems. For example, embellishment is commonly used by marketers of men's and women's toiletries, suggesting that if one uses the product advertised, she or he will become more attractive to someone of the opposite sex. Outright deception is totally unethical and, in most jurisdictions, against the law.

Puffery is sometimes defended by advertisers, who say that everyone else does it, or that consumers can decide for themselves if a product is the "best." Since puffery is a claim based on opinion and thus cannot be substantiated, it cannot be considered deceptive under the law. For example, a computer diskette manufacturer made the following claim: "Somebody has to be better than everybody else." This claim cannot be proven true or false. Most "puffs" are harmless exaggeration such as "this auto's engine purrs like a kitten" or "this golf putter will make your stroke as smooth as a baby's skin." But the potential exists for unethical (and even arguably illegal) puffs in advertising.

This debate concerning the ethics of persuasive versus informative advertising has raged for a long time. A common advertising position is that *all* advertising is persuasive because its intention is to sell products. Some philosophers view all persuasive advertising, because it reduces the consumer's autonomy, and any advertising, informative or persuasive, for unsafe or unhealthy products (e.g., cigarettes and handguns) as unethical. Obviously, not everyone holds this view; the advertising community staunchly defends its right to advertise any legal product.

Advocacy (supporting a cause or position) is central to advertising, whether for companies, political candidates, or religious or cultural organizations. Its primary purpose has always been to advocate a point of view or a behavior change in the audience. To achieve this objective, advertising makes use of drama, words, symbols, music, pictures, and demonstrations to make its point.

The advocacy role for advertising leads to most of the issues already discussed. Although opinion polls would indicate consumers do not necessarily appreciate advertising's advocacy position, they are realistic enough to understand the purpose of ads is to sell products. Still, they are justifiably skeptical of much advertising. However, most buyers accept the advocacy role *as given* and believe intrusion and inconvenience may be balanced by the fact that advertising subsidizes most mass media. Without advertising, the newspaper, television, and radio industries would be radically different from what exists today and would likely be prohibitively expensive.

Two persuasive advertising techniques have caused substantial discussion and debate. *Ambush marketing* is used around major sporting events such as the Olympics, World Cup, and Super Bowl. Each of these big events has major sponsors, and in the case of the Olympics, companies pay millions over several years for the right to use the Olympic rings. Other firms like Nike are not "official" sponsors but "ambush"the event by advertising heavily before and during the event and also use billboards and other promotions near the venue. The ethical question involves whether the consumer can distinguish between the sponsors and ambushers.[14] Often, they cannot. The second practice that is seen every election year in the United States and now in Australia as well as other countries is *negative advertising*. This practice refers to pointing out the weaknesses of the competing candidate(s) rather than emphasizing the experience or credentials of the office seeker. (Many papers on this topic are available on the Web.) Much has been written pro and con about this practice. The unfortunate truth is that such ads seem to work with voters and consequently are used rather frequently. **What is your view on the ethics of these two advertising strategies?**

In conclusion, consumers should be able to make decisions based on their own desires, not those created by persuasive appeals. One might thus contend that persuasive advertising is acceptable if it does not coerce a consumer's choice. Yet some puffery or embellishment remains problematic when directed to a market that may not understand all the implications of a message, such as children or immigrants.

Emphasizing Insignificant Differences

The use of emotional and self-expressive benefits can cause ethical dilemmas when an attempt is made to communicate differential benefits when they really don't exist.[15] When products are physically and functionally identical, marketers regularly try to create imagery that conveys some emotional or self-expressive benefits. This is particularly common in the fashion and fragrance industries.

The ethical question here is particularly difficult to engage. Legitimate questions arise about what should count as a real difference, particularly the extent to which imagery itself can be considered "real." Distinct brands are sometimes positioned to target specific demographic or lifestyle groups by differentiating them through the creation of very different images. For instance, Clairol has successfully marketed its hair care products by appealing to women's sense of beauty and esteem. If the underlying physical products sold are functionally similar, if not identical, is it unethical to attempt to differentiate these products through image only? To answer "yes" is to condemn much of branded advertising.[16] To answer no, however, suggests that, in attempting to convince consumers to buy their brands, companies are free to create broad kinds of imagery with impunity.

Agency-Client Relations

The advocacy inherent in advertising has ethical implications of another type. An ad agency is an *advocate* for the company whose products it represents. This is a contractual, usually intermediate term, arrangement. Clients do not switch advertising agencies often because it is costly in terms of continuity in ad campaigns and requires establishing new working relationships, as well as starting another learning curve with a new agency.

One useful distinction for assessing the ethical responsibility of an advertising or public-relations agency is to differentiate between a technician's and an advisor's role. The *technician* can be viewed as giving advice only on the message content, appropriate audiences, and media. This approach would place the agency in what is almost an employee's role with a loyalty obligation to the client organization. An *advisor* perceives duties to the client to include the obligation to act on behalf of a larger constituency, viz., the client's customers. Thus, advisors are remiss if they fail to point out shortcomings in company decisions that might adversely affect those customers. This advisor role in advertising agency ethics involves taking on more of a stakeholder perspective.[17] For example, executives at Leo Burnett or Hill & Knowlton who handle a fast-food account may take it as their responsibility as advisors to question the client's managers about the fat and sodium content of certain heavily advertised menu items.

Two ethical principles useful for examining the advocacy role of advertising agencies are the *veracity* and the *hierarchy* principles.[18] The veracity principle states that an advocate should always be truthful. Not only should an agency following this principle not lie or distort, it should also avoid using manipulation in making arguments. Possibly, one could interpret this to mean the ad or public relations agency then should not use strong social acceptance or ageist appeals if the intention is to manipulate consumers. The hierarchy principle entails the agency deciding that its primary role is a broad advisory one that takes into consideration various stakeholders.

The advisor role is likely more ethically justifiable and would probably ensure a cooperative, rather than subservient, position for the agency, *if* the agency has the leverage to make it work. Advocacy is a fact of life in advertising. To heighten the ethical sensitivity of advertising, the advocacy role must be tempered by some of the techniques suggested earlier. The "anything goes" philosophy in the name of advocacy seems outdated; agencies, their clients, and the media should recognize higher obligations inherent in being an effective advocate for the long run. However, as Exhibit 5-2 discusses, ad agency executives may not "see" ethical issues clearly. The ethical imperative most frequently encountered in client-agency relations is that agencies should not take on work for companies selling products competing with those of existing clients. Recent changes in both the advertising agency and client business structure (e.g., mergers) have complicated this rule's observance. Many firms have diversified and agencies have aligned such that the opportunities for potential conflicts of interest have increased, and, accordingly, client-agency relationships are often jeopardized. The two central questions in this continuing struggle seem to be:

- Are clients becoming unreasonable by telling their agencies more and more product categories are "off limits"?
- Are agencies wrong in demanding a softening of the traditional conflict policy by their clients as their own interests spread?

Although there is no universal solution to these problems, clients do use words such as "trust" and "loyalty" as virtues that they are looking for in their agencies. They want to be able to share confidential information and enter into a partnership arrangement with the ad agency. Both sides want the potential conflict rules spelled out, so that they understand what is expected. When an agency is attracted to a prospective client and knows this could cause trouble with a current client, advertisers need to be notified, explaining the circumstances. The client can then decide whether the conflict is problematic and, if so, give the agency a choice between resigning or not. In apparently enlightened situations, agencies get the okay to "pitch" a competitor. If the agency loses, clients may "let bygones be bygones." However, the implied insult of pursuing a more attractive competitor may destroy or weaken the original relationship.

Advertisers' Ethical Responsibility to Audiences

How much responsibility advertisers should exercise toward audiences would likely elicit a spectrum of opinions from *some* responsibility to an *extreme* amount, depending on whether the respondent was an advertising person or a consumer advocate. Since advertising is typically directed at a mass market using mass media, the utilitarian argument (essentially that the majority of consumers benefit from advertising) is a strong and intuitively appealing one. The educated adult consumer seems equipped to deal with most advertising. However, several significant groups appear to require special attention—children, the elderly, and "market illiterates."

Exhibit 5-2   Advertising Agency Executives' Views on Ethics

Over fifty ad agency executives were interviewed regarding their views about ethical issues in advertising. A majority saw few ethical problems facing advertising. Their views are characterized as exhibiting moral muteness and moral myopia.

Moral Myopia

This view described ad agency personnel who had difficulty seeing ethical issues or seeing them clearly. Several manifestations of moral myopia were found. Actual verbatim responses are shown for each category.

> **Consumers are smart**—"Consumers are really smart, really astute. . . . I feel like I am so unpowerful that if I were unethical in my [creative] presentation [of the advertising message] and were I to oversell, I would be found out so incredibly quickly."
>
> **Passing the buck**—"We're more sheep than we are shepherds. We follow the trends. We don't create them. We're too scared to create them; our clients are too scared to create them."
>
> **What is legal is moral**—"I think this is probably one of the most ethical businesses there is. It is so regulated. Everything that we do has to go through our lawyers to make sure that it's conforming to law, and then our client's lawyers, and then we have to send it through to the networks and their lawyers. . . . It's really hard to be unethical in this business even if you wanted to."
>
> **Ostrich syndrome**—"I think that if I did a little bit more digging into a company's connections . . . then yes, I'd probably have a problem working on it."

Moral Muteness

It is distinguished from myopia since this concept refers to individuals who recognize ethical issues but remain silent and avoid confronting them personally or organizationally. The various types of muteness expressed by respondents are as follows:

> **Compartmentalization**—"I know that things go on. When I'm at home all of these things sicken me, really. But when I'm here, it's different because I'm so into creatively what I'm doing it's like a different picture."
>
> **Client is always right**—"So the last thing that you want to do is make them [the client] feel uncomfortable about what they're doing and what their beliefs are."
>
> **Ethics is bad for business**—"Unfortunately, the solution [to ethical dilemmas] is often to do even less interesting advertising that's even more acceptable to the masses by offending no one."

Pandora's box syndrome—"When you start looking for ethical issues, they are everywhere. . . . You open up a can of worms that just goes on and on and on. . . . You could get so bogged down in wondering if what you are doing is right that you would end up not doing anything."

Moral Imagination

A number of respondents, but a minority of the ones studied, did advocate a morally grounded approach to advertising ethics. They exhibited three characteristics that differentiated them from the others.

Recognition of ethical issues—"Whenever we get a sense that [a promise that can't be fulfilled] is in the back of a client's mind, we point it out, and it usually goes away."

Communication about ethics—"And we try to be very clear with our clients, from the first time that we meet them, about what we stand for. That it's about the work, and they need to be able to not just tolerate, but welcome and encourage, bone honesty. And we're going to give them our opinion, and they're not always going to like that."

Saying no to clients—"It's OK to get fired. It is OK to resign."

Source: Minette E. Drumwright and Patrick E. Murphy, "How Advertising Practitioners View Ethics: Moral Muteness, Moral Myopia and Moral Imagination," *Journal of Advertising* (Summer 2004), 7–24.

Children

Many public and consumer interest groups (such as Campaign for Tobacco Free Kids—www.tobaccofreekids.org) have noted advertising's unique responsibility toward children. Observers contend some ads aimed at children are simply too violent. They object to advertising potentially unsafe products to children and adolescents, for example, guns in Boy Scout magazines or tobacco and alcohol products appearing in media such as *Rolling Stone* read by many teens. They also question whether younger children understand the difference between advertising and program content, that is, the use of cartoon characters (e.g., Teletubbies and SpongeBob SquarePants) as product representatives. Some argue these efforts manipulate impressionable children. **Should media managers allow the programming of violent shows targeted at children?**

The advertising industry has been active in the self-regulation of advertising to children. This is necessary because the United States has fewer governmental restrictions on advertising to children than most western nations. The Children's Advertising Review Unit (CARU), established in the early 1970s by the Better Business Bureau, monitors advertising directed to children under age 12 and seeks modification or discontinuance of ads it finds to be inaccurate or unfair.[19] Its Web site features recent press releases, case reports, and the "Self-Regulatory Guidelines for Children's Advertising" updated in 2003. The AAAA's position is that advertising self-regulation provides adequate safeguards against advertising abuses; that advertising does not harm children and that, therefore, there is no need to further protect them from it; and, if a program has "too many" commercials, children will stop watching it. In sum, market forces will serve the interest of children by naturally regulating what is broadcast to them. This interpretation, of course, implies that advertisers, agencies, and media as well as parents understand an obligation to protect children and youth from their vulnerability to self-destructive messages.

Seniors

Until recently, older Americans were ignored or stereotyped by advertisers. Now, seniors live longer, and many engage in active and affluent lifestyles. This has made them particularly good targets for advertising products such as hair-care products, denture creams, pharmaceuticals associated with the aging process, financial services, and travel packages. For many seniors, television is a principal companion and the primary source of news and product information. Telemarketing programs have frequently targeted this population. The psychological vulnerability of many in this population implies the need for special care with respect to accurate disclosure of product and pricing information because high percentages of older consumers may be misled by advertising.

Market Illiterates

As was discussed in Chapter 2, many consumers with limited education, language capability, and consumption experience are naive in understanding the sometimes exploitive ways of the marketplace. The burgeoning number of immigrants to the United States, including undocumented residents, suggests the size of this segment has grown and will continue to grow. In their purchasing habits, immigrants tend to be more national brand loyal, more likely to buy home remedies, and not as nutrition conscious as those who are more market literate. The policy of "mainstreaming" or deinstitutionalizing many people who are mentally ill or retarded, placing them in independent living situations, undoubtedly adds to the number of unsophisticated who may be susceptible to unethical appeals.

The responsibility for market illiterates is not necessarily with advertisers any more than it is primarily a government, education, or health care community issue. However, market illiteracy is a significant long-term ethical challenge if these vulnerable consumers are misled by advertising or if ads contribute to other social problems. The business community can offer avenues for these consumers to become more market literate. For example, some supermarket chains provide extensive consumer education aimed at all consumers, but especially at those in less privileged areas. The difference principle, introduced in Chapter 1, suggests marketers have a special obligation to low income and otherwise disadvantaged consumers. All firms should better understand the needs and information processing capabilities of older consumers before targeting them in their advertising.

The Role of the Media in Advertising Ethics

Advertising is the principal source of revenue for most newspapers, magazines, broadcast networks and stations, and many Internet sites. Given media dependence on advertisers, the relationship among advertisers, agencies, and media can become ethically strained in many ways.

The categories of media are print, broadcast, outdoor, and direct, including mail, telemarketing, and Internet or online marketing. Each presents some unusual specific issues, and a few ethical concerns pervade media. (Since Internet advertising raises a number of special cases, it is covered separately later in this chapter.)

Print

Newspapers and magazines make up the first group. Newspapers tend to specialize in informative advertising—classified ads and display ads featuring special sales for food, clothing, and other retailers. Although "small print" restrictions on advertised specials raise questions, newspaper advertising content is seldom challenged on ethical grounds. One type of newspaper ad that may prove troublesome is the so-called "advertorial," which is intentionally made to look like a news story. Although these ads must be clearly labeled "advertisement," the small print may be missed by some readers, especially the elderly. One possibility would be that publishers consider using a larger typeface for such ads than legally required.

Magazines (with the exception of the newsweeklies) are often targeted to specialized audiences with a greater interest in a specific subject—skiing, farming, or architecture. Thus, magazine advertisers can use more sophisticated, customized messages in appealing to their target market. Since the persuasive content of magazine advertising is higher and informational content is often lower than newspapers, ethical questions about status-oriented messages are more common, and the FTC adopted a policy many years ago of requiring documentation for claims. Since newspapers and magazines do not have a captive audience for their ads and readers are free to skim or ignore them, print advertising is not viewed as highly intrusive. The point about advertorials needs to be stressed for magazines too, because they tend to be used more frequently in this medium. An illustration of how to overcome potential ethical issues was depicted in an 18-page "Special Advertising Section" for Greater Milwaukee, Wisconsin, in *Forbes* magazine. Each page carried a number and "ADVERTISEMENT" as headers. (The marketing strategy aspect was also well done with short columns by local CEOs with adjoining ads for their company.)

Broadcast

Advertising in broadcast media, in contrast to print advertising, is perceived as very intrusive and is regularly questioned on ethical grounds. Programs are too often interrupted by commercials, often at a perceived higher audio pitch. Since messages are typically fleeting in broadcast media, advertisers usually rely on persuasive and emotional appeals rather than "just the facts." Therefore, consumers are generally more confused about the messages conveyed by television advertising. On the other hand, advertisers defend this type of promotion by contending that consumers want to be "entertained," especially when they watch television. Also, broadcast media are classified as "low involvement"; the audience is not actively seeking information. Therefore, advertisers feel they must enchant, startle, trick, or cajole the consumer into paying attention to commercials. For these reasons and others, television and, to a lesser extent, radio advertising bears a larger burden of criticism and responsibility from an ethical standpoint.

Outdoor

Billboards necessarily carry little information and, therefore, are seldom challenged for being deceptive. However, liquor and tobacco companies are frequent users of billboard ads. Further, outdoor billboards arguably are a form of "aesthetic pollution" detracting from the natural beauty of the environment. Other forms of billboard advertising are transit advertising, found on and in buses and subways, and the increasing use of "rolling billboards" on semitrailers, city buses, and even personal vehicles. Combined with the occasional use of barn-side ads, the complaint that advertising is a blight on the outdoor environment has more than a little validity.

Direct Marketing

This medium is targeted to individual consumers and can be personalized, thanks to computer technology. Some ethical abuses associated with direct marketing are product misrepresentation, pirating, and unauthorized use of lists, order fulfillment, unauthorized billings, and "negative option sales" (unless you decline, we assume you want . . . to join our book club, subscribe to this magazine, etc.). Since so much of it goes directly into the wastebasket, direct mail houses have resorted to making messages appear "official." Envelopes sometimes look as if they come from the government or carry a statement that the recipient has won something. (One such envelope even looks like it contains a tax refund check!) The sheer volume of direct mail advertising, facilitated by preferential postage rates, poses an environmental threat in terms of both resource use and disposal.

Telemarketing programs now aided by computerized messaging are most notable because of how they intrude on ordinary lives. Whose dinner isn't interrupted several times each month by offers to replace windows—on your new house—or clean the carpet—when you have tile or hardwood floors? Also, despite regulations forbidding the practice, telemarketers sometimes pose as researchers. (A separate, follow-up call or visit to a respondent whose answers fit a good prospect's profile skirts the FTC prohibition of this form of representation.) As mentioned earlier, these tactics, along with outright misrepresentation, have led the FTC to create a do-not-call/mail registry system, which allows people to opt out of any list. However, charities and other not-for-profits such as volunteer fire departments, often heavy users of telemarketing, are exempt from this restriction, as are off-shore operators.

The reverse of these "phone-out" programs are those (via direct mail, print, or broadcast media) inviting "phone-ins." While most phone-in programs are quite proper as they offer consumers the choice of calling or not—an option denied in phone-out programs—some are highly deceptive in their construction. A most egregious example is a direct mail piece announcing "you may be a winner"—of a new truck or $50,000, or so on—"Call (900) XYZ-1234." The call winds up being costly, for example, $7.50, and, as far as we know, nobody ever wins—the marketer receives the major portion of the phone charge. One elderly woman ran up a phone bill of over $800 in one month responding to this kind of offer. Several years ago, AARP launched a major effort to educate consumers and regulators about these abuses. But some marketers are very creative in their use of technology and work around regulations. **What do you think of this kind of program?**

The Direct Marketing Association has issued extensive "Guidelines for Ethical Business Practice"[20] covering mail, phone, and online media, but the industry still receives much criticism for the intrusive and deceptive nature of many direct marketing programs.

General Concerns

The media's sales objective of selling more time or space frequently conflicts with advertisers' requirements for effectively reaching their markets.

What should media reps do if they know the demographics of the customer's market more closely fit the audience of another magazine or even another medium? Should they decline business and send the potential customer to a "friendly" competitor? Furthermore, should media resist the tendency of agencies to recommend excessive advertising to their clients (when they are paid on a commission basis)?

Broader concerns between media and advertisers present even more difficult problems. Social critics contend most media have been "captured" by advertising, and, as a result, editorial content may be skewed, suppressed, or downplayed. While there is little hard evidence to support this position, the perception remains that the advertising and editorial sides of media may not be independent. Several specific questions relate to this issue:[21]

- Should media attempt to accommodate more advertisers, either by adding more advertising pages or reducing the length of commercials, so that more ads may be run?
- Should media create new marketing entities (home buying services, network news breaks) largely for the purpose of selling more advertising?
- Should media content or programming be arranged largely for the benefit of the advertiser?
- Should publishing or broadcasting ventures be undertaken *mostly* because of market-dominated criteria?
- Should publication of a newspaper or magazine be stopped entirely due to weakened advertising without questioning readers about their willingness to pay more to keep it in circulation?

Media executives should follow ethical principles in order to answer these questions. Undoubtedly, there are additional issues that can be raised such as what products should be advertised and how messages should be constructed to be more ethical.

ETHICS IN INTERNET ADVERTISING AND MARKETING

The Internet has been one of the big developments of the late twentieth and early twenty-first centuries. Its growth is nothing short of phenomenal. In 2002 there were 619 million users involved in nearly $6.8 billion in Internet-based commerce around the globe.[22] Usage is expected to grow to 1.5 billion people by 2007.[23] The Internet has many of the advantages of several of the media examined earlier—it has color and sound, can be interactive, and can reach a broad audience for a relatively low cost. In some ways it resembles direct marketing, but in others it has characteristics of both TV (visually appealing) and magazines (can contain much copy). The amount spent on

Internet advertising is projected to grow from $5.5 billion in 2002 to almost $16 billion by 2007.[24] The Internet is the latest and arguably most powerful in a progression of media—telegraph, telephone, radio, television—that eliminate time and space obstacles to communication. Addressing ethical concerns in this medium is a major challenge for marketers. These issues are intrusiveness, deception, violations of privacy, the promotion of controversial products, and consumer ethics in this new media.

The Web differs from most other advertising media. It easily spans countries and continents. Therefore, the types of country or regional regulation or self-regulation available for other types of advertising do not exist for this new medium. This does not mean regulators are unaware of the problem. As mentioned earlier in this chapter, the FTC has taken a strong stance on Internet privacy in recent years. The difficulties in finding a common ground for copyright protection, defamation, free speech, and libel thus far have been unsurmountable. See Exhibit 5-3 for a list of international rules covering the Internet.

Intrusiveness

Probably the most irritating and ethically suspect practice associated with Internet marketing is *spam*. Internet users coined this pejorative term to describe the instance where the burden of selectivity shifts from the sender to the recipient. In the United States, bills have been introduced in Congress and several state legislatures to limit spammers and their activities. The activities of these firms are often rather ingenious, and offshore computers are used to generate lists of individuals to spam. Other intrusive features of Internet advertising are banner or "pop up" ads. All these types of Internet advertising communicate selling propositions usually viewed as unacceptable in more traditional media.

Online Privacy

The privacy of information available on the Internet is an area of concern for consumers and regulators. Privacy has both legal and ethical elements. Some of the legal statutes that protect consumers and data are not particularly effective in the online world. The use of *cookies* (not the ones you eat) has led to marketers having extensive ability to "track" consumers as they surf the Internet. Unless savvy users know how to disable the cookies, they automatically record activity without any user action. **Is this an ethically justifiable practice?**

Companies have responded to consumers' concerns about privacy by posting privacy policies on their Web sites. Unfortunately, many are written in legalese and are indecipherable by the average consumer. Furthermore, a

EXHIBIT 5-3   A Web of Laws

A look at some of the major international rules—either passed or pending—that cover the Internet:

The World Intellectual Property Organization (WIPO)

Two WIPO treaties, laid down in Geneva, adapted copyright rules for e-commerce. Before, copyright laws covered only physical copies and broadcasting. Now books, songs, and films distributed online are protected. Countries also agreed to pass laws to outlaw cyber-piracy of CDs and DVDs, as well as hacking into online music and film subscription services. The treaties, now ratified by 41 countries, went into effect in 2002.

- cipo.int/treaties/ip/wct/index.html
- wipo.int/treaties/ip/wppt/index.html

The Digital Millennium Copyright Act

The 1998 law adapted U.S. legislation to the WIPO treaties.

- copyright.gov/legislation/dmca.pdf

The European Union's Electronic Commerce Directive

This directive, handed down in 2000, gave online businesses assurance that they would have to comply with laws only where they are based, rather than face rules in 15 different countries.

- europa.eu.int/smartapi/cgi/sga_doc?smartapi!prod!CELEXnumdoc&lg=en&numdoc=32000L0031&model=guichett

The European Union's Rome II Directive

This could allow consumers to sue e-businesses in their home country, undermining the legal certainty of the Electronic Commerce directive. Online businesses fear they will have to comply with 15 different laws on defamation and product liability.

- europa.eu.int/comm./justice_home/unit/civil/consultation/index_en.htm

Hague Convention on International Jurisdiction and Foreign Judgments in Civil and Commercial Matters

A treaty that would assure people that if they win a judgment in one country, it will be recognized and enforced in other countries. A draft treaty in 1992 sought to set global standards for defamation, libel, and copyright on the Internet. Debate now focuses on business-to-business commercial contracts. An accord is possible in 2004.

- www.hcch.net/e/workprog/jdgm.html

Source: Matthew Newman, "So Many Countries, So Many Laws," *Wall Street Journal,* April 28, 2003, R8.

study by the Annenberg Public Policy Center of the University of Pennsylvania found that many users are under mistaken assumptions about their privacy on the Web.[25] For example, almost 60 percent of adults who use the Internet at home mistakenly believe that Web sites with privacy policies are not gathering or sharing personal information, even though the fine print of the policies generally allows the companies to do so.[26]

Much has been written about online privacy in both the scholarly and academic press in recent years. Only one major piece of legislation has passed in the United States. It is the Children's Online Privacy Protection Act (recall Chapter 2 discussion), which protects young users (twelve and younger) from providing information to marketers that may be private or does not have the consent of a parent. On the self-regulatory front, a growing number of Web sites feature a third-party seal—BBBOnline, Truste, or others that verify the site are following certain practices that maintain consumer privacy. However, much activity still occurs outside of this kind of certification. (You may want to click on the privacy policy of your favorite Web site. Can you understand your rights?) Finally, one of the authors and a colleague developed an ethical responsibility continuum that incorporates corporate business and ethical policy and US and EU public policy. On the privacy front, the European Union has been much more activist in protecting consumer information than has the United States.[27] Exhibit 5-4 shows this continuum.

Promotion of Questionable Products

The seamier side of the Web is that it has been used for promoting a number of controversial products, including pornography, gambling, and financial service products of dubious merit. A recent survey of marketing executives disclosed that security of online transactions, fraud, protection of privacy, pornography, plagiarism, and targeting children were among their most frequent concerns.[28] (Pornography may be the largest "product category" of spam, followed closely by financial service products of dubious value. And pornographic Web sites are reportedly the most populous, having often captured respectable sounding URLs; once entered (even in error), they sometimes capture your home page and are difficult to remove.) To these might be added the growth of online gambling sites (typically operated from offshore locations) and the difficulties associated with developing an effective regulatory strategy. Finally, the Internet is a source for many kinds of information and has created a "digital divide" between young and old, wealthy and poor, and developed and less developed nations.

Regarding self-regulation, the American Association of Advertising Agencies, the Direct Marketing Association, and Better Business Bureau have

EXHIBIT 5-4   Ethical Responsibility Continuum

| | Business Orientation | | Societal Orientation | |
Theories	Corporate Business Policy	Corporate Ethical Policy	U.S. Public Policy	EU Public Policy
Managerial egoism[a]	X			
Utilitarianism[b]	X	X		
Stakeholder theory[c]	X	X	X	
Virtue ethics[d]		X	X	
Integrative social contracts theory[e]		X	X	
Duty-based theories[f]			X	X
Power and responsibility[g]	X	X	X	X

[a]Managerial egoism: Executives take steps that most efficiently advance the exclusive self-interest of themselves or their firm. The X is placed under corporate business policy because the sole motivation is to further the firm; trade-off incentives are offered for the purpose of obtaining consumer information that is viewed as the property of that company.

[b]Utilitarianism: Corporate conduct is proper if a decision results in the greatest good for the greatest number of people. Self-regulatory advocates maintain that consumers are not hurt by corporations' collection and use of personal information but are annoyed (the costs are low); furthermore, the information allows for a wide assortment of product choice (benefits are great).

[c]Stakeholder theory: Organizations affect and are affected by several stakeholder groups. On the continuum, this theory ranges from corporate business policy, because of the effect of corporate actions on consumers (e.g., incentive trade-offs), to corporate ethical policy, because of the positive influence of privacy statements and privacy audits on many stakeholders, to public policy, because government and society are seen as important stakeholders.

[d]Virtue ethics: Balance in the relationship between the online marketer and the consumer should be achieved for the market system to work effectively. Thus, corporations and public policy makers need to move toward the ethic of the mean in the privacy debate.

[e]Integrative social contracts theory: This theory presupposes that the Internet community precedes the development of rules of conduct, public policy, or "microsocial contracts." Corporate ethical policies assume that the corporation's participation in the development of social rules would necessitate transparent ethical practices.

[f]Duty-based theories: The normative nature of these theories means that they are used to policy makers in determining the company's absolute duties to consumers. If the duties of fidelity, beneficence, and nonmaleficence are violated in the course of Internet marketing, greater participation by regulatory agencies in the United States and Europe can be expected.

[g]Power and responsibility equilibrium: Corporate power and responsibility must be approximately equal for Internet marketers to be effective. In the long run, those who do not use power in a way that society considers responsible will lose it. This covers the entire continuum, because it incorporates organizational stakeholders and includes the multiple public policy perspectives.

Source: Eve M. Caudill and Patrick E. Murphy, "Consumer Online Privacy. Legal and Ethical Issues," *Journal of Public Policy & Marketing* 19 no. 1 (Spring 2000): 16.

all added guidelines for online marketing to their advertising statements, and even the Pontifical Council for Social Communications of the Roman Catholic Church has produced a report entitled "Ethics in Internet"—available, appropriately, on the Internet.[29] Many states have also enacted regulations governing the medium. However, concerns for freedom of speech and access, the anonymity of online agents, and the global character of the medium effectively place the burden for consumer protection on individuals in the online audience. Here the legitimate concern parallels the previous discussion about the vulnerability of some segments—children, elderly, and market illiterates—and the relevance of fairness in addressing this concern.[30]

Issues of Consumer Ethics

A discussion of ethics in Internet marketing and advertising would not be complete without mentioning the ethical responsibilities of consumers. Many teenagers (and older folks too) now download music from the Internet. Some employees spend time at work surfing the net (and even visiting pornographic sites). The sharing of computer software is commonplace. What are the ethical principles one can apply to these actions? As the teenage sons of two of the authors commented about downloading music—"Dad, everyone does it." Consumer ethics, as well as marketer ethics, need to be raised to have a more equitable and ethical system.   **In your opinion, what are consumers' ethical responsibilities?**

POSITIVE DEVELOPMENTS AND FUTURE CHALLENGES FOR ETHICS IN ADVERTISING

Several developments have occurred that may signal a more ethical posture by the advertising community. At the same time, there are areas of emerging concern for advertisers in the twenty-first century. We begin with the good news. At least five significant favorable trends are occurring with respect to ethics in advertising.

First, some advertisers have made genuine efforts to promote more positive images. Women are now depicted more frequently in professional and business roles. Advertisers not only want to avoid exploitation of women, but also obviously want to target them as consumers. For example, Ford broke with tradition by hiring actors who reflect average customers rather than utilizing beauty queens at a recent auto show. However, while substantial progress seems to have been achieved, there remains substantial room for improvement. Other groups are also being portrayed more favorably by advertisers. For instance, older Americans (partially because of the fact that the baby boomers are moving into this group) are being used as spokespersons for many consumer products. Asian, African, and Hispanic Americans now appear in many ads. Also, more handicapped (including the hearing impaired) are depicted in more and more advertisements. International advertisers have generally followed this trend.

Second, increasing specialization in mass media via cable television and specialized magazines means abuses associated with mass market advertising are less likely to happen due to the more defined audiences for these media. Messages intended for one market are less likely to offend those not targeted. But a cautionary note should be sounded: while the major television networks have elaborate guidelines and strict standards for advertising to children, independent stations and cable companies tend to have looser or no controls at all.

Third, many companies have shifted more of their promotional budgets from advertising to sales promotion techniques such as coupons and rebates or pricing discounts to retailers. This is, of course, not good news for the advertising industry, which has been criticized for ineffective communication. Other promotional approaches seem to be better able to generate sales and market share. It would seem that the advertising community might be more receptive to changing its creative and *ethical* stance if it felt consumers would be more likely to be influenced by advertising. (Unfortunately, these alternative promotional concepts are also open to ethical challenge.)

Fourth, advertisers seem to be more responsive to consumer complaints regarding the program content of the shows they sponsor. This may lead advertisers and their agencies to take a closer look at the quality and type of TV and radio programming they support. In certain instances, advertisers or the media have withdrawn ads after receiving only a relatively small number of complaints.

Finally, advertising self-regulation and government regulation is alive and well throughout the world. One study evaluating advertising self-regulation in twelve countries indicated that its purpose is "more moral/ethical than disciplinary."[31] In the United States, the FTC and state consumer protection offices seem to be increasingly more active in regulating advertising (see www.ftc.gov for examples). Recently, firms in the brewing, food, tobacco, automobile, and airline industries were prosecuted for ad claims. While political priorities and sentiments will surely vary from time to time in local, national, and international jurisdictions, it appears that an overarching policy supporting "truth in advertising" is firmly entrenched.

However, three areas continue to present particular ethical challenges to advertisers. The first is "infomercials." These half hour or longer shows follow several formats—talk show, news, or entertainment. They carry innocuous titles such as "Consumer Challenge" and sometimes feature celebrities as spokespersons. Infomercials are a booming business. Undoubtedly, the growth of cable television along with local companies eager to generate revenues outside of prime time programming, adds to the significance of the ethical (and possibly legal) questions about whether consumers, especially market illiterates susceptible to financial injury, are misled into thinking these infomercials might be legitimate programs. Evidence suggests TV stations have inadequate safeguards in place to deal with infomercials. While the broadcast industry has proposed disclosures at the beginning and end of each such program and the FTC has pursued a few infomercial cases against advertisers, ethical duties should be spelled out more clearly.

A second growth area is "green marketing." The sometimes dubious health claims of the past are now being replaced by environmentally oriented messages. Marketers have begun using adjectives such as "biodegradable" or "recyclable," promoting the environmental compatibility of their products, even when benefits are minimal. State and federal agencies are prosecuting the most egregious violations. Many marketers want to contribute to a cleaner natural environment and to reduce packaging in the solid waste stream. However, promoting unjustified environmental benefits is not the way to accomplish this goal.

As noted, the third major concern in the early twenty-first century encompasses the whole range of issues we have discussed that relate to the growing use of the Internet and online marketing. The absence of effective national or global regulation has invited an invasion of questionable practices and practitioners. Banner ads, pop-ups, and spam e-mail are viewed as intrusive and communicate selling propositions that would never be accepted in more public or regulated circumstances. In the future, both ethical marketers and consumers as well as improved regulatory mechanisms are surely called for.

ADVERTISERS AND ETHICAL PRINCIPLES IN ACTION

To understand how ethical issues are addressed by advertisers, some questions must be asked about the values inherent in the advertising community. What do advertising people consider unethical? What is the prevailing professional ethic of advertising? Some sense of this ethic can be ascertained by looking at the codes of ethics promulgated by the American Association of Advertising Agencies (AAAA) and the American Advertising Federation (AAF). In the spirit of all these As, recall that one of the ABCs in Chapter 1 is "above the law." Both codes contain the following provisions:

- False and misleading statements are prohibited.
- Testimonials that do not reflect the real opinion of individuals involved are forbidden.
- Price claims that are misleading are not allowed.
- Statements or pictures offensive to the public decency are to be avoided.
- Unsubstantiated performance claims are never to be used.

Such admonitions serve as absolutes in guiding advertising practice. In effect they become the lowest common denominator in shaping the professional ethic of advertising practitioners. One major disadvantage of the approach used in the AAAA and AAF codes is that their prohibitions are formulated in terms of "negative" absolutes—in other words, practices that formulators of advertising should not engage in. These negative absolutes have value because they suggest (for example) that to be ethical, advertisers should not lie to customers, should not steal competitor ideas for their own campaigns, should not cheat the media, and so on. However, some observers of the advertising industry have suggested that "positive" absolutes, which stress the meritorious duties advertisers ought to engage in, provide a more inspirational avenue for shaping advertising practice. An example of a positive meritorious duty would be the "principle of fairness." Applied to advertising, it might be stated as follows: "Advertisers must be fair in their dealings with consumers, clients, suppliers, vendors, media, employees, and agency management."

Ethical Principles for Advertising

The dominant perspective used by most managers to evaluate advertising ethics is utilitarian. Most advertising practitioners feel that the benefits of promoting products in our consumption-oriented society justify the social costs of advertising. Interestingly, the critics of advertising also sometimes use consequences to evaluate advertising. One consequentialist point of view is that "if consumers don't like the advertising, they won't buy the product—and the ad sponsors will be punished at the cash register." Many business executives defend advertising on the grounds that it communicates with the mass market and, therefore, contributes to the well-being, if not happiness, of large numbers of consumers. For example, advertising Toyota automobiles not only informs consumers about the features of the cars, but also stimulates demand for this brand and thereby lowers the cost for everyone.

The other category of philosophical theories used to evaluate ethics in advertising is duty based. Applying Kant's well-known categorical imperative to advertising, one could state that "advertising should never treat its audience or spokespersons as merely means." Persuasive advertising, which attempts to change attitudes and values in order that a product solves a heretofore unrecognized problem, may assault individual dignity. For example, blatant sex appeal advertising would probably not meet this imperative of *never* using women (or men) as means to an end. A TV ad campaign to which this principle might be applied is the controversial Miller Lite sex-appeal wrestling match commercial used by SAB Miller in 2002 and 2003. Applying the principle, one would contend that, while the use of such blatant sex appeals constituted a memorable television commercial, the salacious portrayal of sparing and scantily clothed women featured in the ad was an inappropriate means for seeking economic success.

Advertising may be also analyzed as duty based especially when references are made by defenders of advertising to the Golden Rule and Kant's so-called *absolute* duties. That is, advertisers subscribe to moral principles that are negatively stated, for example, do *not* lie to customers or clients, do *not* steal competitors' ideas, and do *not* cheat the media. However, advertising practitioners may be less likely to follow the so-called *meritorious* duties, which are positive in tone, for example, always tell the whole truth to client and customers, come to the aid of a failing supplier, and routinely inform the media of an upcoming change in a promotional campaign. Exercising such positive meritorious duties would be more in line with the virtue ethics theory examined in Chapter 1.

The *principle of fairness* is an embodiment of a meritorious duty, and implies that advertisers should take fairness into consideration in their day-to-day dealings with customers and clients. As mentioned earlier, "fairness" to stakeholders (e.g., clients, customers, suppliers, vendors and media, employees and agency management, and even other agencies) presents ongoing challenges to ad agencies.

However, it is difficult to apply moral imperatives to many specific situations. For example, most advertising practitioners would agree with the guideline that testimonial ads should not use celebrity spokespeople to endorse products they have never used. Suppose, however, a company hires a well-known actor who has never previously used a particular product but upon signing his endorsement contract honestly concludes that the product is a superior one. Is this a misleading use of testimonials? The case is debatable.

The conclusion we draw is that ethics in advertising, in proper perspective, is founded on several moral philosophies. Therefore, advertising agencies, the media, and product/brand managers should consider using multiple philosophical perspectives in evaluating the impact of their advertising. Conversely, information directed at assisting choice, solving real needs and consumer problems, irrespective of its commercial motivation, serves consumer goals and is, therefore, of positive ethical value according to this view. We advocate greater use of "moral imagination" by those involved in advertising (recall Exhibit 5-2).

IDEAS FOR ETHICAL MARKETING

Four suggestions are offered for improving the ethics of advertising.

First, all businesses involved in advertising and public relations should develop specific ethical principles for their operations. Advertisers, advertising and public-relations agencies, and the media should spell out the principles by which they operate. One reason for the strong criticism of advertising appears to be its "anything goes" attitude. For example, companies that advertise should make clear what type of advertising content fits the company's image and the type of media and programs they will and will not support. In examining many codes of conduct over the last several years, we found few that spell out a particular company's ethical perspective on advertising, even though many firms spend millions of dollars on promotion. Similarly, agency executives should formulate and express the principles by which they operate. Agencies must be prepared to *walk away* from potential clients because of ethical concerns, but a rationale needs to be developed and articulated for substantiating this position. The public-relations industry has focused on ethics education, strong sanctions against code violators, and professionalism to enhance its ethical posture. In fact, the public-relations industry held a "World Festival" on Ethics in Public Relations in Rome during June 2003. An outcome was a "Global Protocol on Ethics."[32] At the same time, television media have cut costs by reducing the number of employees in their standards departments. It seems even more imperative, then, that the principles to which the media subscribe in their relationship with advertisers be clearly delineated. One agency's principles of operation are shown in Exhibit 5-5. Corporantes, Inc. articulates both personal and organizational values and attempts to live them with strong CEO leadership by Ron Nahser.

Second, the advertising community should push for revised association codes. Most ethical problems perceived by ad executives relate to fairness in dealing with various stakeholders in formulating advertising campaigns. Yet the codes of four major advertising industry associations deal principally with the content of advertising and not fairness in business dealings. The industry also needs to think more explicitly about fairness to the consumer, seemingly ignored by ad executives. Leaders of these associations should consider code revisions, both to overcome this deficiency and to reflect newer challenges. It seems ironic that there is also a problem with communication. Advertising associations could exert a leadership role if they were to develop meaningful and helpful ethics statements for their members. We commend the American Marketing Association (which has many advertising members) for not only revising their overall code (see Exhibit 1-3), but also having adopted a "Code of Ethics for Marketing" on the Internet shown in Exhibit 5-6.

Third, an ethical ombudsman for the advertising industry should be considered. This individual could be employed by one or more advertising associations in order to monitor advertising, and sit in on deliberations of the National Advertising Review Board and similar groups. The ethical ombudsman would represent the consumer in the advertising transaction and would introduce the sometimes missing dimension of fairness. The establishment of

Exhibit 5-5   One Firm's Statement of Values

CORPORANTES

Our purpose is to help our clients uncover and implement outstanding ideas to help their businesses grow, benefit the user, and contribute to the well-being of society.

To achieve this, we ignite our clients' sustainable competitive advantages to grow their market positions.

OWN WHO YOU ARE®

We do this by living certain deeply held, shared values.

Personal Values	Organizational Values
ATTITUDE	GROWTH
INTEGRITY	FAIRNESS
HARD WORK	RESPONSIBILITY
TALENT	RESPECT

"A **Value** is any belief, principle or virtue held so deeply,
(consciously or unconsciously)
that it guides our behaviors, decisions and actions."

We are passionate about our work.

Function effectively in groups.

"Gladly learn and gladly teach." (Chaucer)

Wish to be recognized and fairly
compensated for our outstanding work.

November 21, 1980 (Updated March 31, 2004)

Reprinted by permission of Corporantes, Inc.

Exhibit 5-6   American Marketing Association Code of Ethics for Marketing on the Internet

Preamble

The Internet, including online computer communications, has become increasingly important to marketers' activities, as they provide exchanges and access to markets worldwide. The ability to interact with stakeholders has created new marketing opportunities and risks that are not currently specifically addressed in the American Marketing Association Code of Ethics. The American Marketing Association Code of Ethics for Internet marketing provides additional guidance and direction for ethical responsibility in this dynamic area of marketing. The American Marketing Association is committed to ethical professional conduct and has adopted these principles for using the Internet, including on-line marketing activities utilizing network computers.

General Responsibilities

Internet marketers must assess the risks and take responsibility for the consequences of their activities. Internet marketers' professional conduct must be guided by:

1. Support of professional ethics to avoid harm by protecting the rights of privacy, ownership and access.
2. Adherence to all applicable laws and regulations with no use of Internet marketing that would be illegal, if conducted by mail, telephone, fax or other media.
3. Awareness of changes in regulations related to Internet marketing.
4. Effective communication to organizational members on risks and policies related to Internet marketing, when appropriate.
5. Organizational commitment to ethical Internet practices communicated to employees, customers and relevant stakeholders.

Privacy

Information collected from customers should be confidential and used only for expressed purposes. All data, especially confidential customer data, should be safeguarded against unauthorized access. The expressed wishes of others should be respected with regard to the receipt of unsolicited e-mail messages.

Ownership

Information obtained from the Internet sources should be properly authorized and documented. Information ownership should be safeguarded and respected. Marketers should respect the integrity and ownership of computer and network systems.

Access

Marketers should treat access to accounts, passwords, and other information as confidential, and only examine or disclose content when authorized by a responsible party. The integrity of others' information systems should be respected with regard to placement of information, advertising or messages.

Source: AMA Web site—MarketingPower.com; for full AMA Code of Ethics, see About AMA page. Reprinted by permission of the American Marketing Association.

an ethical ombudsman program would help implement both of these ideas for ethical action by forcing agencies to rethink their practices and by making their ethics codes more specific. Such a program promises several benefits. Ethical issues would be raised that are not currently addressed. Also, the presence of an ombudsman should heighten the consciousness of ad practition-ers and result in a greater sensitivity to ethical issues. In addition, the ethical ombudsman would ensure that the corporate culture includes ethical thinking.

Fourth, ethical questions about advertisements and advertising strategies need to be more frequently asked. A final and related proposal is for advertisers and agencies to develop an ethical questions checklist for mutual consideration. Exhibit 5-7 contains questions about the impact of advertising on stakeholders and deals with some of the fairness issues outlined earlier. We contend the process of asking these questions would be more important than the specific answers and highlight the importance of ethics in advertising. (We discuss some other possible questions in the Ethical Audit section of Chapter 7.) This type of evaluation would also allow advertisers to see that their agencies follow the ethical principles set down by the company. The exercise could also protect ad agencies, since they would better know client expectations. Ad campaigns should communicate client values, reducing the expensive, time-consuming, and emotionally draining prospect of developing alternative campaigns due to ethical deficiencies.

CONCLUDING COMMENT

Advertising is an important institution in our society. It provides information to buyers, supports news and entertainment media, and contributes to economic efficiency. The most obvious forms of deception and unfairness in advertising are governed by industry self-regulation, governmental controls, competition, and the professional ethics of the ad industry. But we believe

Exhibit 5-7   Advertising Ethics Checklist

In judging whether a certain ad or advertising strategy is ethical, many factors must be considered. The following questions cover many issues and may serve as a preliminary checklist:

General

- What does the advertiser intend to accomplish?
- Are the effects of this advertising potentially detrimental to the individual and to society as a whole?
- Are these effects accidental, or do they result almost necessarily from the techniques used?

On Technique

- Does the ad provide information, or does it appeal only to status and emotions?
- If the latter is true, does the ad attempt to bypass the individual's judgment?

On Content

- Is the information in the ad truthful?
- Are relevant (material) facts omitted?

On Psychological Effects

- Does the ad seriously disturb the existing psychological position of the person without sufficient reason?
- Does the ad appeal to purely materialistic, sexual, or selfish values?

On the Advertised Product

- Does the ad lead to the misallocation of individual resources relative to the person's basic needs?
- Does it encourage an abusive use of any particular product?

On Social Consumption

- Does the ad and the product advertised lead to a waste of natural resources?

Final Judgment

- When the intent and techniques are not troublesome in and of themselves, and where the harmful effects are not necessary, are there other effects that outweigh the harmful effects?

Source: Adapted from Thomas J. Garrett, *An Introduction to Some Ethical Problems of Modern Advertising* (Rome: Gregorian University Press, 1961), 180. Reprinted by permission.

ethical standards in the industry can be raised, producing many benefits for all concerned. Because advertising is such a dynamic exercise in commercial persuasion, undertaken for the primary purpose of selling specific products and services, it undoubtedly will continue to generate controversy—and provide opportunities for thoughtful professionals to apply ethical reasoning to specific problems as they arise. We now move to an examination of another major promotional technique used by marketers—personal selling—and the ethical questions that arise from it.

Chapter Six

Personal Selling Ethics

Scenario 1

Anne McGilvray is a sales representative for a cookie and cracker company. While working in the field on the final day of the sales period, she receives an emergency cell phone call from her office. Her supervisor wants to remind her that it is the last day of the third quarter and as of that morning she is 8 percent below her quota. The branch is also 3 percent below its cumulative quota, and no one, including her supervisor, will receive a quarterly bonus if this difference is not made up. He tells Anne he would be willing to send out extra delivery trucks that day and to do whatever it took to make quota.

Anne has tried in her time with the company to build positive relationships with her customers and did not want to do anything that would jeopardize these alliances. However, she also felt the need to please her supervisor and coworkers who are relying on her to help them all achieve quota. She knows that some other sales representatives have padded the end-of-quarter figures by preshipping pallets of products that they know will be demanded in the next period. She considers this alternative. Another possibility is just calling her best accounts and explaining the situation. She feels that some of them may be willing to take extra products to help her out but isn't sure it will be enough to make quota. She also knows that if she asks her accounts to take extra products and they say "no," she cannot slip a few extras on the order hoping it will go unnoticed.[1] **What should Anne do?**

Scenario 2

Mike O'Brien is a new regional sales manager for a U.S.-based construction equipment company with responsibilities for the Asian and Eastern European markets. Thanks to a multimillion dollar loan from the World Bank, one of the less developed nations in Africa is shopping for equipment to improve its currently primitive road system. Mike's company, along with several others around the world, has been invited to submit a proposal. Mike is responsible for coordinating the development of the offer, which is also to include a longer term parts and service contract. In his first meeting with the government minister responsible for the purchase, Mike was made aware that whoever got the contract would be expected to pay the minister U.S. $100,000 and a 10 percent commission on future parts and service revenues. Mike has no doubt that some foreign companies bidding for the business will have no hesitation about making this kind of commitment, but Mike's company is bound by the Foreign Corrupt Practices Act (and some of his competitors by OECD guidelines) and has a policy forbidding bribes. Mike's experience before his current assignment was calling on contractors in the United States and coordinating military purchases in Europe. He has no experience with this kind of situation but knows getting this contract would be a major deal, both for the company and his personal commission income. **Should Mike pay the bribe? What other options does he have?**

These scenarios present two ethical dilemmas confronting sales representatives. Personal selling accounts for over 16 million jobs in the United States.[2] For every position in advertising, there are over 30 jobs in personal selling. Many organizations employ salespeople. They may be called customer representatives, service agents, or even counselors in nonprofit settings. While reliable estimates of expenditures for sales management and personal selling are not available, financial outlays for these activities undoubtedly exceed the amounts spent on advertising, product development, or any other major component of marketing. Moreover, selling is the typical entry-level position for marketing graduates. Selling, which involves direct contact with the buyer and requires extensive product knowledge, provides the necessary experience for advancement into marketing management and top organizational positions. The express purpose of most personal selling is to convince customers that the salesperson's product or service represents the best solution to their needs. Because of its financial magnitude and persuasive aspects, personal selling generates many ethical questions.

To say that salespeople don't exactly enjoy a positive image among American consumers is an understatement. Issues such as poorly informed salesclerks, who may be condescending or engaged in other activities while waiting on consumers, continue to bother high percentages of buyers. Also, highly aggressive sales representatives in the automotive and technology industries often "put off" consumers with their behavior.

It is just as difficult on the other side of the sales exchange. Salespeople often feel strong pressure to succeed because sales results are linked to organizational rewards and advancement. For example, upon attainment of the annual quota, a sales representative may receive a $5,000 bonus. Being close, but not at, this goal could influence year-end selling tactics as in Scenario 1. In normal selling situations, temptations occur that arguably may hurt the customer, but would benefit the salesperson.

In this regard, the following ethical questions face all sales reps:

- To what degree does a sales representative owe *disclosure* to a customer?
- Is it appropriate to *oversell* a customer for the purposes of "making quota"? Is this practice acceptable if the sales representative believes overstocking the customer will not create a long-term problem for the buying organization?
- Is it acceptable for salespeople to use *white lies or misrepresent* the seller to increase the probability of a sale if they believe misrepresentation will not hurt the potential buyer?

Exhibit 6-1 presents some "benchmark" data that answer the last question and gives insight into a sample of salespeople in the United States. As the exhibit indicates, this story is a "bad news/good news" one. We are encouraged that a majority (but wish it were a higher percentage) do have processes to deal with ethical issues. We would caution the reader to not generalize to all salespeople in all industries in all countries from this limited survey.

In this chapter, we explore the ethical underpinnings of such questions. We also review the major laws governing personal selling, the "gray areas" of sales most likely to raise ethical questions, and issues confronting sales managers. We conclude with several suggestions for modifying the organizational selling process having the potential to improve ethics in selling.

EXHIBIT 6-1   **Ethics in Selling: A Survey of** *Sales and Marketing Management* **Readers**

A survey by *Sales and Marketing Management* magazine of 316 sales and marketing managers yielded some interesting results regarding ethics in selling. It turns out to be a bad news good news story. Here are the results:

Lying

47 percent of sales managers suspect that their salespeople have lied on sales calls

45 percent of managers have heard their sales reps lying about promised delivery times

20 percent of sales managers have overheard their team members give false information about the company's service

16 percent have never heard one of their salespeople make an unrealistic promise to a customer

Competitors

78 percent of sales managers have caught a competitor lying about their company's products

Status of Ethics

36 percent said salespeople now conduct business in a less ethical manner than they did five years ago

36 percent also believe there's been no change at all

Good News

56 percent of companies have a process in place that enables salespeople to alert managers to ethical breaches

What conclusions do you draw from this survey?

Source: Erin Strout, "To Tell the Truth," *Sales and Marketing Management* (July 2002). For more detail about the statistics and company example, see the article.

WHY PERSONAL SELLING PRESENTS PARTICULARLY DIFFICULT ETHICAL QUESTIONS

Ethical conflicts and choices are inherent in the personal selling process because sales representatives must balance the interests of the seller they represent and the buyer they serve. Salespeople face many of the same general ethical issues any other marketing manager encounters. Yet they usually do not have the organizational support structure afforded to other company employees. Few salespeople ever have the luxury of contemplating the ethical propriety of their actions. Sales reps often operate in relative isolation, in circumstances subject to constant change, and under great time pressure. Finally, their results are often "evaluated" by sales managers looking at sales call reports submitted from the field. Such "paper-driven evaluations" contribute to a perceived distance between managers and reps.

The dynamic and autonomous nature of the selling process requires salespersons to make instantaneous choices about what to do when faced with particular dilemmas. For example, most salespeople cannot interrupt their discussions with a customer to make a phone call and ask their supervisors if it is okay to overstock one of their accounts "just enough to make quota." This autonomous aspect of most selling activities necessitates anticipation, if ethical principles are to guide the sales process. (We do recognize that cell phone and laptop computers have helped sales reps become more connected, but they still operate on their own much of the time.)

The pressures on the sales force take many forms. For example, heavy travel schedules may tempt people to inflate expense reports. Long periods away from the home office, sometimes in a foreign country, create special problems. While on assignment, salespeople become conditioned to utilizing company resources as if they were their own. Or the provision of a gift—even a *very large gift*—to an organizational buyer may seem small after spending months (even years) on an account that could mean a commission worth thousands of dollars or more.

Theories of sales motivation recommend rewarding superior *performance*. The resulting behavior that occurs in securing sales may be counter to organizational ethics and culture. In other words, companies that give lip service to ethical selling may in fact counteract that by only rewarding sales results. Many sales reps have been tempted to sell unneeded products because their compensation was based on commission or to overpromise delivery or product performance when a sale might otherwise be lost.[3] Selling in the financial services sector is especially problematic because of client desires for above average returns and their lack of sophistication and experience in evaluating questionable claims.[4] Some companies are beginning to question a heavy reliance on commission-based selling. For example, Home Depot pays its sales staff a generous hourly fee but no sales commission to discourage overselling. Some important guidance for the personal selling process is contained in Exhibit 6-2.

EXHIBIT 6-2   **Ethical and Legal Reminders for Salespeople**

- Use factual data rather than general statements of praise for the product during the sales presentation. Avoid misrepresentation.
- Thoroughly educate customers, before the sale, on the product's specifications, capabilities, and limitations.
- Do not overstep authority, as the salesperson's actions can be binding to the selling firm.

- Avoid discussing these topics with competitors: prices, profit margins, discounts, terms of sale, bids or intent to bid, sales territories or markets to be served, rejection or termination of customers.
- Do not use one product as bait for selling another product.
- Do not try to force the customer to buy only from your organization. Offer the same price and support to all buyers who purchase under the same set of circumstances.
- Do not tamper with a competitor's product.
- Do not disparage a competitor's product without specific evidence for your statements.
- Avoid promises that will be difficult or impossible to honor.

Source: T. N. Ingram, R. W. LaForge, R. Avila, C. Schwepker, and M. Williams, *Sales Management: Analysis and Decision Making,* 5th ed. (Chicago: Dryden Press, 2004), 173.

SELLING AND THE LAW

The first guiding principle for any sales representatives is that they should follow the law. The law is the lowest common denominator of ethical behavior (recall "Above the Law" from Chapter 1). Ideally, ethical conduct exists at a level well above that required by law. Many situations occur where sales representatives are accused of being "unethical" when the conduct in question is actually *illegal.* The following legal strictures attempt to constrain dubious selling efforts.

Federal Regulations

The Clayton Act (1914) and the Robinson-Patman Act (1936) restrict price reductions and promotional concessions. The Clayton Act prohibits tie-in sales whereby a customer, in order to purchase desired items, is required to buy other, unwanted products. Robinson-Patman states that selling firms cannot *indiscriminately* grant price concessions even when important customers demand larger discounts in order to retain their business. Such discounts are not legally allowed. The seller must grant equivalent discounts to all buyers. Unusual discounts or allowances can only be given if they are made available to all other customers or if there is a compelling cost differential to justify the discounting practice.

Various other unfair selling practices are illegal under the Federal Trade Commission Act (1914) and the Wheeler-Lea Amendment (1938). While these statutes do not define "unfair competition," a large body of case law has developed over the years. The following sales practices would clearly be legally dubious: making false, deceptive, or disparaging statements about competitors or their products; having a buyer provide *kickbacks* to secure a critical supply or component; presenting rebuilt or secondhand products as new; engaging in *industrial espionage* to learn competitive trade secrets; or making false or *misleading claims* about services that accompany the product.

State and Local Regulations

Several aspects of the selling process are governed by state or local law:

The Uniform Commercial Code (UCC)

The UCC regulates business contracts in most states, and spells out the various rules of contract law that apply to selling. While the laws governing selling vary somewhat from state to state, most include provisions for an *implied* warranty and a maximum allowable percent of interest when a sale is financed. Salespeople are also subject to legal sanctions if they do not understand the difference between *puffery* (i.e., statements of subjective opinion concerning a product or service) and statements of *fact* concerning product performance characteristics.

Cooling Off Laws

These statutes protect buyers from unscrupulous door-to-door and telemarketing sales representatives, which often subject consumers to undue pressure. Under these laws, customers normally have three days to inform the seller that they have changed their mind; they may void the contract, return any merchandise, and obtain a full refund where the purchase commitment was greater than $25. These laws also apply to purchasing and refinancing mortgages since some selling is involved.

Green River Ordinances

Named for Green River, Wyoming, where this regulation was first enacted, these laws require nonresidents selling goods or services to people in a particular community to register with local authorities, thereby eliminating so-called "fly-by-night" con artists and scam operators. (It should be noted, however, that these ordinances are most often adopted under pressure from local merchants and, thus, often serve to block legitimate as well as questionable parties from doing business.)

Based on the earlier discussion, one can see that many selling practices are controlled by existing *law*. Sales representatives engaging in conduct that violates existing legislation are, in all likelihood, knowingly breaking the law. Other sales practices, however, while not illegal, are certainly subject to question. It is to these that we now turn our attention.

THE GRAY AREAS OF SELLING

Several categories of personal selling behavior fall into "shades of gray." These include sales representatives' use of company assets, dealings with customers, relationships with competitors, conflicts of interest inherent in the selling process, and the issue of paying bribes or "grease" in foreign markets where such payments are customary.

Company Assets

The nature of personal selling often requires salespersons to use company resources when interacting with potential buyers. This may lead, for example, to padding expense reports and the personal use of company-supplied automobiles, fax machines, cell phones, and supplies. Abuses of this kind raise ethical "red flags" and result in substantial organizational costs. Companies rightly hold that they do not wish to add bogus expenses to the already considerable costs of approved selling activities. Some sales reps feel they have the right to inflate reported expenses when various business-related expenses are not reimbursed (e.g., certain gratuities). Others also believe using a company vehicle (without reimbursement) is acceptable because separating business and personal travel is often difficult. No simple answers exist concerning when use of company assets becomes unethical. However, sales organizations should have appropriate and detailed guidelines to govern behavior in situations that invite abuse.

Relationship with Customers

Among the potentially unethical personal selling tactics included in this category that are not necessarily illegal are (a) *overstocking* a customer because the sales rep wishes to win a sales contest or meet a quota; (b) *overselling*, pushing a more expensive or complex product than a customer needs; (c) *overpromising* a delivery, hoping the order will not be canceled when the unattainable delivery date is not met; (d) *overtelling*, sharing information obtained in confidence (such as secrets picked up from a customer); and (e) *underinforming*, failing to convey facts that may be pertinent to a customer's purchase decision but which are not advantageous to the seller. Organizations should take steps to make clear that these practices are not allowed.

A key customer-related issue is that of disclosure. Selling messages commonly include only positive information about products and services, assuming competitive messages provide the whole story about the range of products available to meet particular needs. But a particular seller's offerings are likely to have shortcomings as well as strengths that may be salient in customer choices. If so, the obligation *to the customer* requires information about those shortcomings so that a reasonable judgment can be made.[5] (The practical payoff to that disclosure is customer trust, confidence and relationship building.)

While having policies to deal with these issues does not *guarantee* ethical behavior, at least the company makes its position clear concerning the appropriateness of certain practices. Greater policy clarity is needed with respect to allowing the buyer's personality to affect terms of price, delivery, and other aspects of the sale; charging a less competitive price when the selling company was the sole source; and providing "purchase volume incentive bonuses" for larger buyers. Even when a selling ethics statement is in place, it may be worthwhile to periodically ascertain from the sales force (either through a meeting, formal survey, or a focus group) areas where further guidance is needed.

Exhibit 6-3 depicts the selling philosophy of a Midwestern investments counseling firm. This message is played when a caller to the agency is placed

---

EXHIBIT 6-3   The Healy Group Philosophy

At The Healy Group, we serve the interests of our clients, providing them with financial security and lasting value . . . we will be here not only when clients need us, but when they want us.

We maintain unquestioned financial integrity and strength, because to provide security for others, *we* must be strong.

We keep the promises that we make . . . our word is our bond!

Every member of The Healy Group pledges to adhere to only the highest standards of ethical conduct, fulfilling client's needs and wants responsively and efficiently with products of value and superior service.

You'll find that we'll steer you away from financial fads and gimmicks, preferring instead to engineer tried and true financial solutions and options.

At The Healy Group, we treat people with dignity while valuing diversity because "together we are better."

Source: The Healy Group, Inc. www.healygroup.com (2003). Reprinted with permission.

"on hold" and is displayed at the office. One of the authors asked this agency for a quote on car insurance (because he had multiple male teenage drivers), and the premium continued to go up without any claims. One of its salesman reviewed the policy and his advice was to "stick with you current policy, because it gives you the best deal." So, this company appears to follow its statement even to the extent of turning away potential business. **Have you had a similar experience with a salesperson or company?**

Relationships with Competitors

While sales representatives may not interact directly with competitors, their presence is always felt. It is often necessary to make product comparisons—disparagement of competitive offerings should be avoided, and they should be based on objective and accurate information. Claims of superiority should refer to a certifiable track record. Two other practices in this category are almost always unethical. First, *product tampering* with the competitors' offering—a practice usually occurring in retail stores or at trade shows—constitutes unfair competition and may be subject to legal sanction. A second dubious practice is *spying* on competitors. It is tempting to use whatever means available to obtain valuable competitive intelligence, and astute sales representatives will fearlessly probe buyers for information regarding competitors' price offerings or new product attributes. However, obtaining such information by subterfuge (e.g., taking competitive information from a buyer's desk) is unquestionably unethical. (Recall our discussion of competitive intelligence gathering in Chapter 2 where specific guidelines were offered.)

Relationships with Fellow Workers
and Supervisors[6]

Salesmen and -women have ethical responsibilities to their peers and to sales managers, because salespeople work not only alone but also as part of a team. However, individual rewards usually provide stronger motivation than group rewards. Sales representatives may try to take business away from colleagues, for example, when they sell to customers in another (maybe an adjacent) territory. This issue gets especially muddy with buyers having multiple locations and occurs because the sales compensation system promotes it and fails to reward teamwork adequately. When sales are slow, as in a recession, infighting for leads and sales can be especially problematic and calls for strong efforts by sales managers to define territorial responsibilities clearly and to both invite and respond to complaints.[7]

Given the isolation of some sales reps, they usually have great latitude in reporting their activities to supervisors. For instance, they may claim they made ten calls on Friday when they actually made five morning calls and took the afternoon off (for golf or tennis?) or omit the fact that five calls were via telephone merely "checking in," rather than actually visiting the account as expected.

Conflicts of Interest

A conflict of interest is frequently inherent in the selling process, as salespersons are intermediaries between the companies they represent and the buyers they serve. The desire to make a sale collides with other duties, particularly when commission is the principal form of compensation.[8] Some sellers, such as travel agents and stockbrokers, are faced with conflicting allegiances, because their compensation may come from someone other than the client with whom they are working. A typical example is real estate sales. Individuals looking for a home usually work with a realtor and place considerable confidence in his or her judgment. Yet they must know full well that the commission is paid by the seller of the house and, therefore, that the agent's first loyalty is to the seller. (Some states require affirmative disclosure regarding whether the realtor, in a particular relationship, is functioning as a buyer's or seller's agent. Nonetheless, the agent's commission is typically paid by the seller.) In summary, honesty and fairness are perhaps the key virtues for salespeople to adhere to in their relationships with customers, coworkers, and employers.

Gifts and Entertainment

Gifts and entertainment are often subject to detailed scrutiny, yet they play a legitimate role in the selling process. Most salespeople feel that giving small gifts, like coffee mugs, and providing lunches and some forms of entertainment are a perfectly normal part of the sales process and do not necessarily raise ethical questions. Especially at holiday time, giving gifts to customers is a tradition in America and in many other countries too (see Exhibit 6-4 for an international example). In business-to-business selling, salespeople and purchasing agents often develop a close working relationship, and gifts are an expression of appreciation for past and, perhaps, future business. The ethical question regarding gift-giving, of course, is: *When* does a gift become a bribe? Most buying organizations probably do not object to some of their purchasing representatives receiving a gift-wrapped bottle of wine at Christmas time. However, at what point does the value of a given gift cross the ethical line? For example, a company branded pen and pencil set may be considered acceptable; a pair of midfield tickets for a National Football League game or an international soccer match might be debatable; a color television set for the purchasing agent's den is extremely questionable; and the provision of sexual favors by call girls, arranged and paid for by the seller, is undeniably unethical.

EXHIBIT 6-4   Business Gift Giving in Ireland

In a series of in-depth interviews with top managers at several multinational companies based in Ireland, five open-ended questions were asked. One dealt with a specific ethical issue facing the respondent or his firm.

Gift giving and receiving came up once in response to this question about a specific ethical issue. The Managing Director (MD) who broached it indicated that he had been invited to things that were "more than a bottle of whiskey or a dinner." His response was to decline or to pay his own way so as to avoid the appearance of compromising himself. He also mentioned that it is sometimes difficult to say no in Ireland because he may know the person offering the gift very well due to the small size of the business community.

Two other interviewees brought up the area of gifts in the context of corporate policies and statements. One MD said he writes a note to all employees around Christmas reminding them the company has a firm policy that they should not accept any gifts from suppliers. The other individual commented that it is a custom in Ireland to provide gifts to business contacts. In his organization the purchasing department, shipping department, and finance office often receive such gifts. He conveyed the company position on this area: "During the holidays our policy is that no individual employee can accept such a gift. What we do with them is we turn all the gifts to the personnel department and they put everyone's name in a hat and draw out names and the gift goes to that individual." It was my experience that this practice was somewhat common with a number of medium and large businesses including one of the largest banks having a raffle of Christmas gifts. The resale of some gifts has been a problem in Ireland for some time. A retired CEO told me that his company placed its logo on all gifts before they were given to any customers or suppliers.

Source: Patrick E. Murphy, "Top Managers' Views on Corporate Ethics," *Irish Marketing Review*, 8 (1995): 68.

The difficulty, then, is establishing exactly where the ethical line should be drawn. The United States Internal Revenue Service limits the amount deducted for business gifts to any one individual to $25 annually. Many organizations, such as Wal-Mart, do not allow their purchasing agents or employees to give or receive *any* gifts. From the standpoint of helping shape a sales representative's judgment, firms should have an explicit written policy concerning gift giving and receiving. Exactly what goes into this policy depends on the culture and the tradition of the industry and corporation. However, time-tested guidelines suggest that (a) inordinately expensive gifts be avoided, (b) gifts should never be given *before* a buyer does business with an organization, (c) one should avoid giving gifts to the buyer's spouse or significant other, and (d) an explicit dollar limit should be placed on all gifts.

With respect to entertainment, virtually all salespeople agree that taking a customer to lunch is a reasonable, often expected, aspect of conducting business, though "an evening on the town" may be questionable. As with gifts, the fundamental issue is determining when entertaining is intended to influence a buyer to make a purchase for reasons other than the merits of the organization's offerings—product suitability, service, and price. When negotiating for multimillion dollar equipment contracts, it is common for top executives of the buying organization to be flown to the seller's headquarters for product demonstrations and briefings. Yet some companies and government agencies require such trips to be paid for from the buyer's budget. Again, it is best for organizations to have explicit, written policies about the types and value of permissible entertainment. What is considered acceptable may depend on the situation, but, as noted previously, some practices are never appropriate. Clearly, entertainment is meant to obligate the buyer in some way, to smooth the pathway for subsequent sales. On the other hand, more and more companies, on both the buying and selling side and especially where government contracts are involved, are placing severe restrictions on entertainment, requiring the cost of meals to be shared or prohibiting typical activities such as golf outings and sporting event attendance.

Bribery and Facilitation

While bribery and some grease/facilitation payments are forbidden in the United States and in most advanced economies, they may be accepted as customary in some less developed markets. It appears that the greater the cultural and economic differences between nations, the more striking the ethical differences confronting businesses. Because of the widespread acceptance of cultural relativism, many organizations have been criticized for engaging in practices in foreign (i.e., international) markets that are illegal in their home country. The most widely debated instance of this kind involves the question of the payment of bribes.

The controversy surrounding the Foreign Corrupt Practices Act (FCPA) of 1977, which applies to U.S.-based organizations, illustrates the problem of cultural relativism. This law prohibits unreported payments to foreign officials in order to obtain contracts for overseas business. For each violation— that is, the payment of a bribe—the culpable U.S. organization is subject to a $1 million fine.[9] In addition, managers responsible for violations are subject to a $10,000 fine per incident and up to five years in prison. The law does distinguish between so-called "grease payments" or facilitation—small sums given to minor officials to expedite the purchase process, that is, to get them to do their normal job in issuing permits, getting shipments unloaded, and so on— and bribery—large amounts of money to get officials to take an action they would not normally take, that is, to obtain special favors. Many organizations contend that such payments are standard in some countries. In other words, all grease payments and many bribes should be viewed as "customary" from an economic standpoint and should simply be considered as a cost of doing business.

Because of widespread criticism of the FCPA based on the prospect of placing U.S. firms at an economic disadvantage compared with other transnational marketers, the act was amended in 1988. Permissible payments were more broadly and clearly defined. These include payments for routine government actions, such as processing papers, stamping visas, and scheduling inspections. Thus, spending money related to smoothing the bureaucratic process is now perfectly legal. Nonetheless, an increasing number of companies prohibit *any* of these payments anywhere, large or small, whether to obtain business or simply to expedite imports or exports. In 2002, bp (British Petroleum) announced that it would no longer offer facilitation payments anywhere in the world, strengthening the firm's long-standing position against bribery.

The Organization for Economic Co-operation and Development (OECD) passed an antibribery statute in 1999 which was signed by 34 countries. This convention, that has been enacted, in the meantime, as national law in most OECD countries, is similar to the FCPA, and obligates companies from developed countries not to engage in bribery and corruption of government and other officials. The organization publishes an "Annual Report on the Guidelines for Multinational Enterprises" that has a special focus on enhancing the role of business in the fight against corruption (see www.oecd.org for further information). Another organization that has been instrumental in the fight against bribery and corruption is Berlin-based "Transparency International" (TI—www.transparency.org) which has chapters in the United States and many other countries. In fact, TI publishes an annual Corruptions Perceptions Index and a Bribe Payers Index that rank countries according to receiving and paying bribes, respectively.

Why do businesses persist in making these questionable payments? The case for bribery includes contentions that it is (a) an accepted practice in many countries, (b) merely a kind of commission to intermediaries, and (c) necessary to secure business and compete effectively against other companies allegedly willing to make such payments. The arguments against bribery are that it (a) is inherently wrong, (b) fosters corrupt governments and business practices, and (c) deceives stockholders concerning expenses being reported as legitimate costs of doing business.[10] In many cases, one could also argue that bribery violates the fairness principle. That is, business should be obtained on the basis of objective merit, not paying for favors. Such payments distort economic value by adding to the cost of doing business, most often in poor nations which are the least capable of bearing added costs. To the extent that purchases based on bribery result in less than the best deal otherwise available, an opportunity cost is borne by affected stakeholders—customers, shareholders, citizens, and so forth. Finally, the absence of transparency in these payments, i.e., they are typically made in secret, provides a further argument against their propriety.

Looking forward, the conflict between cultural relativism (recall the discussion in Chapter 1) and universalism as moral philosophies by which bribery and "grease" are evaluated is likely to persist, especially in the face of increasing globalization. As discussed earlier, more multinational corporations are adopting worldwide standards that limit or prohibit such payments and most nations with significant foreign trade activity have adopted some form of the FCPA into law.

When Sales Reps Are Most Pressured to Compromise Their Ethics

As considered generally in Chapter 1, sales reps will be more likely to cross ethical lines when certain opportunities to engage in unethical behavior exist. Similarly, if they realize the likelihood of being caught is low or their behavior will lead to a substantial reward, the probability of acting improperly increases. One can also speculate that the larger the extent to which a given sales representative has developed his/her ethical sensitivities (i.e., higher in the moral development level), the less the likelihood of engaging in unethical selling practices. These factors come into play for *all* marketers. However, several issues directly impact the conduct of sales representatives because of their selling tasks. We speculate, for example, that sales representatives will be pressured to act unethically when:

- Competition is intense.
- Economic times are difficult.
- Compensation is based primarily upon commission.
- Questionable dealings are a common industry practice (e.g., kickbacks or expensive entertainment).
- Policies and codes of ethics are either absent or not enforced.
- Corporate sales training is abbreviated.
- They have limited experience.

Some of these propositions have been systematically studied.[11] Highly competitive markets and tough economic times seem to make unethical choices more probable, while experience and close supervision are associated with ethical actions. Some industries like construction and waste management appear to be plagued with questionable practices. It follows that management should recognize and try to control those organizational factors that may tempt sales reps into violating ethical norms.

SALES MANAGEMENT ETHICS

A discussion of the special ethical responsibilities of sales managers is warranted. Many ethical issues confronting sales managers are the same as those facing any administrator—applying principles of fairness to employing, compensating, promoting, disciplining, and firing personnel. However, the tendency to treat top sales performers who engage in unethical behavior more leniently than others is apparently common.[12]

Further, many actions related to sales management fall under legal jurisdiction. For example, the Equal Employment Opportunity Act forbids discrimination against employees on the basis of race, sex, age, and religion, and successful lawsuits for other forms of unfair treatment are common. Prompt reimbursements for authorized sales force expenses and the accurate and timely payment of salary, commissions, and bonuses are legal, as well as ethical, responsibilities implicit in honest compensation management. However, four decision areas are particularly relevant to sales management and pose ethical concerns: managing sales territories, setting sales quotas, controlling sales messages, and sexual harassment.

Managing Sales Territories

The character of the territory assigned to a sales rep is a major determinant of that person's potential sales success and, consequently, his or her compensation. Therefore, assigning and staffing territories should be undertaken with special care. When it is necessary to reassign territories, loss of income or increased responsibilities for the individuals affected must be taken into consideration. Also, certain accounts become important enough over time to be designated "house" or "national accounts," handled exclusively by top managers or headquarters personnel. In such situations, sales managers should provide early notice to sales reps that have to make up for the lost business. When such account reassignments occur, managers should consider allocating new accounts or expanding the individual's territory, and, even, continuing at least some level of commission on purchases by the reassigned account. It is also a sales manager's responsibility to ensure that one salesperson does not encroach (poach) another representative's territory, depriving him/her of potential sales.

Setting Sales Quotas

Often commissions and bonuses make up much of a salesperson's compensation—and meeting or exceeding sales quotas is a key factor in determining one's compensation. When sales quotas are perceived as unfair, pressures for unethical behavior increase. If the sales force regularly falls short of established quotas, or the sales force perceives the quotas as being unattainable, morale declines. While reviewing methods used to establish sales quotas is beyond the scope of this book, such decisions should be made with concerns for equity, that is, fairness among members of the sales force based on realistic assessments of potential.

Controlling Sales Messages

Sales managers bear a special responsibility for product misrepresentation or communications that unfairly disparage competitors. The sales manager is typically responsible for approving and distributing promotional materials developed by headquarters as sales aids and for training and evaluating members of the sales force. These tasks should be carried out with a view to their ethical implications—accuracy, justice, and consequences for stakeholders. Exhibit 6-5 delineates some fine points in distinguishing between proper and improper communications. **Which point in Exhibit 6-5 do you think is most important?**

EXHIBIT 6-5   **A Checklist to Ensure Ethical Communications**

- Review promotional materials and sales literature before distribution to minimize the possibility that defamatory material is inadvertently circulated.
- Tell salespeople not to repeat unconfirmed trade gossip, particularly about the financial condition of a competitor.
- Tell salespeople to avoid statements that may be interpreted as damaging to the reputation of any business or individual.
- Ensure that salespeople avoid making unfair or inaccurate comparisons about a competitor's product. Mere "puffing" or claiming superiority over a competitor's product is not disparagement as long as the comparison attempts to enhance the quality of your product without being unfairly critical of the competitor's.
- Avoid sending customers written comparisons of competing products. One way to make comparisons is to include scientific facts or statistical evidence documented or prepared by an independent research firm supporting factual claims.

Source: R. E. Anderson, J. E. Hair Jr., and A. J. Bush, *Professional Sales Management* (New York: McGraw-Hill, 1988), 569–70.

Sexual Harassment

A significant trend in the late twentieth and early twenty-first centuries is the "feminization" of the sales profession due to the increased number of women joining companies in a selling capacity. Questions that arise from this development are, Will the increased number of women change the ethics of the sales field? Do women entering sales have a distinctly different moral orientation from men? Results from a study of females and males engaged in selling indicate "that women reach ethical judgments with more concern for feelings and relationships and less concern for rules and rights."[13]

One important ethical issue facing sales organizations employing more women employees is sexual harassment. The term is legally defined as unwanted conduct of a sexual nature that is severe or pervasive enough to create a hostile or intimidating work environment. According to government statistics, the number of individuals (both men and women) claiming to being sexually harassed at work doubled from the middle to late 1990s. The law defines two types of sexual harassment: (1) quid pro quo—sexual favors are a requirement—or appear to be a requirement—for advancement in the workplace; and (2) hostile work environment—a worker has been made to feel uncomfortable because of unwelcome actions or comments relating to sexuality. The second type is more difficult to determine because the *perception* of a remark, gesture, or stare may be quite different between two people (generally a male and a female).

Although sexual harassment presents a problem in any occupation, saleswomen are especially at risk because of the nature of selling. As discussed earlier, they are often isolated in the field and likely dependent on only one person in the organization—the sales manager. Salespeople are expected to entertain clients outside the office, attend conventions (where alcohol may flow freely) and social events that are lengthy and unmonitored, and meet with customers individually. Women also make up a minority of the sales force, and it has traditionally been a male-dominated profession. One of the authors recently gave a presentation to a sales group from the wine and spirits industry and only four of the 85 salespeople were women. In a report by *Sales and Marketing Management,* over 60 percent of the women and nearly 10 percent of the men indicated they had been sexually harassed at some point in their career.[14]

Women and men may be sexually harassed by other salespersons or the sales manager. An even more difficult situation emerges when the harasser is the customer. How should companies and sales managers respond when complaints occur? Just as firms make a strong stand against improper requests for special concessions like unjustified price breaks and unauthorized payments, companies must react strongly when a member of the sales force is sexually harassed by a customer. As organizations are moving more to relationship selling and close contact with customers, this issue is one that demands salespersons and managers take great pains to keep the relationship on a cordial, but professional, level.

It does not require great moral imagination to recognize that mixing sex and sales is wrong and an unacceptable business practice. No woman or man should have to endure the indignity of an unwanted sexual relationship or required flirtation to keep either a customer or a job.

DIRECT MARKETING AND SELLING

Although the field of direct marketing (telemarketing, direct mail, catalog, direct response on TV, and online) spans several areas of marketing, selling plays an integral role in many of them. Whether it is an outbound telemarketer or a catalog employee who only takes incoming calls, ethical issues do arise. The fact that, in most instances, consumers cannot physically examine the merchandise before buying creates a special responsibility on salespersons to be informative, forthcoming, and transparent regarding prices, shipping fees, and other charges.

Several ethical issues arise in direct marketing and selling. They are irritation, unfairness, deception, abuses of privacy, and pressure. Direct marketing organizations have responded with guidelines for these issues.

Irritation, Unfairness, and Deception

Direct marketing and selling excesses can annoy and/or offend consumers. Especially bothersome are telemarketing calls (now restricted in the United States by Do Not Call lists). Some sales pitches can confuse and mislead consumers. Misrepresentation, for example, of the portion of donations going to charity in a fund-raising campaign conducted over the phone has been found to be the basis for refunds and even punitive damages.[15] Although some consumers have responded to these problems by conducting transactions over the Internet, direct sales can still be effective through the call-in centers that are used extensively by airlines, hotels, and certain clothing marketers.

Invasions of Privacy

Information collected from consumers during telemarketing and catalog purchases is collected and used by marketers. As noted in the advertising chapter, consumers are leery of providing detailed information and are suspicious of how it might be used. Database marketing has many advantages for companies. However,

> Many critics worry that marketers may know too much about consumers' lives and that they may use this knowledge to take unfair advantage of consumers. At some point, they claim, the extensive use of databases intrudes on consumer privacy.
>
> For example, they ask, should AT&T be allowed to sell marketers the names of customers who frequently call the 800 numbers of catalog companies? . . . Is it right for credit bureaus to compile and sell lists of people who have recently applied for credit cards—people who are considered prime direct-marketing targets because of their spending behavior? Or is it right for states to sell the names and addresses of driver's license holders, along with height, weight, and gender information, allowing apparel retailers to target tall or overweight people with special clothing offers?[16]   **What do you think?**

Perceived Pressure

The field of direct marketing and selling has a history of putting pressure on consumers. From the bygone days of the door-to-door salesmen in the 1950s to twenty-first-century telemarketers who won't take no for an answer, consumers have perceived undue pressures to buy in order to get the salesperson to terminate the interaction. In fact, Kirby salespeople still use such tactics to sell their expensive (over $2,000) vacuum cleaners. One of the primary reasons for the cooling off laws mentioned earlier in the chapter is to allow consumers to void contracts that they feel pressured into accepting.

Response of Direct Marketers

Due to these and other ethical questions about their industry, both the Direct Marketing Association (DMA) and the Direct Selling Educational Foundation (DSEF) in the United States have been active in promoting ethical practices. The DMA (www.the-dma.org) has instituted the Privacy Promise, and the DSEF has published Ethical Standards Salespersons Should Follow (www.dsef.org). Companies that are members of these organizations are as concerned as consumers that some unethical direct marketers are ruining the reputation of the industry.

IDEAS FOR ETHICAL MARKETING

The following suggestions are offered to help sales managers establish and maintain an organizational climate more likely to support ethical conduct by sales personnel.

First, develop, circulate, and publicize a detailed and explicit sales ethics policy statement. Topics covered in this statement should address the major questions that arise in interactions with buyers—obligations to customers and competitors, gift giving, entertainment, and bribery. This policy should provide as much detail as the organization's selling experience allows. One of the best is the statement shown in Exhibit 6-6 by Integrity Systems®. In fact, this firm, by its name and actions, is strongly committed to ethical selling. Policy statements should also address special product-related issues. As examples, selling farm agricultural chemicals may pose special obligations concerning safety disclosure, and pharmaceutical reps have a duty to both physicians and patients to highlight a new drug's potential side effects. The statement should also make clear that ethics policies will be enforced, and disciplinary actions resulting from policy violations should be visible. In fact, a seven-step process for structuring a global sales organization to incorporate ethical and legal conduct is shown in Exhibit 6-7. While some organizations apparently rely on religious or spiritual beliefs to govern their actions,[17]

EXHIBIT 6-6   Integrity Systems®

Integrity Selling®: Statement of Values and Ethics

1. Selling is a mutual exchange of value.
2. Selling isn't something you do to people; it's something you do for and with them.
3. Developing trust and rapport precedes any selling activity.
4. Understanding people's wants or needs must always precede attempts to sell.
5. Selling techniques give way to values-driven principles.
6. Truth, respect, and honesty provide the basis for long-term selling success.
7. Ethics and values contribute more to sales success than do techniques or strategies.
8. Selling pressure is never exerted by the salesperson. It's exerted only by customers when they perceive they want or need the item being recommended.
9. Negotiation is never manipulation. It's always a strategy to work out problems—when customers want to work out the problems.
10. Closing is a victory for both the salesperson and the customer.

Integrity Systems® and Integrity Selling® are registered trademarks owned by Integrity Systems, Inc. All rights reserved. The Statement of Values and Ethics is copyrighted material from Integrity Selling®. Used with permission.

EXHIBIT 6-7   Steps for Initiating a Global Ethical Sales Structure

1. **Establish Specific Standards of Conduct for the Sales Organization.** Even though an organization might have an overall organizational code of conduct, it is important to create standards for behavior within the sales function. Because salespeople and sales managers have more direct contact with customers and competitors, the situations faced are often different than those confronted by other employees in the firm.
2. **Appoint a Sales Manager as a Compliance Officer.** Many organizations have an ethics officer or compliance official for companywide behavior. This is an appropriate policy, but the sales organization needs someone within its management structure to be responsible for ethical compliance by salespeople and sales managers.
3. **Address Ethical Propensity in the Sales Organization Hiring Process.** Although an organization must use legal and acceptable procedures in the recruiting and hiring process, it is important that due diligence is taken in evaluating potential employees for the sales organization.
4. **Provide Ethics Training to Salespeople and Sales Managers.** The situations faced by salespeople and sales managers are often complex, especially in different international markets. Even individuals who want to behave in an ethical manner may not realize the ethical implications of some actions, or even if they do, may not know what the acceptable behavior should be.
5. **Monitor Behavior of Salespeople and Sales Managers.** The saying "what gets measured gets done" applies here. The sales organization should establish ongoing procedures to continuously audit the ethical compliance of salespeople and sales managers.
6. **Enforce Sales Organization's Ethical Standards.** The ethical code must be enforced and disciplinary action taken when violations occur. This approach should be communicated throughout the sales organization and understood by all.
7. **Develop Ethical Culture within the Sales Organization.** The sales organization needs to develop an ethical culture that promotes continuous improvement in ethical sensitivity and behavior. Although the previous six steps will help establish this culture, more needs to be done. Top levels of management throughout the firm must constantly communicate the ethical standards in both word and deed. The sales organization must also recognize and reward those who engage in ethical behavior.

Source: O. C. Ferrell, T. N. Ingram, and R. W. LaForge, "Initiating Structure for Legal and Ethical Decisions in a Global Sales Organization," *Industrial Marketing Management* 29 no. 6 (November 2000): 562–63.

written policies that are frequently communicated, modeled, and enforced are also effective means of ensuring ethical conduct.

Second, sales quotas should always be realistic. Pressure to attain sales quotas that are not realistic creates an environment in which salespeople are likely to rationalize unethical conduct (discussed in Chapter 1). Exaggerating product characteristics, overselling, and bribery or kickbacks may be viewed as a necessary means to make sales and meet quotas. Sales managers also have the responsibility of monitoring sales force behavior. This traditionally includes occasionally accompanying reps on calls, actually reviewing the call reports most organizations routinely require, and setting a climate where open, forthright discussions can occur. Individuals who have historically submitted questionable expense vouchers or accumulated extraordinary sales only during contest periods are candidates for special attention. Prudential scrutiny may lead to purging members of the sales force that might later cause embarrassment or even legal action against the organization because of unethical actions.

Third, sales managers should encourage sales representatives to seek assistance when they face an ethically troublesome issue. As noted previously, sales representatives operate with much more independence than most other employees. However, this independence may foster a climate that creates a moral vacuum. Sales reps should be encouraged to consult sales managers by cell phone when confronted with an ethical issue in the field. Some organizations should designate someone who can be approached with ethical concerns. The idea of a "sales chaplain" has been suggested as a mechanism for providing ethical guidance realm. This chaplain could be a retired sales executive or someone trained in ethics and familiar with the organization whose role is to provide ethical guidance and counsel on issues that less experienced salesperson may not have previously encountered. Other possibilities are discussed in Chapter 7.

Fourth, if ethical problems persist in the selling environment, management should take proactive measures. If unethical sales conduct is a persistent problem in an industry—for example, if kickbacks or payoffs are customary—top management should consider meeting with competitors to hammer out an industrywide code of sales ethics that will level the competitive playing field. Working with competitors to improve the ethical climate in an industry does not violate federal antitrust law. The defense industry, one certainly deserving of censure for past unethical selling practices, has attempted to develop consistent industrywide practices since the mid 1980s.

Ethical abuse may stem from many factors, such as continuing unethical sales practices by competitors or improper requests by buyers. If sales reps become aware of continuing abuses and their immediate supervisor provides no help, there should be a mechanism by which they can "blow the whistle." See Exhibit 6-8 for a whistle-blowing incident. Such a mechanism allows employees to approach someone—the sales chaplain mentioned

EXHIBIT 6-8   A Salesman's Whistle-Blowing Tale

Douglas Durand became vice president of sales for TAP Pharmaceutical Products, Inc. in 1995. Several months after joining the firm, Durand found himself listening in disbelief as his sales staff openly discussed how to bribe urologists. In his 20 years as a pharmaceutical salesman, Durand had never experienced anything like this. With a numbers-driven corporate culture as its basis, TAP salespeople were encouraged to lure doctors with "discounts, gifts, and trips." Durand later stated that TAP employed no internal legal counsel because it would be viewed as "a sales-prevention department."

Enticed with a $140,000 salary and promised a $50,000 bonus, Durand initially attempted to counter the abuses, offering an extra year's salary to those who kept accurate records—an effort quickly curtailed by senior management. Growing increasingly concerned, Durand began to privately document TAP's abuses, even going so far as to seek the assistance of a Philadelphia lawyer with ties to an assistant U.S. attorney specializing in medical fraud.

These efforts soon became a "six-year quest to expose massive fraud at the company." In over 200 pages of notes, Durand compiled abuses that ultimately led to a "guilty plea" by TAP. In October 2001, after two years of negotiations, federal prosecutors announced a record $875 million fine against the company for conspiring with doctors to cheat the government. For his role, Durand received 14 percent of the settlement as is permissible under the federal whistle-blower statute.

Today, after collecting his $77 million, Durand is "more than happy to have left the industry behind." He has retired to West Florida. As a reluctant millionaire, Durand continues to make weekly shopping trips with his parents to Wal-Mart and he and his wife "continue to clip grocery coupons from the Sunday newspaper."

Source: Adapted from Charles Haddad, "A Whistle-Blower Rocks an Industry," *Business Week*, June 24, 2002, 126–30.

---

earlier or some other ethical ombudsman—in confidence. This person should be able to help resolve situations that have been reported repeatedly when the immediate supervisor seems unwilling or unable to do that. It is critical that protection from retribution against an employee who has bypassed the chain of command should be built into the whistle-blowing mechanism. For example, United Technologies, a firm in an industry with a history of ethical and legal scrapes with the government, has now established a corporate ombudsman position that includes confidentiality of any employee that comes forward as part of its mandate. Furthermore, UT also has an ethics officer and an ongoing training program.[18]

A Framework to Evaluate Sales Ethics

Beyond these organizational measures, four guidelines might be useful to the individual sales representative facing an ethical dilemma. Although limitations to any procedural approach exist, we recommend the proportionality framework.[19] While some experts have called for a more comprehensive normative approach, this approach was designed with the decision maker in mind. Thus, we endorse it as a starting point for the action-oriented and pragmatic sales rep. The following points capture the highlights of this approach.[20]

 1.   Actions with ethical ramifications have at least three components: (a) the intent behind the action, (b) the action itself (the means), and (c) the outcomes that flow from that action. In considering the ethical propriety of an action, one must consider all three components. Thus, scrutiny of what the sales rep *does* (the action) alone is too limited. One must also look at the intent preceding the action and any subsequent outcomes.

 2.   If the action results in a substantial negative outcome for any stakeholder, it is almost always unethical. For example, if a salesperson engages in bid-rigging (the means) with the outcome of driving competition from the marketplace, the action is unethical (a significant negative outcome), even though the by-product may be the provision of some product to customers at a currently lower price (a good outcome). Similarly, even if a sales rep has made full disclosure (an appropriate means), it would probably be unethical to sell a buyer a product that had attributes that the buyer simply did not need (a negative outcome).

 3.   If there are unintended side effects (outcomes) to an action taken by a salesperson and these side effects cause a *major* negative outcome, the action is almost always unethical. Suppose the sales representative of a pharmaceutical firm has been providing experimental drugs to a research institute to be used in animal research. In the course of the sales process, the salesperson learns that the drugs are to be used on human subjects. In such an instance, it may be unethical to go ahead with the transaction, because the side effects of the sale could produce significant negative consequences for other individuals (the unsuspecting human subjects). Major negative side effects, even if unintended, must be avoided.

 4.   Almost any action can have unintended side effects. He or she may take an action having side effects if the foreseen consequences of that side effect are *minor*. For example, in making a sale to a buying organization, a sales rep may learn that the sale will result in a competing salesperson losing a sales contest involving an overseas trip. Obviously, it would still be ethical for the salesperson to complete the transaction even though there would be a

negative consequence for his or her counterpart. Minor negative side effects, when not the purpose of the action, can be tolerated.

Clearly, this framework still requires judgment. What constitutes a *major* versus a *minor* negative outcome? If a sales rep anticipates side effects, does this mean they are intended? For example, suppose a salesperson realizes that making a large sale will cause another seller, desperately hoping for the contract, to file for bankruptcy. Does this mean that sales rep has caused a major negative outcome? Certainly not, as many other factors would have contributed to the insolvency. Still, the model provides only limited guidance. In addition, the framework depends on the ability to recognize an inherent impropriety as well as the likelihood of negative outcomes. Thus, the workability of this framework depends on the individual's moral sensitivity, sophistication, and imagination. And the model is meant to be applied to actions of a questionable nature. For example, if the actions taken by a salesperson are honest, well intentioned, and totally professional, there is little to be gained in calculating possible side effects and unintended outcomes. These limitations aside, however, the sketched approach does come to grips with the primary ethical components of decisions sales reps must make in the field.

CONCLUDING COMMENT

In this chapter, we have described the key factors that cause ethical difficulties for the sales force, and we discussed the major areas of ethical conflict occurring in selling situations. We reviewed the laws regulating personal selling and constraining the actions of salespeople and we also proposed "Ideas for Ethical Marketing" to provide guidance to sales personnel. In the final analysis, the necessity of making ethical judgments cannot be eliminated from the marketplace. Many of the organizational approaches discussed elsewhere in the book can overcome some of the ambiguity that sales reps encounter when facing an ethical question. However, the persuasive nature of the selling process often includes, as part of its residue, tough ethical cases that are difficult to confidently resolve.

Chapter Seven

Implementing and Auditing Ethical Marketing

Scenario 1

Andrew Gales, chief ethics officer of Sonic Company, was facing a serious situation. Despite instituting a strong ethics code in the 1980s and joining with other defense contractors and airplane manufacturers for a major initiative in corporate ethics, Andrew was confronted with reports that a few Sonic employees had engaged in corporate espionage against a major competitor. Although several employees were previously fired over the incident, a new internal investigation showed that a handful of those involved were still at the company. This fact could jeopardize future defense contracts.

He also learned of recent allegations that one of Sonic's top executives had "tampered with" a government official. The news media had picked up the story and reports said that improper contact was made with a current Sonic employee while he was still an employee of the U.S. government. So, added to the espionage charge was this current one that might undermine the company's position with its largest customer since it was a major defense contractor.

Andrew was scheduled for a meeting with the CEO on Tuesday. He was reviewing his thick file folder about the espionage episode and government contracts. He wondered how the company, already with a strong commitment to ethics, could reassert the importance of ethical behavior. He needed to come up with a convincing strategy for the CEO. **What should his plan be?**

Scenario 2

Harry Kraemer, CEO of Baxter International, faced a tough ethical dilemma in late 2001. (Kraemer had worked his way up the ladder at Baxter and was the lead person in the early 1990s when Baxter unveiled its Shared Values program. He resigned as CEO in early 2004.) Baxter had purchased a company in Sweden that made renal dialysis machines. Several deaths of patients occurred using the machine in Spain, but all the individuals were elderly, and initially the incidents were not a cause for alarm.

Studies that were done after the deaths in Spain exonerated the dialyzers. However, a number of patients in Croatia being treated on the same equipment subsequently died. Later, said Stan Heller (president of Baxter Renal Division), "I knew that there was too much there to be a coincidence." The filters in Croatia were probably manufactured around the same time as the ones in Spain. What's more, the recent deaths had occurred at six locations and the patients weren't all elderly. The clustering in two different countries was highly unusual. Something was wrong with the filters.

Suddenly, Baxter's world exploded. The deaths were front-page news every day in the Croatian newspapers. The Croatian health ministry, like regional officials in Valencia, refused to release the used filters to Baxter for testing. The possibility of tampering was broached.

The U.S. business press didn't report much on the situation. News of the deaths was soon eclipsed, first by the profound tragedy of September 11 and then by the opening bars of Enron's opera of greed and deceit. Over the next few weeks, though, a total of 53 deaths in the United States and six other countries would be linked circumstantially to Baxter's filters. It wasn't certain until later that the filters were to blame. To this day, it isn't clear exactly what went wrong.

But what was certain was this: Baxter and its CEO, Harry M. Jansen Kraemer Jr., faced a moment of truth. How Baxter responded would leave a lasting imprint on the company's relationships with patients and doctors, with employees, and, of course, with investors. The episode would, for better or worse, open a window onto Baxter's corporate soul.[1] **What were Kraemer's options?**

These scenarios illustrate why ethics should be *implemented* in the daily operations of a corporation. We believe marketing managers working in the areas examined previously (new products, distribution, advertising, international, etc.) need guidance from their firm to deal with ethically troublesome issues. *Corporate ethics statements, ethics training programs,* and an *ethical questions checklist,* all implicit in the scenarios, can help lead to ethical actions that provide necessary direction. The crucial question addressed here is: How can companies incorporate the ethical dimension into their marketing decision making?

In this chapter we outline several avenues to instill ethical values into marketing organizations. First, we suggest formal corporate policies, such as ethics statements (i.e., codes, credos, or values statements) and ethics programs for managers and employees. These structural mechanisms can enhance ethical decision making. We then encourage the nurturing of a corporate culture that places a premium on ethical action. Third, we envision that these steps would include an audit involving "check" questions to assure routine considerations of ethical issues. Finally, we provide several ideas for ethical marketing and close with comments to spur future thinking about ethics in marketing.

ORGANIZING FOR MARKETING ETHICS IMPLEMENTATION

Implementing marketing ethics entails both establishing policies that promote ethical decisions *and* creating a corporate culture conducive to ethical behavior. Managers need to ensure these policies are carried out, and an ethical culture is reinforced. In practice, enacting ethical marketing policies includes several responsibilities in managing product, price, distribution, and promotion. Exhibit 7-1 presents a summary of these elements. We first turn to the issue of formal corporate policies and their role in improving organizational ethics.

Formal Corporate Policies

Companies that sustain concern for ethical marketing have instituted several formal policies ensuring that this topic is regularly discussed. The most prevalent approach is a corporate ethics statement. Such statements are important because they are public manifestations of organizational commitment to ethics. Four types of ethics statements are commonly used.

Corporate Credos

The first is a corporate credo—a one-page (or less) document that lists corporate beliefs and/or responsibilities to stakeholders. Because of its brevity, a credo works best in firms with a cohesive corporate culture where a spirit of open and frequent communication exists. This approach may be less useful for multinational or recently merged companies. In addition to

Exhibit 7-1   Implementing Marketing Ethics

Organizing Ethical Marketing Policies

Structure: The Formal Organization	Culture: The Informal Organization
Corporate Credo	Open and Candid
Corporate Code	Family Values
Communicated	Principles
Specific	Atmosphere/Ambience
Pertinent	
Enforced	
Revised	
Values Statement	
Promoted	
Reinforced	
Internet Privacy Policy	
Ethics Training Programs	

Enacting Ethical Marketing Policies

Implementation Responsibilities	Implementation Tasks
Leadership—Integrity	Product Alteration
Delegation—Trust	Price Negotiation
Communication—Openness	Place Determination
Motivation—Reward and Punishment	Promotion Presentation

the acclaimed Johnson & Johnson credo (see Exhibit 1-2), two other exemplary credos are worthy of comment.

The oldest corporate credo is "The Penney Idea" of J. C. Penney Company. It originated in 1913 and is shown in Exhibit 7-2. In fact, the initial corporate name that founder J. C. Penney selected for his retail outlets were the "Golden Rule Stores." Why? He believed strongly that the application of and adherence to the Golden Rule concept should pervade his company's business decisions. "The Penney Company adopted these principles in 1913 and they have been a guideline for conducting business since that date. We do not have any plans to discontinue the use of these principles as we still find them to be effective in today's working environment."[2] A more recent example is the Cooperative Bank headquartered in Manchester, England. The firm has used its Ethical Policy for over a decade as a "positioning" strategy to differentiate the firm from other U.K. financial institutions. Two of its most interesting policies deal with human rights and arms trade (see www.cooperativebank.co.uk/ethics/ethicalpolicy.html).

EXHIBIT 7-2   **The Penney Idea (Adopted in 1913)**

1. To serve the public, as nearly as we can, to its complete satisfaction.
2. To expect for the service we render a fair remuneration and not all the profit the traffic will bear.
3. To do all in our power to pack the customer's dollar full of value, quality, and satisfaction.
4. To continue to train ourselves and our associates so that the service we give will be more and more intelligently performed.
5. To improve constantly the human factor in our business.
6. To reward men and women in our organization through participation in what the business produces.
7. To test our every policy, method, and act in this wise: "Does it square with what is right and just?"

Reprinted by permission of J. C. Penney Company, Inc.

Codes of Ethics

Codes of conduct (or ethics) are a second, and more prevalent, type of ethics statement. Over half of all firms and over 90 percent of *Fortune* 500 companies have a formal ethics code.[3] Most codes address such issues as conflicts of interest, treatment of competitors, privacy, gift giving, and political contributions. Codes of conduct/ethics are perceived as an effective way to encourage ethical corporate behavior, especially in large corporations with far-flung operations. However, critics believe codes are really only public-relations documents—nothing more than "motherhood and apple pie statements" that fail to meaningfully address significant managerial issues.

We believe that codes are useful but need to be tailored to critical marketing functions. That is, codes should go beyond platitudes and delve into substantive marketing issues facing the particular firm. Some companies have a customer relations section in their codes, but few have sections on marketing. Energy East, an energy company headquartered in Binghampton, New York, is an exception. Its "Code of Conduct" has a section on "Sales Practices."

> Marketing and selling activities should be predicated upon the superiority of the products and services that Energy East has to offer. In making comparisons to competitors, care must be taken to avoid disparaging a competitor through inaccurate statements. In addition, our credibility with our customers depends on our ability to fulfill our commitments. We must not make promises unless we are reasonably confident that we will be able to keep them.[4]

For companies contemplating or maintaining a marketing code of conduct, we offer the following suggestions.[5] (Another list of considerations in developing an effective code is shown in Exhibit 7-3). Any marketing code of ethics should be:

Communicated. To be understood and appreciated, the code should be publicized to the entire firm. New employees are usually asked to read and "sign off" on the code during their orientation. However, the code is quickly forgotten if it is never mentioned again. Firms should regularly communicate with their personnel about the code and promote it in departmental memos and meetings. Some organizations, including HCA—a national health care provider—require that employees read and affirm their commitment to the code on an annual basis. In addition to being communicated internally, the code should also be disseminated *publicly* to a firm's stakeholders. We are aware of many codes (including those of large firms) that are exclusively internal documents. If the code is worth having, it should be made widely available. Otherwise, it gives the impression that the firm has something to hide or is using the code exclusively as a legalistic crutch.

Specific. To avoid vagueness, the code should offer (wherever possible) detailed guidance to sales and marketing executives. The code should not use words such as "nominal," "token," or "modest value" when dealing with the giving and receiving of gifts. For example, Donnelly Corporation's code says, "If you can't eat it, drink it or use it up in one day, don't give it or anything else of greater value." Recent data indicate that only about half of companies that have codes even now offer guidelines on "Industry Specific Information."[6]

Pertinent. To have maximum effectiveness, the code should deal with issues central to the industry for which the code is written. Each organization has certain areas that are particularly susceptible to ethical abuse, and these concerns are ones on which the code should focus. For instance, toy companies should make special provisions for protecting the safety of children. Mail order and Internet firms should address their return policies and how they handle merchandise damaged in shipping. Major e-marketers are now making it easier to return merchandise by offering free shipping or pickups for returns. Companies that spend millions of dollars on promotion and advertising need to detail their advertising philosophy, as well as what program vehicles or media they will or will not use. Target Corporation is one of the few that has an advertising section in its code.

Enforced. To gain the respect of managers and their subordinates, the code of marketing conduct must be enforced. Sanctions should be specified

EXHIBIT 7-3   **Basic Concepts of a Code of Conduct by Hong Kong Ethics Development Centre**

Uniqueness

For a code of conduct to be effective, it has to be developed by the company to suit its own needs and aspirations. A code must also be consistent with the culture of that company. It is not desirable nor possible to lay down a single model code suitable for all business corporations. A code of conduct is therefore unique and tailor-made for the company concerned.

Open Process

The development and implementation of a code of conduct is an open process carried out in a transparent and high-profile manner. This facilitates staff consultation. It also sends the right signal to those within and outside the company that it abides by a certain standard of behavior in its operations.

Consistency in Standards

Values and principles embodied in the code should be consistent. Double standards undermine management's credibility, cause confusion and erode the effectiveness of the code.

Evolutionary

A code of conduct should address the present day issues, concerns and situations faced by a company. An effective code of conduct evolves over time. It needs to be regularly reviewed to meet with the changes in a company's internal and external environments which may pose new legal and ethical considerations. The way in which the code is reviewed should also be transparent and mentioned explicitly in the code.

Easily Understood

Whatever contents a company decides to include in its code of conduct, they should be written in a manner and style that can be readily understood.

Enforcement

A code of conduct will not serve any useful purpose if it is not effectively enforced. Having the corporate will and determination to do so is the basic requirement. If necessary, supporting mechanisms in terms of drawing up related procedures, delegating responsibilities and creating new organizational set-ups need to be put in place.

Source: Hong Kong Ethics Development Centre, 1997, 11.

and punishments meted out. Particular sanctions for a given violation depend on its severity. For example, padding an expense account for the first time may result in a salesperson losing commissions temporarily, while a manager who induces employees to use bait-and-switch tactics might be dismissed. Specifically, Baxter's code states that violators' employment will be terminated. The last section in Exhibit 7-3 adds further guidance on enforcement. We would add that the best companies offer multiple avenues for reporting code violations (i.e., 800 number, ethics officer, supervisor, ombudsman, or top manager).

Revised. To remain current, credos and codes should be revised periodically. They need to be living documents to reflect changing worldwide conditions, community standards, and evolving organization policies. For example, Caterpillar Corporation has revised its code five times since instituting it in 1974. Johnson & Johnson held a series of meetings in the late 1970s to challenge the company corporate credo. What emerged from the meetings was that the document in fact functioned as intended. A slightly reworded, but substantially unchanged, credo was reintroduced in 1979. Weyerhauser's code is now in its sixth edition.

Values Statements

Many companies have set out their corporate values in a systematic manner that makes reference to quality, customers, and a range of employee issues. In fact, we believe customer commitment/focus should be the dominant moral value driving marketing organizations. Values statements often stem from the company's mission and give direction to it. While these statements are not exclusively devoted to ethics, they do provide insight as to how companies integrate ethical issues with their operating principles. Values statements speak of a firm's being ethical and fair, with an emphasis on integrity, teamwork, trustworthiness, and openness in communication.

Values statements are intended to set out the guiding principles of the firm, and organizations often list them in concert with their mission statement. A number of companies make reference to the values espoused by their founders as ones that have withstood the test of time. The most frequent criticism of values statements is that companies do not live up to them or that they have no practical impact on the organization. We encourage students and prospective employees to prioritize their personal values. They should then look for employers whose values are consonant with theirs. Sometimes, marketing staff must learn to compromise with the company on some of the less important values.

Although many corporations have had a statement of values in place for some time, the 1990s saw a resurgence in them. In fact, a study by one of the authors found that the percentage of large U.S.-based companies with values statements jumped from 53 percent in 1992 to 63 percent in 1997 and to 68 percent in 2003.[7] The actual number of values can range from three (respect, integrity, and responsibility by Hanna Andersson, the children's clothing manufacturer mentioned in Chapter 1) to ten by Ethan Allen (see http://www.ethanallen.com/).

In addition to the list of factors discussed within the section on codes, we would add two others here:

Reinforced.   If values are to take root in any organization, they must be reinforced especially by the management team—from CEO to vice president of marketing to sales manager and so on. For instance, if integrity is listed as a core value of a company (and it often is), the use of white lies and frequent product embellishment by salespeople would violate this value. Unless management takes a strong stance against what some would perceive as these trivial violations, the value of integrity will likely not be evident in the firm.

Promoted.   A company code of ethics can be communicated widely, but it is difficult to envision promoting a code in a marketing sense. A values statement (and/or credo), however, because of its brevity, lends itself to promotion on the Web site, framed posters, small cards, and other public displays. For example, Xilinx, a Silicon Valley software company, spells out a word that is familiar to everyone with its values. The word is CREATIVE (C = customer focus, R = respect, E = excellence, A = accountability, T = teamwork, I = integrity, V = very open communication, and E = enjoying our work). Probably the best example of both promoting and reinforcing corporate values is at GSD & M, a major ad agency in Austin, Texas. In the foyer of its new building (constructed in the late 1990s), the seven values (Integrity, Restlessness, Freedom, Responsibility, Curiosity, Winning, and Community) are literally chiseled into the floor of the company. (See Exhibit 7-4.) This permanent display of GSD & M's values serves as a daily reminder not only for visitors and clients coming to the office, but also employees who walk past/over them regularly.

Internet Privacy Policies

This is the newest type of ethics statement and various consumer groups expect one to be present as a matter of forthright business practice. Internet privacy policies outline the company's position on what the firm will do with information collected from consumers. In the last several years, the vast majority of the firms with Web sites have posted a privacy statement on the company Web site. Such a statement is a legal requirement for all financial

EXHIBIT 7-4   GSD & M Values

You have to stand for something. Even if you're an advertising agency. Even beyond the work. We knew that from the very beginning. And we all kind of know the things we believe in, but we only recently defined—and literally carved in stone—our core, authentic values: principles we do not compromise. Under any circumstances. Ever.

We have a set of core values, a set of principles we believe in. Community— we're all in this together and everyone's important: clients, vendor partners, us. Curiosity—there's got to be a better way. Winning—play hard; play fair; play to win. Freedom & Responsibility—success is in your hands. Restlessness— What's next? Integrity—Do the right thing.

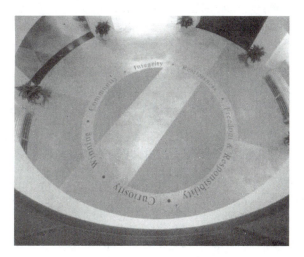

Source: GSD & M company documents. Reprinted with permission.

services firms. One of the biggest stimulants to the posting of privacy statements was IBM's announcement in 1999 that it would do e-business only with firms that had a privacy statement.[8] We view IBM's action as a classic "power-responsibility" move where the company with substantial economic power properly assumes its ethical and social responsibility.

Internet privacy statements have, unfortunately, become largely legalistic documents. The average consumer, even those with a college or graduate education, often has difficulty deciphering what the firm's policy is. Furthermore, a number of publicized cases have been discussed in the media where consumers claim that some firms do not follow their own privacy statements.

If Internet privacy statements are to be "ethical" rather than legal in orientation, we propose that they be relatively short, simple, and easy for the average consumer to understand. Although Mattress.com has lengthened its
privacy statement in the last few years, the policy's eight short sections are
written in plain English (not legalese). They address the information Mat-
tress.com collects, what the firm does with it, and even directly comments on
"cookies" (see http://www.mattress.com/service/privacy_policy.php).

Ethics Training

Another ethics-enhancing corporate policy is the development of ethics
training programs (see Exhibit 7-1). They can provide more specific direction
than credos or codes. Such programs range from a modest effort, such as
having a speaker or panel at a dealer meeting or corporate gathering to an
annual several-day conference. For example, Medtronic, a leading medical
instrument company, annually brings together its top management team for
an ethics workshop.

Ethics training for marketing and other functional areas of the firm has
evolved over the last decade. Now, 88 percent of big companies have ethics
training programs. The two major approaches to training are *compliance*
(following rules and the code) and *values/integrity* (using the credo or values
statement as an aspirational goal). A number of large companies try to
incorporate both types of ethics training (compliance and values) into their
programs. In three separate surveys, over a ten-year period, the number of
firms indicating that they focused on compliance and values jumped from
14 percent to 36 percent.[9] In Scenario 1, it appears that Sonic Company needs
to redouble its ethics training in light of current problems.

There are no guarantees that formal corporate policies will institution-
alize ethics within a firm and its marketing department. Formal efforts
alone—printed policies and training—do not by themselves ensure a corporate environment that both encourages ethical conduct *and* discourages
misdeeds. To achieve that, we need to look at the informal aspects of corporate life—culture, leadership, and managerial style. Additionally, policies
and structures that frame issues such as compensation and employee control
will shape the "character" of a company, its managers, employees, and dealers. Therefore, we now turn to corporate elements that may provide more
continual and longer lasting guidance.

CORPORATE CULTURE: THE INFORMAL ORGANIZATION

Corporate culture (informally defined as "the way we do things around here")
serves as a pervasive informal policy for instilling a higher level of firmwide
ethical commitment. It is one of the major focal points of organizational

analysis in recent times. After nearly 20 years of study, the consensus among informed observers is that corporate culture is explicitly linked with ethics, in the sense that cohesive and strong cultures tend to reinforce ethical behavior. Open communication, a commitment to organizational values, and their connection to community values are hallmarks of such ethically oriented cultures. It seems especially significant that, based on a recent study of 14 organizations by Professor Leonard Berry, a precondition of durable corporate success is values driven leadership.[10] It is the role of the CEO and top marketing executives to ensure that such characteristics exist.

A major dimension of corporate culture has to do with organizational *values*. As noted previously, these are strongly held core attitudes of the firm. One logical way to examine a corporation's values is to liken the obligations of employees to community duties. Typical community values, such as caring for one another and being a good "citizen," easily translate into the corporate setting. This analogy may ease the understanding and integration of ethics into a familial or community management style. We agree strongly with this statement: "As in family life, corporate ethics begins at home, and a corporation that emphasizes ethical behavior within the organization is probably going to insist on ethical behavior and a positive impact on the outside community as well."[11]

Other components of corporate culture relate to the *principles* espoused by firms. Principles refer to the articulation of the atmosphere and ambience of a company. For many firms, ethical principles are implicit. That is, the values have become part of the culture rather than having been included in formal corporate policies. Exhibit 7-5 discusses four principles often followed by firms that place a high value on ethics. Though the writings on which those principles are based were published some time ago, we believe they definitely hold for twenty-first-century marketing managers. **What do you think?**

To create and foster a corporate culture that reduces pressure on managers, a two-pronged approach is proposed: articulation and communication of an explicit managerial ideology and the facilitation of discussions and agreements on moral questions among all organization members. The first component—*communication about ethics*—is achieved by removing ambiguity about the firm's ethical priorities, that is, top management has the responsibility to let its managers and employees know exactly where they stand on key ethical issues, such as dealing with suppliers and promotional policies. The second point—*discussion of ethics*—is accomplished by examining specific moral questions during employee training sessions. Such exchanges may ultimately lead to a consensus on what constitutes morally appropriate behavior for particular situations. The first communication component is prescriptive and directive, while the second is participative and nondirective; yet they are equally important.

A candid and ethical corporate culture exists when communication flows freely within the organization. In such a culture, managers are open to

EXHIBIT 7-5   **Principles for High-Ethics Firms**

After studying twenty-five firms that are recognized for both their economic and ethical performance, Mark Pastin proposed the following four principles for high-ethics firms. They are the following:

Principle 1. High-ethics firms are at ease interacting with diverse internal and external stakeholder groups. The ground rules of these firms make the good of these stakeholder groups part of the firm's own good.

Principle 2. High-ethics firms are "obsessed" with fairness. Their ground rules emphasize that the other person's interests count as much as their own.

Principle 3. In high-ethics firms, responsibility is individual rather than collective, with individuals assuming personal responsibility for actions of the firm. These firms' ground rules mandate that individuals are responsible to themselves.

Principle 4. The high-ethics firm sees its activities in terms of a purpose. This purpose is a way of operating that members of the firm value. And purpose ties the firm to its environment.

Source: Mark Pastin, *The Hard Problems of Management: Gaining the Ethics Edge* (San Francisco: Jossey-Bass, 1986), 221–25.

questions by subordinates; thus, two-way communications must be encouraged and supported. Corporate culture is an elusive concept. In its broadest sense, culture refers to the "corporate air one breathes." And it is important to recognize that organizational culture and ethics are very closely related. Pressures encouraging unethical behavior by marketing employees can often be explained by examining the corporate culture. For example, certain appliance superstores place their employees in an atmosphere of high-pressure selling aimed at manipulating consumers and pitting the representatives against fellow salespeople; sometimes commissions are based on sales of service contracts of dubious value. Yet, these retailers wonder why morale is low and customers are dissatisfied. On the other hand, Cummins Engine of Indiana (see www.cummins.com) has a long-standing culture of commitment to employees in terms of outplacement and training. Although its financial performance has been uneven in recent years, firm loyalty has remained high. This example suggests that marketing managers who want ethics to be a central theme of their organization must make the long-term commitment to instituting and reinforcing a culture where this objective, ethical concern, is a reality.

ENACTING ETHICAL MARKETING POLICIES

Exhibit 7-1 also shows the two components of actually performing ethical marketing implementation. It is not enough to have a structure and culture that support ethical decision making. These organizational dimensions must be combined with implementation responsibilities and tasks, so that managers act ethically when they carry out marketing strategies.

Implementation Responsibilities

Although four managerial responsibilities are listed in Exhibit 7-1, the overarching one in establishing ethical concern is *executive leadership*. There is truth to the view that American corporations are often overmanaged and underled. To counteract this perception, the 1990s witnessed an explosion of discussion on leadership in business organizations. Many of these treatises were little more than cookbooks for success filled with trivial phrases such as lead from the rear, aspire to greatness, toss away the past, and so forth. However, this advice underlines the notion that leadership is more than planning, organizing, and controlling the key functions ordinarily associated with management.

Several significant works linking leadership with ethics did appear during this time. Exhibit 7-6 shows five types of leadership with an ethical foundation. As Bill George, retired Medtronic CEO, indicates in his book, authentic leaders are more interested in empowering the people they lead to make a difference than they are in power, money, or prestige for themselves. Covenantal leadership was popularized by Max DePree, the retired CEO of Herman Miller, who views a leader as having a covenant with the followers (employees) and other stakeholders. Harvard Professor Joseph Badarraco contends that individuals at middle and lower levels of an organization can exhibit "quiet" leadership. Probably the most widely held leadership approach is servant leadership. This notion of "leader as servant" was originally proposed in the 1970s by Robert Greenleaf. TDIndustries of Dallas has incorporated servant leadership into its values statement (see www. tdindustries.com). Following the trend of values statements, a number of CEOs now employ "values-based leadership." As Wim Roelandts, CEO of Xilinx, told one of the authors: "The CEO must also set an example and 'walk the talk.' Regarding our values at Xilinx (see http://www.xilinx.com/hr/culture/index.htm), these can be rather abstract. So I tend to use examples. The values are the glue that keep people together in the organization. They are the underpinnings of good communication. I try to find specific examples of people living the values and use these in my discussions and communication with employees to bring the values home to each employee."

Exhibit 7-6   **Ethical Leadership Approaches**

Types of Leadership	Author	Company Examples
Authentic Leadership	George[1]	Medtronic
Covenantal Leadership	DePree[2]	Herman Miller
Quiet Leadership	Badaracco[3]	
Servant Leadership	Greenleaf[4]	TDIndustries, Service Master, Toro, Vanguard
Values Based Leadership	DeSpain and Converse[5]	Xilinx, Caterpillar

[1]Bill George, *Authentic Leadership—Rediscovering the Secrets to Creating Lasting Value* (San Francisco: Jossey-Bass, 2003).
[2]Max DePree, *Leadership Is an Art* (New York: Dell Publishing, 1989); *Leadership Jazz* (New York: Doubleday, 1992).
[3]Joseph Badaracco, *Leading Quietly* (Boston, MA: Harvard, 2002).
[4]Robert Greenleaf, *Servant Leadership* (New York: Paulist Press, 1977).
[5]James DeSpain and Jane Badman Converse, *And Dignity for All* (New York, Prentice-Hall, 2003).

The one constant in all these writings on executive leadership is that the leader must continually exhibit a high level of *integrity*. A common failing in the recent business scandals is the lack of integrity exhibited by CEOs and other top managers. We believe integrity is an indispensable ingredient in ethical business leadership. That is, leadership is important in all aspects of business, but critical in the ethics area. In Scenario 2, Harry Kraemer must demonstrate ethical leadership at Baxter (to find out what he did, see Web site listed in endnote 1). In fact, integrity can serve as a linch-pin for developing an ethics strategy.

Delegation is one of the necessary managerial responsibilities that follow from leadership. To effect ethical sensitivity, middle and lower level marketing managers must not be placed in difficult ethical situations where their ethical responsibilities are unclear. Ethical guidance, delegated "down the line," is critical. The way we describe delegation is through *trust*. A recent book, *Trust or Consequences*, offers strategies that any company can use to build, strengthen, and even restore the bonds of trust.[12]

Delegation can also have a negative interpretation. Statements such as "I don't care how you do it, just meet or beat your quota," or "Ship more to that customer this month than you did last," or "Find a way to make that person quit" often give subordinates the impression that any tactics can be used to reach organizational objectives. For example, a sales manager who continually raises the quota or reduces territory size of a top performing salesperson puts increasing pressure on the individual to engage in unethical activities such as lavish gift giving or overselling to accomplish sales objectives. If the delegation responsibility is to be dispatched properly, executives must be more explicit about what practices are acceptable and enhance trust in their organizations.

Communication is a third managerial characteristic for ethical marketing policies to be implemented effectively. For communication to occur, the watchword should be *openness* (or transparency as we indicated in the Introduction) between and among marketing managers and their subordinates. This communication can occur "formally" in many ways, including through the ethics code as well as through ethics seminars and training programs. For example, new employees of many companies are asked to read, reflect upon, and then sign the ethics code upon their employment. In many instances, however, little communication follows the initial exposure. To overcome this potential problem, Caterpillar requires its managers to report annually about the implementation of the code within their division or department. This communication is most effective if combined with concrete actions by top marketing managers about ethics.

"Informal" communication is also a potentially effective implementation mechanism. The grapevine can disseminate information that formal channels cannot. For instance, the fact that several salespersons lost a commission for padding their expense accounts may not lend itself to discussion in the company newsletter. However, "word" can get out through informal channels and thereby influence future behavior.

The last, but certainly not the least important, managerial responsibility for successful ethics implementation, is *motivation*. If companies are to be successful in enacting ethical marketing policies, individuals must be rewarded for doing things "right" and penalized for doing them "wrong." This means that higher level executives must look closely at how performance is measured. Jim Collins observed in his book about great companies that strong "core values" serve as the key motivator for employees.[13]

The negative side of motivation—*punishment*—should also not be ignored. For example, marketing personnel who engage in exorbitant entertainment of clients or who informally practice racial or sexual discrimination should be reprimanded (or fired) for these activities. One partial explanation of the mutual funds trading scandals was that top managers did not look closely at the guidelines their associates were following because they were generating large profits for the firm. How did such commissions materialize? Unfortunately in many cases, we now know the answer. Employees are motivated by the expectations communicated by higher level executives. If generating client activity, and hence commissions, is their sole objective, ethical issues will receive only limited consideration. The implication of this point, which also ties into the previously discussed issues of leadership and communications, is that executives concerned with ethical conduct in their organizations must walk the talk. Employees and other stakeholders should regularly be made aware that the CEO and other corporate leaders believe and act in accord with values of truth and integrity, respect for diversity and fairness, and responsibility to communities and for their organization's environmental impact.[14]

Implementation Tasks

The implementation of ethics in marketing ultimately requires relating ethical policies to specific functional areas (e.g., product management, pricing, distribution, and promotion). Because marketing deals with the external firm and customer relationships, many ethical issues occur during the implementation phase. Exhibit 7-1 lists some of the relevant tasks stemming from implementation of a marketing program. This list and the discussion below are illustrative, but by no means exhaustive. These issues suggest ethical *questions* that often arise when executing a marketing campaign.

Product alteration is intended to enhance product value and get the consumer to make the intended purchase. Ethical concerns emerge when minor product adjustments are promoted as being significant. For example, some consumer packaged goods marketers use terms like "improved" or "better tasting" with only minor ingredient changes. Furthermore, the introduction of "me-too" products raises additional ethical issues. For example, how many flavors of toothpaste are really needed? Another product alteration issue relates to the position of product manager. Several questions come to mind. For example, do these fast track individuals (who may be promoted in a few months) make necessary long-term modifications to a brand to ensure its marketplace staying power, regardless of short-term financial performance? Or do they simply undertake cosmetic modifications to improve next quarter's market share or profit picture?

Price negotiation is often at the heart of marketing implementation. Marketing managers who can effectively negotiate on price win many contracts. An ethical problem occurs in this process when one of the participants has more leverage than the other. For example, several years ago, a large midwestern department store chain dealing with a small candy producer told this supplier they would pay 70 percent of the earlier negotiated price and the small firm could keep the business. Or they would pay the full amount of the invoice, but the small manufacturer would lose the account. This approach was little more than extortion. Currently, Wal-Mart and the major auto manufacturers *demand* continuing price decreases by suppliers. The issue of slotting allowances discussed in Chapter 4 is another good illustration. Some of these practices, which have been challenged for being unethical or even illegal, are nonetheless quite common. They might be mitigated somewhat by the smaller firm taking its case to the top echelon of the company that made the threat. Of course, the prospect of squeezing suppliers is a natural outgrowth of the desire to cut costs; though appropriate to a competitive market system and of benefit to most consumers, it raises larger questions of fairness to all stakeholders.

In this era of single sourcing, manufacturers often look at their suppliers as partners rather than adversaries in price negotiation. They emphasize consistent product quality and timely delivery instead of price. For example, while many U.S. distributors were once skeptical of Japanese and other Asian manufacturers, their high-quality products and service responsiveness quickly won the Americans over.

Place determination refers to getting the product where it is demanded in an expeditious manner. Sometimes marketers promise more than they can deliver. For instance, certain suppliers assure one-week delivery, but commonly ship in ten days. This becomes an ethical issue when there is economic or other harm to the client/consumer. In health care or other life-threatening situations, distribution "as promised" is especially critical. Too much promotion by these organizations may heighten the ethical problems they face. Furthermore, some manufacturers may treat some of their retailers unevenly simply to meet their objectives in getting products to the most desirable markets. In the computer software industry, the term "vaporware" has come into prominence because developers often fail to ship the product they promised in a timely fashion. When failure to deliver essential components or repair parts results in downtime, significant economic losses are incurred.

Promotional presentation is another primary function of marketing. Both selling and advertising have persuasive, informative, and reminder components. Persuasive promotions are most often associated with ethical abuses. In selling, ethical problems often arise when persuasion is too intense or competitors are unscrupulous in their appeals. What ethical salespersons should do is ensure that buyers are making decisions on the most relevant evaluative criteria. For instance, if the competitor is stressing price and the salesperson knows that product quality in terms of failure or breakage rates is the most important criterion, the buyer should be informed of this fact. If unethical marketers cannot deliver on their promises, the ethical firm has a good chance to gain the business.

Even if the business is lost when principles are not compromised, opportunities to regain the business often occur. For example, a communications consultant submitted a proposal to a defense contractor, but found the defense company's sole intention was to procure the consulting firm's valuable list of industry contacts. The consultant determined that he would not meet such terms and withdrew from the negotiations. Several months later he was awarded a $50,000 contract from the same defense contractor.

In striving to be ethical, some companies identify acceptable sales and marketing tactics in their code. For instance, Boston Scientific, whose mission is to "improve the quality of patient care and the productivity of health care delivery through the development and advocacy of less invasive medical devices and procedures," makes explicit reference in its code to marketing, advertising and sales practices:

> We believe that enduring customer relationships are based on integrity and trust, and that our marketing, advertising and sales practices must be both legal and ethical. We must work zealously, honestly and in good faith with our hospital and physician partners on behalf of the millions of patients who entrust themselves to that partnership. We must present product information that is truthful, accurate, fully informative and fair. All sales and marketing materials must be based on facts and documented research and include all information required by regulatory agencies (such as the U.S. FDA, the Japanese MHW, or a European Competent Authority). All sales and marketing materials must be pre-approved in accordance with our policies. We do not sacrifice integrity to make or maintain sales. Our marketing and sales activities must not encourage customers, or their representatives, to place their personal interests above those of their employers or patients.[15]

Advertising is one area where persuasion is often criticized for being unethical. (Recall our discussion in Chapter 5.) If the message includes puffery (exaggerated praise for the product) but not deception (which is illegal), it falls into an ethically gray area. One type of advertising that continues to receive growing criticism is advertising to children, especially for fast food and highly sugared products. Furthermore, the ongoing debate about advertising beer and wine on television pits free speech against the potential negative effects of consuming such products, especially when their desirability is enhanced by the questionable lifestyles portrayed in these commercials.

In examining many codes of ethics, we were surprised to find that very few recommend guidelines for ethical advertising. An exception is SUEZ (a French firm), which provides a specific statement on advertising— "Companies should take the necessary precautions to heed regulations and ethical advertising standards to avoid misleading the consumer and engaging in unfair competition. When agency work or trademarks are protected by copyright, companies use them only after investigating the rights of third parties."[16] Consumer products marketers, who spend millions of dollars every year on advertising, should consider developing explicit guidelines for their advertising. Some firms have ad hoc policies regarding sponsorship of shows dealing with sensitive subjects or containing large amounts of sex and/or violence. But more thought should be given to what constitutes an appropriate advertising message and, perhaps, what media should be used.

THE CONCEPT OF AN ETHICAL AUDIT

The dictionary defines an audit as an official examination of records. The purpose of an accounting audit is to examine the financial health of an organization, and it is standard practice in most companies. The objective of a marketing audit is to similarly assess the marketing function. It too has become more widely accepted.

An *ethical audit* for marketing, then, possesses some of the same characteristics as these more traditional audits. It gauges the ethical health of the marketing department and its activities. Like a marketing audit, it should be comprehensive, systematic, independent, and periodic. That is, all major marketing decisions should be evaluated through an orderly sequence of steps in an objective fashion every few years. The audit is consistent with the current call for "accountability" after the business scandals of the last few years. The marketing ethics auditor could be someone from inside the firm who has the necessary expertise and whose background is above reproach. Possibilities for an external ethics auditor include a retired marketing executive, an outside director, or a member of the board's audit committee.

Types of Ethical Audits

Philosophical, functional, compliance, and cultural audits are the four major thematic variations used in conducting an ethical marketing audit for marketing. The *philosophical* approach involves asking questions about the duties to stakeholders in a marketing decision and about whether the decision violates any written or unwritten obligations to these parties. Additional philosophical considerations entail the consequences of marketing decisions. That is, what are the costs and benefits of any marketing action? An assessment of the positive and negative impacts on consumers, employees, and other stakeholders should be conducted. In the final analysis, the company must decide if more people are better or worse off because of the marketing action.

A second type of ethical audit pertains to the *functional* decisions that marketing managers make in devising and implementing marketing strategies. This audit does not explicitly draw on philosophical theories, but reflects them through a battery of questions. A list of marketing audit questions is included in Appendix 7A. The third option is a marketing "compliance" audit that focuses on questions dealing with codes and other formal policies (see Appendix 7B). A fourth possible audit evaluates the corporate context or *cultural* characteristics of the organization in which individuals work. A partial list of ethical audit questions has been generated by the Woodstock Center and is shown in Appendix 7C. The entire battery of questions can be found at http://www.georgetown.edu/centers/woodstock/business_ethics/cmecc.htm.

Company Examples of Ethical Audits

A number of companies, including Johnson & Johnson and AES (see www.aes.com for list of values and description of AES's unique culture), conduct periodic surveys of employees to seek their guidance concerning the status of the company credo or values statement and its implementation. Such general surveys, while useful, are not as comprehensive as a full-blown audit nor do they typically focus on the marketing function. Obviously, different approaches to conducting a comprehensive ethical audit exist.

We are also aware of several companies, including Ford, Nestle, and Shell, that are now producing corporate responsibility or sustainability reports. While these are laudatory activities, they do not focus directly on ethical questions, but often mostly on compliance with acceptable environmental standards. Consequently, we see ethical audits to be a necessary activity for most companies.[17]

Appendix 7A lists questions to be answered in an ethical audit for marketing. This type of audit should put primary emphasis on the integrity of the organization. The questions pertain to many marketing activities within a firm. They are based on our assessment and study of the marketing function and not, unfortunately, on existing audit documents because none are available. Although there are undoubtedly more qualified and complete possible answers to the questions, at minimum a "yes-no" format is recommended to allow managers to compare their answers quickly with their subordinates. For a more in-depth examination, a range of answers (e.g., always, usually, sometimes, rarely, never) could be used.

Questions on Functional Areas

Appendix 7A provides detailed questions regarding the functional areas of marketing. The first bank of questions addresses product issues. Not all these questions are relevant for every company, but they typify questions that product and marketing managers should consider. For example, marketers of consumer packaged goods should pay particular attention to the nature of their product offering. Bankers or investment brokers need to explain the core product; for example, is the financial information consumers receive on a new service purposely vague? Nonprofit marketers such as hospitals and universities should be aware of the ethical ramifications of their service decisions. In sum, ethical questions regarding the viability and configuration of the organization's product assortment should be answered in a straightforward way.

The second section of Appendix 7A deals with pricing issues. The way prices are arrived at often has ethical overtones. The setting of pricing objectives can be legal but not ethical. For instance, a large firm may try to undercut a smaller competitor by just enough to damage the firm, but not enough to cause legal recourse. In other words, the *intent* is predatory even when that purpose may not be provable *de jure*.

The third section pertains to the channel of distribution. Coercion within channels and the markups charged by wholesalers and retailers are issues that come up commonly in evaluating channel members. Marketing managers need to examine these and other relevant channel issues and decide how ethical the firm is in its relationships with channel partners. Of course, the ethical posture reinforced by the corporate culture will probably have much to do with how these and other questions about the marketing mix are answered.

The final section in this portion of the audit deals with promotional questions. Promotion is the most visible area in marketing. Consequently, in large measure because of its inherently persuasive character, ethical questions tend to abound. In addition, the very nature of certain promotional vehicles means that some consumers will find these selling efforts unethical (see Chapters 5 and 6 for a discussion of ethics in advertising and selling). For example, door-to-door selling, pop-up Internet ads, and telemarketing are intrusive and might be questioned on that ground alone, apart from whether selling messages associated with these "media" are deceptive or overly persuasive.

Using the Ethical Audit

The easiest way to employ our ethical audit is to compile the "yes" and "no" answers and calculate percentages in each category. Questions that are not relevant to a particular organization can be eliminated. Companies should strive for 100 percent "yes" answers, or at least more than 90 percent. If the final percentage of yes answers falls below 70 percent, the company should definitely reevaluate the ethics of its marketing. (We use the 70 percent figure somewhat arbitrarily; we want to create some debate as that percentage is the common passing grade in academic programs.) We realize that no firm, however, is perfect, and there are undoubtedly areas where even the most ethical companies can improve. A key value of the audit instrument is to help firms pinpoint those areas where there are ethical concerns.

More than one person's views should be sought in answering these questions. Everyone in a department or division may be asked to fill out the audit and the answers could be compiled by an independent auditor. Areas where the "no" answers dominate could be discussed at a follow-up meeting of the department. For instance, members of the sales force may believe that they are being encouraged to use very aggressive sales tactics to meet sales quotas while the sales managers might not interpret their instructions in this manner. A thorough audit evaluation would allow such differences to surface.

Ideally, an ethical audit should be conducted every year or two. If too long a time elapses, the culture and strategy of the firm obviously can change. Several months after a new manager or parent company takes over would also be a good time for an ethical audit. If the audit is conducted too soon after a change, the new environment will not have had enough time to emerge and have an effect on conduct. As in the case of a financial or marketing audit, the ethical audit should normally not be undertaken only in a time of crisis. For example, just after a lawsuit or court case has been brought by a competitor or a customer is not the best time for an ethical audit. Such an approach has been the knee-jerk reaction of several companies in the investment banking community after being confronted with ethical violations.

IDEAS FOR ETHICAL MARKETING

Marketing organizations should put a formal structure in place to encourage proper conduct. In addition, steps should be taken to develop an informal culture that enhances ethical decision making. Specific guidelines for accomplishing these endeavors have been discussed. In conducting an ethical audit, it is more important to develop and discuss provocative questions than to seek right (i.e., perfect) answers. We agree with Robert Reich, former U.S. Secretary of Labor, who is now a professor at Brandeis University: "Ethics is not a coherent set of answers but a coherent set of questions."

Marketing managers should institute or evaluate current ethics policies. In this regard, we suggest a number of possibilities in this chapter. We assume that most firms have ethical policies in place, but they are not like the Ten Commandments, chiseled in stone (except at GSD & M). Every several years, the corporate code, training programs, and ethical audit mechanisms need to be reviewed. We advocate that ethics materials that pertain exclusively to the marketing department be developed, if they do not already exist.

For the smaller or new firm, the CEO and chief marketing officer can formulate ethical guidelines from scratch. Several models are suggested in this chapter. There is no one best way to implement ethical policies, but care should be taken that the unique aspects of the firm receive consideration.

The ethical component of corporate culture should be assessed. Over the years, various writings on management and corporate culture have labeled the central values of an organization as spiritual values. While we do not attribute undue religious significance to this, it does capture the fact that values encompass the issue of justice in business operations. Surprisingly little attention has been paid to the religious underpinnings of corporate culture and its ethics linkage (recall our discussion of "Religious Models of Marketing Ethics" in Chapter 1). Furthermore, marketing managers should ascertain whether the culture of their firm enhances or impedes ethical decision making by their subordinates.

There are ways for executives to make this tie between ethics and culture explicit. For instance, those previously mentioned implementation responsibilities of leadership, delegation, communication, and motivation are really about creating a climate of trust and commitment within the firm. Top marketing managers can use many methods to nurture the ethical component of their corporate culture. Specifically, Joseph Pichler, former chairman and CEO of Kroger's, shared with us several pithy points about how to create a moral corporate culture (see Exhibit 7-7).

An ethical audit for marketing should be conducted regularly. One barometer of a company's ethical position is an ethical audit. Just as accounting or marketing audits are useful for isolating problems in these functional areas, an ethical audit can provide needed information about troublesome issues. For example, the ethical audit of a firm might pinpoint major differences of opinion between upper and middle management on openness of communication and goal setting. We suggest that the ethical audit instrument (in some form) is a vehicle whose time has come.

CLOSING COMMENTS

To conclude this chapter and the book, we offer several observations we hope will assist marketing managers in practicing ethical marketing in the future. First, *the marketing concept, customer satisfaction, relationship marketing, and supply chain management are fundamentally ethical activities.* Professor Craig

---

EXHIBIT 7-7   Creating a Moral Corporate Culture

- Talk it [difficult issues] out and do it. Actions speak louder than words.
- You have to enforce it. Use the corporate code and spell out expectations.
- Play fair with violators. It is important to follow due process.
- Use *The Wall Street Journal* test. How will this decision read in the paper tomorrow?
- Listen carefully. Use both internal (audit staff) and external (outside directors) channels for communication about ethical issues.
- Manage by walking around. Buy the truck drivers a pizza and walk around the plants to find out what is going on.
- Give employees a sense of ownership. Create a stock option plan and incentive systems for all employees.

Source: Joseph Pichler, former Chairman and CEO of the Kroger Company, personal communication with the authors (January 2004).

Smith of the London Business School has proposed a "consumer sovereignty test" as a guideline that managers can use to evaluate the ethics of many marketing decisions.[18] If any or all marketing practices are to be successful, a sense of trust and fairness must exist among marketers, their customers and suppliers, and the end users of their products. This is not a new idea but one that requires diligence. In fact, we would draw your attention to Exhibit 7-8, which provides some humorous ethical advice on customer satisfaction by one of our favorite writers, Mark Twain.

Second, although we have tended to use well-known and large companies for most of the illustrations in this book, we believe *ethical sensitivity is equally important in smaller firms.* The thrust toward entrepreneurial activity probably means there will be a growing number of small firms in the future. Therefore, more attention must be paid to ethical issues in smaller firms, particularly as they struggle to survive in the competitive climate of the new century.

One of the particularly troublesome outcomes of the scandals that hit business in recent years is how many CEOs who started as entrepreneurs were found guilty of major ethical (if not legal) transgressions. Bernie Ebbers, Ken Lay, and the Rigas family were all entrepreneurs. Their business reputations will always be tainted by the ethical problems that arose once their firms grew and prospered. We believe the entrepreneurial community is dominated by ethical owners and CEOs. However, they must set the ethical climate early in the firm's existence and maintain it.

Third, *a new approach to codes of ethics seems needed.* From our examination of codes over the years, they often appear to be mostly boilerplate. Nearly every code covers the same topics—relationships with employees and suppliers, conflicts of interest, bribery, insider information, and political activities and contributions. We sometimes get the sense that only the company names are changed. At minimum, codes in the future should possess the five characteristics outlined in this chapter—communicated, specific, pertinent, enforced, and revised.

Although few codes actually stand out, Caterpillar's is one we would recommend (see http://www.caterpillar.com/). Caterpillar's code is traditional in the sense that it covers the topic areas noted earlier. However, the code's statements are thorough and concise so that employees can understand the discussion. What is also different is there is a clear-cut explanation for every point that gives the reason for the enactment of this policy. Unfortunately, most firms do not tell us why they institute such policies within the code. Furthermore, Caterpillar has always publicized the code to outsiders. Its stakeholders know Caterpillar managers are proud of their ethical stance and not just covering themselves legally.

Fourth, *ethical issues facing companies in the future will likely require both a philosophical and technical analysis.* Most ethical issues are complex. Therefore, one reaction by firms has been to hire ethicists to help them deal with the

EXHIBIT 7-8   Mark Twain Was an Unsung CS Expert

Mark Twain had an uncanny eye for the preposterous as well as the practical. Even though he lived more than a century ago—and without intending to do so—he provided enduring lessons in customer satisfaction that are applicable in the 21st century.

"Always do right. This will gratify some people and astonish the rest."

The value of a customer satisfaction program is proven: Doing right by customers is the correct (and profitable) thing to do. Additionally, when conducted in a forthright and thorough manner, such a program places your organization in a select group of companies that care and are willing to treat customers with respect.

Providing superior customer satisfaction will gratify your existing customers and astonish your new ones.

"It's noble to be good, and it's nobler to teach others to be good, and less trouble."

Teaching employees how to treat customers by example is inexpensive and less trouble than finding new customers. Any program aimed at customer satisfaction represents an expense, but even a simple approach can be taken, and at a reasonable cost. For example, make customer satisfaction a topic at every meeting and discuss it. Keep customer satisfaction at the forefront; talk about it in the hallways. Make a point of customer satisfaction's importance with recognition, from a simple "Thank you" to a "Thank you" note recognizing a way that they recently satisfied a customer mailed to the employee's home.

"When in doubt, tell the truth."

When in doubt, trust that you've hired the right people, and that they can be trusted. It's not so much that your employees wouldn't *tell* the truth as it's that they don't *know* it. They need to know and understand that their priority isn't the task at hand as much as it's to provide what customers need. Only when you let employees provide immediate assistance will you be able to turn your organization into one that provides genuine customer satisfaction. Employees need to be trained to do this, and something as simple as a one-page guide listing whom to call for which type of problem is a fine starting point.

"It is better to keep your mouth closed and let people think you are a fool than to open it and remove all doubt."

There are times when silence speaks volumes. The best example of the worst in customer satisfaction is any story (you've heard many of them) about the employee who always had the "right" answer and shared it with customers, at the expense of that customer. Even with training, some employees go too far—often with the wrong information—in trying to alleviate a customer's feeling of

(continued)

inadequate service. If you have employees who cannot gauge how far they need to go without your assistance, they have to be retrained. If they can't be retrained, they need to be replaced. Your employees need to know what to say, when to say it and how much to say. They also need to know when to be quiet and ask for help.

"Few things are harder to put up with than the annoyance of a good example."

Don't you just hate it when your spouse is right—again? Still, you can appreciate the value of the difference between the right and wrong answer. By setting an example of superior customer satisfaction you make it difficult for your employees to do anything less. Employees and customers both constantly appraise your demeanor; the former will take it at face value and, one hopes, emulate it, while the latter will appreciate it and ultimately repay it with more business.

Setting standards always is a challenging task; not setting standards is failure.

"I think a compliment ought always to precede a complaint, where one is possible, because it softens resentment and ensures for the complaint a courteous and gentle reception."

There are those times when a customer is wrong. It's not smart to make that distinction immediately, but there are times when the customer has to be "retrained" to your corporate values. This is the time to lead off with how much you value his business, to let him know how important he is to your company's success and to prepare him for the information he needs to become a better customer.

The best way to register a complaint is to get the person on you side first.

"I have never let my schooling interfere with my education."

In the end, you're responsible for the success of your company, the one who has to decide what level of customer satisfaction is required, how to train for it and how to nurture it. It usually requires a generous serving of knowledge learned in school and out in the real world, and you decide how much from each is appropriate.

The truly educated are the ones who know that their education is not complete.

Source: Roger Morey, "Mark Twain Was an Unsung CS Expert," *Marketing News*, May 7, 2001, p. 16. Reprinted with permission by the American Marketing Association.

---

issues and set up ethics training programs. However, this is probably not enough for the future. For example, many environmental and solid waste problems caused by consumer and industrial waste require sophisticated technical advice on recycling vis-à-vis landfill disposal. Consumer packaged goods companies are now examining the biodegradability of their packaging. These issues require engineering and scientific, as well as ethical, advice. The "right" decision may not be clear until the scientific evidence is factored in. Therefore, we advocate the use of both ethical and technical analyses to help illuminate the difficult choices ahead for marketing and top management.

Fifth, *marketing's role in society and in dealing with societal issues should be examined from an ethical standpoint.* Marketing as a business practice has made major contributions to society over time and sometimes is judged harshly from an ethical viewpoint. However, the benefits of modern marketing in the business sector outweigh the costs in most observers' minds.[19] The beneficial B from the ABCs of marketing ethics is relevant here.

However, major social issues facing the world, including AIDS, illegal drug use, deteriorating primary and secondary education, racism, and the widening gap between the rich and poor, are evident. Marketing has been effectively, if not always ethically, used to promote a number of social causes. Issues such as AIDS and drug testing, as well as support for education and social services, will continue to be major concerns throughout the foreseeable future. We believe that managers should view these areas as not just social issues, but ethical ones as well.

At minimum, more informed discussion and debate about social issues must occur, not only in the boardrooms but throughout entire companies. Solutions will not be forthcoming without commitment by large numbers of individuals acting within companies or in civic and religious groups. In addition, a more creative relationship between business and the government will have to be developed to find a way to share the costs of dealing with public welfare issues. Marketing principles, such as market segmentation, positioning, and customer orientation, can be applied to alleviate some of society's major social ills. Ethics, however, should play a central role in evaluating all marketing techniques in this realm.[20] More generally, studies in the field of macromarketing tend to analyze marketing practices on the basis of their fairness and their impact on the environment or disadvantaged from an ethical perspective.

Sixth, the *notion of whistle-blowing in marketing and business needs objective analysis.* Many corporate and marketing critics argue strongly for the right of disgruntled employees to "blow the whistle" when they observe wrongdoing. (We touched on this subject briefly in Exhibit 6-8.) The reality of the situation is that most whistle-blowers pay a high price for raising ethics issues—ostracism, demotions (and often firing), inability to gain employment in other firms, and so on. More attention now is being paid to this idea. For instance, *Time* named three female whistle-blowers its "Persons of the Year" for 2002.[21] There is little doubt that some (and maybe many) middle- to high-level executives in the companies mentioned in the Introduction knew about the wrongdoing at their firms. Yet, hardly any spoke up. One suggestion is that the whistle-blowers receive 10 percent of all fines and legal awards imposed on the company or individual executives.[22] The U.S. government does have a whistle-blower protection and compensation program for those who come forward. We believe that more innovative thinking needs to be done both inside companies and outside to encourage and reward constructive dissent.

Finally, *a dynamic tension will always exist between ethics and competition.* This issue, in various forms, always arises. Many opinions are expressed as to what energizes a marketplace economy, but certainly self-interest is there somewhere. Corporate advocates for market economies, now dominant throughout the world, laud competition and then spend much of their time and effort trying to find a shelter (i.e., sustainable competitive advantage) from it. Antitrust laws in the developed countries set the boundaries of the playing field for marketers, but there are many strategic (both legal and illegal) avenues to get around competition.

Since competition is a most powerful force, we need to insist that managers are aware of ethical ramifications so the dynamic tension is balanced and competition is fair. (Recall our discussion of the "ethic of the mean" in Chapter 1.) In other words, we are faced with a formidable task of creating a system where the selfishness of competitive aggression can create marketplace innovation, while at the same time tempering the ethical abuse that can come with the desire "to win at all costs." We should rely on self-control and self-regulation, as well as some government intervention but not too much. Otherwise, we create public demand for an inferior economic alternative (e.g., witness the failed planned economies of Eastern Europe). Our responsibility as marketing professionals is to deal with the tension generated by competition and ensure that ethics is always brought into the debate. If we succeed, the result should be a more vigorous and ethical marketplace where managers choose the higher road.

Appendix 7A:
Marketing Functions Audit

A. ETHICAL QUESTIONS RELATING TO THE PRODUCT

Core Product

	Yes	No
Is there an underlying benefit to the product?	____	____
Are benefits accurately communicated?	____	____

Product Offering

	Yes	No
Does the package adequately present the size or components of the product?	____	____
Are the brand name and manufacturer clearly spelled out on the label?	____	____
Does the label contain adequate amounts of information for safe consumer use?	____	____
Is after-sale service promised with adequate provisions to deliver it?	____	____
Is the warranty, including restrictions and requirements, clear to consumers?	____	____

B. ETHICAL QUESTIONS IN PRICING

Pricing Objectives

Does the company consciously set pricing objectives to not damage competitors?	____	____
Do marketers who convey a discount image do so accurately (i.e., try not to add expensive services and accessories that inflate the final price)?	____	____
Are only major product changes promoted to the media as innovations?	____	____

Pricing Methods

Is the price discrimination that the marketer practices always justifiable? (For example, do professionals avoid charging more to people they know can or will pay more?

In competitive bidding, does the firm not attempt (by lawful means) to find out what another firm bid? Do they also avoid lowballing (bidding the first contract low in hopes of recovering on later contracts)?

In markup pricing, does the marketer promote only accurate sales percentages (e.g., refrain from advertising large, i.e., 50 percent, discounts from the normal selling price)?

Pricing Decisions

Does the marketer promote only one line as its highest quality (e.g., he or she does not try to differentiate on only cosmetic differences or a different package that distinguishes it from the middle price line)?

Does the firm always justify its flexible pricing (i.e., different prices for differing customers)?

Are loss leaders beneficial to consumers (rather than an expensive version of bait and switch)?

C. ETHICAL QUESTIONS IN DISTRIBUTION

Channel Questions

Do large channel members avoid coercing smaller ones in selling or buying products?

Do manufacturers try to build relationships with their intermediaries rather than seek new channels to force traditional channel members to take small markups?

Are smaller wholesalers or retailers banding together to influence public policy to protect them from larger channel members?

Wholesaling

Do wholesalers avoid keeping products in reserve for larger customers while not adequately serving smaller customers?

Do the services rendered relate to the quantity of products purchased?

Retailing

Does the retailer avoid special (lower quality) merchandise
used for sales?

Does the commission system discourage salespeople from
using high-pressure sales tactics?

Are salespeople instructed to "trade up" customers only when
the buyers express interest in the more expensive product?

Physical Distribution

Are cost minimization decisions arrived at in a manner equitable
to all parties?

Are conservations and pollution considerations important
in deciding among modes of transportation such as trucks,
trains, planes?

D. ETHICAL QUESTIONS ABOUT PROMOTION

Advertising

Does advertising promise only what it can deliver?

Is embellishment (i.e., exaggerated product benefits)
discouraged?

Do ads promote significant facts (as opposed to leaving
them out) about the products?

Are claims based on unbiased research results?

Sales Promotion

Are products properly represented at trade shows and
exhibitions?

Are samples or premiums only promoted when they have
significant value?

Publicity

Do organizations rely on newsworthiness rather than influence
to get publicity?

Are only major product changes promoted to the media as
innovations?

Personal Selling

Does the organization discourage salespeople from using
high-pressure selling techniques?   ——   ——

Do salespeople avoid utilizing questionable psychological
pressure to close the sale?   ——   ——

Sales Management

Do sales managers monitor expense accounts and watch out
for inflated expenses and padding of these accounts?   ——   ——

Are territory quotas adjusted to economic conditions rather
than automatically inflated every year?   ——   ——

Public Relations

Does the public-relations department share valuable
information with the media even if it is sometimes negative?   ——   ——

If negative stories about the organization appear, does the
public-relations department avoid retaliation at a later time?   ——   ——

Source: Adapted from Gene R. Laczniak and Patrick E. Murphy. *Ethical Marketing Decisions: The Higher Road* (Boston: Allyn and Bacon 1993), 303–309.

Appendix 7B:
Ethical Compliance Audit

ORGANIZATIONAL QUESTIONS*

YES   NO   1. Does the company have a code of ethics that is reasonably capable of preventing misconduct?

YES   NO   2. Does the board of directors participate in the development and evaluation of the ethics program?

YES   NO   3. Is there a person with high managerial authority responsible for the ethics program?

YES   NO   4. Are there mechanisms in place to avoid delegating authority to individuals with a propensity for misconduct?

YES   NO   5. Does the organization effectively communicate standards and procedures to its employees via ethics training programs?

YES   NO   6. Does the organization communicate its ethical standards to suppliers, customers, and significant others that have a relationship with the organization?

YES   NO   7. Do the company's manuals and written documents guiding operations contain ethics messages about appropriate behavior?

YES   NO   8. Is there formal or informal communication within the organization about procedures and activities that are considered acceptable ethical behavior?

YES   NO   9. Does top management have a mechanism to detect ethical issues relating to employees, customers, the community, and society?

YES   NO   10. Is there a system for employees to report unethical behavior?

YES   NO   11. Is there consistent enforcement of standards and punishments in the organization?

YES   NO   12. Is there a committee, department, team, or group that deals with ethical issues in the organization?

YES   NO   13. Does the organization make a continuous effort to improve its ethical compliance program?

YES   NO   14. Does the firm perform an ethics audit?

EXAMPLES OF SPECIFIC ISSUES THAT COULD BE MONITORED IN AN ETHICS AUDIT**

YES	NO	1.	Does the firm lack systems and operational procedures to safeguard employees' individual ethical behavior?
YES	NO	2.	Is it necessary for employees to break the company's ethical rules in order to get the job done?
YES	NO	3.	Is there an environment of deception, repression, and cover-ups concerning events that would embarrass the company?
YES	NO	4.	Is there a lack of participatory management practices that allow ethical issues to be discussed?
YES	NO	5.	Are compensation systems totally dependent on performance?
YES	NO	6.	Is there sexual harassment?
YES	NO	7.	Is there any form of discrimination—race, sex, or age—in hiring, promotion, or compensation?
YES	NO	8.	Are the only standards about environmental impact those that are legally required?
YES	NO	9.	Do the firm's activities fail to show any concern for the ethical value systems of the community?
YES	NO	10.	Are there deceptive and misleading messages in promotion?
YES	NO	11.	Are products described in misleading ways or without communicating their limitations to customers?
YES	NO	12.	Are the documents and copyrighted materials of other companies used in unauthorized ways?
YES	NO	13.	Are expense accounts inflated?
YES	NO	14.	Are customers overcharged?
YES	NO	15.	Is there unauthorized copying of computer software?

*A high number of YES answers indicates that ethical control mechanisms and procedures are in place within the organization.

**The number of YES answers indicates the number of possible ethical issues to address.

Source: O. C. Ferrell, J. Fraedrich and L. Ferrell, *Business Ethics: Ethical Decision Making and Cases,* 6th ed. (Boston, MA: Houghton Mifflin Company, 2005), 202–203.

Appendix 7C:
Ethical Climate Audit

A. Does top management have a common understanding of and strong commitment to ethical values? (4 questions)

B. Do management's actions and policies reflect the organization's ethical values? (2 questions)

C. Do employees throughout the firm share management's ethical values and commitment? (6 questions)

D. Do managers at all levels work to build shared ethical values? (7 questions)

E. Does management provide employees with ethical guidance when needed? (5 questions)

F. Are ethical considerations included in personnel decisions? (3 questions)

G. Does the firm's system of rewards include ethical accountability? (6 questions)

H. Does the organization have a procedure for identifying and dealing with ethical violations? (4 questions)

I. Does the organization have designated personnel whose job it is to monitor and promote an ethical climate? (2 questions)

J. As a result of all the above, does every employee consider ethical conduct, supervision, and guidance part of the job? (1 question)

Source: http://www.georgetown.edu/centers/woodstock/business_ethics/cmecc.htm.

Notes

Chapter One: Ethical Reasoning and Marketing Decisions

1. Gerry Khermouch and Jeff Green, "Buzz Marketing," *Business Week*, July 30, 2001, 50–56.

2. Chris Adams, "Xenical Ads Avoid Listing Unpleasant Side Effects," *Wall Street Journal*, April 3, 2001, B1 and B6. For a followup, see Vanessa Fuhrman, "Roche Attempts to Beef Up Sales of Diet-Drug Xenical," *Wall Street Journal*, February 21, 2002, B3.

3. Patrick E. Murphy, *Eighty Exemplary Ethics Statements* (Notre Dame, IN: University of Notre Dame Press, 1998): 106–7.

4. Thomas A. Klein and Robert W. Nason, "Marketing and Development: Macromarketing Perspectives," in *Handbook of Society and Marketing*, ed. Paul N. Bloom and Gregory T. Gundlach, 263–97 (Thousand Oaks, CA: Sage, 2001).

5. Robert C. Solomon and Fernando Flores, *Building Trust in Business, Politics, Relationships, and Life* (New York: Oxford University Press, 2001): 40–43.

6. James M. Carman and Luis V. Dominguez, "Organizational Transformations in Transition Economies: Hypotheses," *Journal of Macromarketing* 21 no. 2(December 2001): 164–80.

7. One of the most persistent twentieth-century critics of the marketing system was John Kenneth Galbraith. His influential books were *The Affluent Society* (New York: Houghton Mifflin, 1958) and *The New Industrial State* (New York: Houghton Mifflin, 1967).

8. Edward R. Freeman, *Strategic Management: A Stakeholder Approach* (Boston, MA: Pitman, 1984): 46. See also Kenneth E. Goodpaster, "Business Ethics and Stakeholder Analysis," *Business Ethics Quarterly* (January 1991): 53–73.

9. Archie B. Carroll and Ann K. Buchholtz, *Business and Society: Ethics and Stakeholder Management*, 5th ed. (Cincinnati, OH: South-Western College Publishing, 2003).

10. Lawrence G. Foster, *Robert Wood Johnson: The Gentleman Rebel* (State College, PA: Lillian Press, 1999).

11. Robert C. Solomon, *The New World of Business: Ethics and Free Enterprise in the Global 1990s* (Lanham, MD: Rowman & Littlefield, 1994).

12. See *The Shell Report*, 2003 at www.shell.com (accessed December 31, 2003).

13. Patricia H. Werhane, *Moral Imagination and Management Decision Making* (New York: Oxford University Press, 1999).

14. Patrick E. Murphy, "Corporate Ethics Statements: An Update," in *Global Codes of Conduct: An Idea Whose Time Has Come*, ed. O. Williams, 295–304 (Notre Dame, IN: University of Notre Dame Press, 2000).

15. James Rachels, "The Challenge of Cultural Relativism," in *Moral Relativism*, ed. P. K. Moser and T. L. Carson, 53–65 (New York: Oxford University Press, 2001); Norman Bowie, "Relativism, Cultural and Moral," in *Encyclopedic Dictionary of Business Ethics*, ed. P. H. Werhane and R. E. Freeman, 551–555 (Malden, MA: Blackwell, 1997).

16. Joseph Des Jardins, *An Introduction to Business Ethics* (New York: McGraw-Hill, 2003): 18–19.

17. Norman E. Bowie, "Challenging the Egoistic Paradigm," *Business Ethics Quarterly* (January 1991): 1–21.

18. Jeremy Bentham, *An Introduction to the Principles of Morals and Legislation* (New York: Hafner Publishing, 1984); and John Stuart Mill, *Utilitarianism* (Indianapolis, IN: Hackett Publishing, 1979).

19. Immanuel Kant, *Grounding for the Metaphysics of Morals* (1785; Indianapolis, IN: Hackett Publishing, 1981).

20. Norman E. Bowie, "A Kantian Approach to Business Ethics," in *A Companion to Business Ethics*, ed. R. E. Frederick, 3–16 (Malden, MA: Blackwell Publishers, 1999). See also Norman E. Bowie, *Business Ethics: A Kantian Perspective* (Malden, MA: Blackwell Publishers, 1999).

21. John Rawls, *A Theory of Justice* (Cambridge, MA: Harvard University Press, 1971).

22. John Paul II, "Centesimus Annus," *Origins* 21 no. 1(May 16, 1991): 1, 3–24.

23. Thomas Donaldson and Thomas W. Dunfee, *Ties That Bind: A Social Contracts Approach to Business Ethics* (Boston, MA: Harvard Business School Press, 1999).

24. Thomas W. Dunfee, "Business and Ethics," in *Modern Business Law and the Regulatory Environment* (New York: McGraw-Hill, 1997).

25. Alasdair MacIntyre, *After Virtue*, 2d ed. (Notre Dame, IN: University of Notre Dame Press, 1984).

26. Aristotle, *Nicomachean Ethics* (New York: MacMillan Publishing, 1962).

27. Aristotle, *Ethics* (London, UK: Penguin Books, 1976): 94.

28. Patrick E. Murphy, "Character and Virtue Ethics in International Marketing: An Agenda for Managers, Researchers and Educators," *Journal of Business Ethics* 18 (1999): 107–24.

29. "Economic Justice for All: Catholic Social Teaching and the U.S. Economy," *Origins* 16 no. 4(November 27, 1986): 409–55.

30. A more thorough examination of the marketing implications of the U.S. Bishops Economic Letter may be found in Thomas A. Klein, "Prophets and Profits: Macromarketing Implications of the 'Pastoral Letter on Catholic Social Teaching and the U.S. Economy,'" *Journal of Macromarketing* 7 no. 1(fall 1987): 59–77. For more information on Catholic social thought and business, see H. J. Alford, and M. J. Naughton, *Managing as If Faith Mattered* (Notre Dame, IN: University of Notre Dame Press, 2001).

31. See, e.g., Meir Tamari, *In the Marketplace: Jewish Business Ethics* (Southfield, MI: Targum Press, 1991); Moses L. Pava, "The Substance of Jewish Business Ethics," *Journal of Business Ethics* 17 no. 6(April 1, 1998): 603–17; David Vogel, "How Green Is Judaism?—Exploring Jewish Environmental Ethics," *Business Ethics Quarterly* 11 no. 2(April 2001): 349–63; and Hershey H. Friedman, "The Impact of Jewish Values on Marketing and Business Practices," *Journal of Macromarketing* 21 no. 1(June 2001): 74–80.

32. Matthew W. Seeger and Robert R. Ulmer, "Virtuous Responses to Organizational Crisis: Aaron Feuerstein and Milt Cole," *Journal of Business Ethics* 31 (2001): 369–376.

33. Mohammad Saeed, Zafar U. Ahmed, and Syeda-Masooda Mukhtar, "International Marketing Ethics from an Islamic Perspective: A Value-Maximization Approach," *Journal of Business Ethics* 32 no. 2 (July 2, 2001): 127–42; see also Rafik Issa Beekun, *Islamic Business Ethics* (Herndon, VA: International Institute of Islamic Thought, 1997).

34. Daryl Koehn, "Confucian Trustworthiness and the Practice of Business in China," *Business Ethics Quarterly* 11 no. 3 (July 2001): 415–29.

35. Francisco J. Varela, *Ethical Know-How: Action, Wisdom, and Cognition* (Stanford, CA: Stanford University Press, 1999).

36. Victor Wee, "Buddhist Approach to Economic Development," in *Buddhist Perspective in the Face of the Third Millenium,* Proceedings of the Year 2000 Global Conference on Buddhism, (Buddhist Fellowship, 2001). See also Bodhipaksa, "Reinventing the Wheel: A Buddhist Approach to Ethical Work," in *Spiritual Goods: Faith Traditions and the Practice of Business,* ed. Stewart W. Herman with A. G. Schaefer, 33–54 (Bowling Green, OH: Philosophy Documentation Center, 2001).

37. Miller, Debra and William Miller, "Defining Business Success," spirituality. indiatimes.com/articleshow/37572573.cms, accessed December 22, 2003.

38. Ibid.

39. L. Kohlberg, "Stage and Sequence: The Cognitive Development Approach to Socialization," in *Handbook of Socialization Theory and Research,* ed. D. A. Goslin, 347–480 (Chicago: Rand McNally, 1969). Kohlberg's approach has been challenged by Carol Gilligan, *In a Different Voice: Psychological Theory and Women's Development* (Cambridge, MA: Harvard University Press, 1993).

40. D. Narváez and J. Rest, "The Four Components of Acting Morally," in *Moral Development: An Introduction,* ed. W. M.

Kurtines and J. L. Gewirtz, 385–99 (Boston: Allyn and Bacon, 1995).

41. Shelby D. Hunt and Scott Vitell, "A General Theory of Marketing Ethics," *Journal of Macromarketing* 6 no. 1(spring 1986): 5–16; Shelby D. Hunt and Scott Vitell, "The General Theory of Marketing Ethics: A Retrospective and Revision," in *Ethics in Marketing,* ed. N. Craig Smith and John A. Quelch, 775–84 (Burr Ridge, IL: Irwin, 1993); S. J. Vitell, G. P. Paolilla, and J. L. Thomas, "The Perceived Role of Ethics and Social Responsibility: A Study of Marketing Professionals," *Business Ethics Quarterly* 13 no. 1(January 2003): 63–86.

Chapter Two: Ethics in Researching and Segmenting Markets

1. Dan Morse, "Trade Group's Ad Citing Gallup Survey Angers Pollster," *Wall Street Journal,* March 31, 1998.

2. Daulatram B. Lund, "Deontological and Teleological Influences on Marketing Research Ethics," *Journal of Applied Business Research* (spring 2001): 75.

3. Allan J. Kimmel, ed., "Deception in Marketing Research and Practice," *Psychology and Marketing* 18 no. 7(July 2001).

4. A cookie is an interactive data file, placed on the computer's hard drive after the user connects to a particular Web site, and used to record the visitor's activities while connected to the site.

5. Patrick E. Murphy, "Privacy in Market Research," in *Excellence in International Research,* ed. Maureen Shepstone, 293–311 (Amersterdam, The Netherlands: Esomar, 2001).

6. Kirsten J. Means, "The Business of Ethics and the Ethics of Business," *AMS News* (January 1991): 16.

7. Ibid.

8. Morse, "Trade Group's Ad."

9. William R. Dillon, Thomas J. Madden, and Neil H. Firtle, *Marketing Research in a Marketing Environment,* 2d ed. (Homewood, IL: Irwin, 1990): 41.

10. Susan Warren "I-Spy. Getting the Low-down on Your Competition Is Just a Few Clicks Away," *Wall Street Journal,* January 14, 2002.

11. Ibid.

12. Robert C. Solomon and Fernando Flores, *Building Trust in Business, Politics, Relationships, and Life* (Oxford, NY: Oxford University Press, 2001): 28.

13. George Brenkert, "Marketing and the Vulnerable, "*Business Ethics Quarterly,* Ruffin Series, no. 1 (1998): 7–20.

14. Statistics are from James U. McNeal, "Tapping the Three Kids' Markets," *American Demographics* 20 (April 1998): 37–41.

15. Commissioner Kathleen Q. Abernathy, "Children's Television" Programming and Commercial Limits," www.fec.gov/commissioners/abernathy/news/childrenstv .html. Accessed on January 15, 2004.

16. For a discussion of these issues, see Lynn S. Paine, *Value Shift* (New York: McGraw Hill, 2003): 59–60.

17. Eve M. Caudill and Patrick E. Murphy, "Consumer Online Privacy: Legal and Ethical Issues." *Journal of Public Policy and Marketing* (spring 2000): 7–19.

18. William M. Savina, "Protecting On-line Privacy," *Marketing Management* (September/October 2002): 62.

19. Leslie Earnest, "Tweens: From Dolls to Thongs; Marketers Dangle Glittery Goods to Lure Preteen Girls with Spending Power. But Some Adults Say It's Too Much, Too Soon," *Los Angeles Times,* June 27, 2002.

20. Center on Alcohol Marketing and Youth, "Alcohol Advertising and Youth" (2003), www.camy.org/factsheets. Accessed on January 12, 2004.

21. Clifford G. Christians, Mark Fackler, Kim B. Rotzoll, and Kathy B. McKee. *Media Ethics: Cases and Moral Reasoning,* 6th ed. (New York: Longman, 2004).

22. M. Viswanathan, J. A. Rosa, and J. E. Harris, "Decision Making and Coping by Functionally Illiterate Consumers: Understanding a Reaching an Underserved Market Segment," Working Paper, University of Illinois, 2003, 16.

23. Al Ossip, "Ethics-Everyday Choices in Marketing Research," *Journal of Advertising Research* (October–November 1985): RC10–RC12.

24. Bill MacElroy, "New Techniques and Technologies: Best Practices and the Future of Online Research." Presentation to AMA School of Marketing Research, June 2003.

25. Diane K. Bowers, "A Snapshot of U.S. Research," *Marketing Research* (fall 1999): 35. For additional observations on this topic, see Robert F. Lusch and Matthew O'Brien, "Fostering Professionalism," *Marketing Research* (spring 1997): 25–31.

26. Alvin A. Achenbaum, "Can We Tolerate a Double Standard in Marketing Research?" *Journal of Advertising Research* (June–July 1985): RC3–RC7.

Chapter Three: Product Management Ethics

1. http://www.toy-tia.org/industry/publications/fbcurrent/safety.htm.

2. Lynda J. Oswald, *The Law of Marketing* (Cincinnati, OH: West, 2002), Chapter 10.

3. Sholun Freeman, "Raising the (Roll) Bar on SUV Safety," *Wall Street Journal,* October 24, 2002, D1 and D4; Milo Geyelin and Jeffrey Ball, "How Rugged Is Your Car's Roof?" *Wall Street Journal,* March 4, 2002, B1.

4. John Carey, "Gas-Guzzlers Are Safer? Pose Bank," *Business Week,* September 9, 2002, 96–97.

5. http://www.iacc.org.

6. Oswald, *Law of Marketing,* 176.

7. "A Basketball Star from Shanghai Is Big Business," *Wall Street Journal,* October 22, 2002, A10.

8. Lynette Knowles Mathur, "The Impact of International Gray Marketing on Consumers and Firms," *Journal of Euro-Marketing* 4 no. 2(1995): 39.

9. Kirk Davidson, *Selling Sin: The Marketing of Socially Unacceptable Products,* 2nd ed. (Westport, CT: Quorum Books, 2003).

10. Alison Beard, "Tobacco Spending on Ads Hits High," *Financial Times*, June 13, 2003, 17; http://www.adage.com. Accessed June 30, 2003.

11. "Cigarette Smoking-Attributable Mortality and Years of Potential Life Lost: United States, 1990," *MMWR Morb Mortal Wkly Rep*. 42 (1993): 645–49.

12. Richard W. Pollay and Timothy Dewhirst, "Filter, Flavor . . . Flim-Flam, Too!: Cigarette Advertising Content and Its Regulation," *Journal of Public Policy & Marketing* 8 (1989): 30–39; Rick Pollay et al., "The Last Straw? Cigarette Advertising and Realized Market Shares among Youths and Adults, 1979–1993," *Journal of Marketing* (April 1996): 1–16.

13. Elise Truly Sautter and Nancy A Oretskin, "Tobacco Targeting: The Ethical Complexity of Marketing to Minorities," *Journal of Business Ethics* 16 no. 10(1997): 1011–17.

14. *Central Hudson Gas & Electric Corporation* v. *Public Service Commission of New York*, 447 U.S. 557, 100 S.Ct. 2343, 65 L.Ed.2d 341 (1980).

15. Frances Williams, "Tobacco Control Treaty 'Set for Approval,'" *Financial Times*, May 16, 2003, 5.

16. P. M. Fischer, M. P. Schwartz, J. W. Richards Jr., A. O. Goldstein, and T. H. Rojas, "Brand Logo Recognition by Children Aged 3 to 6 years: Mickey Mouse and Old Joe the Camel," *Journal of the American Medical Association* (December 11, 1991): 3145–48; "R. J. Reynolds to Drop Joe Camel," www.facts.com/wnd/camel.htm. Accessed January 5, 2004.

17. Frank B. Cross and Brenda J. Winslett, "Export Death: Ethical Issues and the International Trade in Hazardous Products," *American Business Law Journal* (fall 1987): 487–521.

18. Christina C. Berk and Christopher Lawton, "Diageo to Provide Content Labeling on Alcohol Drinks," *Wall Street Journal*, December 18, 2003, B8.

19. www.learner.org/exhibits/garbage.

20. For an excellent ethical analysis of the Valdez, see Michael G. Bowen and F. Clark Power, "The Moral Manager: Communicative Ethics and the Exxon Valdez Disaster," *Business Ethics Quarterly* (April 1998): 97–115.

21. Thorstein Veblen, *The Theory of the Leisure Class: An Economic Study of Institutions* (New York: Mentor Books, 1899, 1953), chaps. 4, 7.

22. Linda F. Golodner, "Healthy Confusion for Consumers," *Journal of Public Policy & Marketing* 12 no. 1(1993): 130.

23. Roger Parloff, "Is Fat the Next Tobacco?" *Fortune*, February 3, 2003, 50–54.

24. Andrew Abela, "Additive versus Inclusive Approaches to Measuring Brand Equity: Practical and Ethical Implications." *Journal of Brand Management* 10, nos. 4–5(2003): 342–52. This section was prepared by Professor Abela based on this article and other sources.

25. David A. Aaker and Erich Joachimsthaler, *Brand Leadership* (New York: Free Press); Berry, Leonard L., "Cultivating Service Brand Equity," *Journal of the Academy of Marketing Science* 28 no. 1(2000): 128–37.

26. K. K. Holliday, "Putting Brands to the Test," *US Banker* (December 1997); "Keeping Promises: Today's Currency—Tomorrow's Future of Branding," *Discount Store News*, September 7, 1998; K. Cleland, "Clinton 'Brand' Needs a Marketing Overhaul," *Advertising Age's Business Marketing* (November 1994); M. Hewett, "Broken Promises That Can Damage Trust in the Brand," *Marketing* (August 1996); K. Zhivago, "The Promise Keepers," www.marketingcomputers.com (August 1998); Andrew Abela, *When a Brand Is a Promise: Building Firm Credibility by Integrating Strategic and Ethical Aspects of Brand Management* (Charlottesville, VA: Darden Business School, 2002).

27. Hilary Cassidy, "Playing with a New Attitude," *Brandweek*, June 30, 2001, 26–30; Naomi Klein, *No Logo: Taking Aim at the Brand Bullies* (New York: Picador, 1999).

28. Matthew Hart, *Diamond: A Journey to the Heart of an Obsession* (New York: Walker & Co., 2001); Stefan Kanfer, *The Last Empire: De Beers, Diamonds, and the World*

(New York: Farrar, Straus, Giroux, 1993); Ana M. Perez-Katz, "The Role of Conflict Diamonds in Fueling Wars in Africa: The Case of Sierra Leone," *International Affairs Review* 11 no. 1(2002): 160–75.

29. John Seabrook, *Nobrow: The Culture of Marketing—The Marketing of Culture* (New York: Alfred A. Knopf, 2000): 75.

30. P. Schweitzer and R. Schweitzer, *Disney, The Mouse Betrayed: Greed, Corruption and Children at Risk* (Washington, DC: Regnery Publishing, 1998).

31. Dan Bischoff, "Consuming Passions," *Ms.* (December 2000/January 2001).

32. Dana James, "Lighting the Way," *Mobility News*, April 1, 2002, 11.

33. Michael P. Mokwa, "Ethical Consciousness and the Competence of Product Management," in *Philosophical and Radical Thought in Marketing*, ed. A. F. Firat, N. Dholakia, and R. Bagozzi (Lexington Books, 1987).

Chapter Four: Ethical Issues in Distribution Channels and Pricing

1. Paul Klebnikov, "Coke's Sinful World," *Forbes*, December 22, 2003, 86–92.

2. Keith Johnson, "European Offers Online Deals to U.S. Climbers," *Wall Street Journal*, July 8, 2002, A14.

3. Stefan Fatsis, "The Barry Bonds Tax: Teams Raise Prices for Good Games," *Wall Street Journal*, December 3, 2002, D1, 8.

4. Scenario developed from following sources: Vanessa Fuhrman and Scott Hensley, "Price Controls in Europe Draw Drug Makers' Criticism," *Wall Street Journal*, December 13, 2001, B4; "Industry Suit to Block Michigan's Plan on Price Cuts for Drugs May Send Message," *Wall Street Journal*, December 3, 2001, A2, A4; Thomas M. Burton, "Lilly to Discount Drugs for Elderly on Low Incomes," *Wall Street Journal*, March 5, 2002, B1, B4; Scott Hensley, "Pfizer Offers Seniors a Flat-Fee Drug Plan," *Wall Street Journal*, January 16, 2002, B14.

5. Graham Wood, "Ethics in Purchasing: The Practitioner's Experience," *Business Ethics: A European Review* (April 1995): 95–101.

6. Thomas A. Klein, *Ethical Purchasing Practices in Canada* (Toronto, Ontario: Purchasing Management Association of Canada, 1996).

7. See, e.g., Barry Meier, "Ethics Standards Overhaul Urged for Hospital Buying Groups," *New York Times*, October 24, 2002, C3; "Purchasing Ethics Need an Update for 21st Century Imperatives," *Supplier Selection and Management Report*, September 1, 2002, 1–2.

8. Craig R. Carter, *Ethical Issues in Global Buyer-Supplier Relationships. Focus Study.* Center for Advanced Purchasing Studies, 1998.

9. Adapted from Daniel M. Traub, "Purchasing Ethics: A Management Introduction," Paper submitted in partial fulfillment of the requirements for MBA Marketing Ethics Class, May 2002.

10. Julie S. Roberts, "Navigating the Ethics of E-Commerce," *Purchasing Today* (December 2001): 28.

11. Damon Francis, "Buyers Revisit Ethical Policies," *Purchasing Magazine Online*, April 5, 2001.

12. Robert Landeros and Richard E. Plank, "How Ethical Are Purchasing Management Professionals?" *Journal of Business Ethics* 15 no. 7(July 1996): 789–803.

13. Federal Trade Commission, "Slotting Allowances in the Retail Grocery Industry: Selected Case Studies in Five Product Categories," (November 2003) at ftc.gov/op/2003/11/slottingallowance.htm. Accessed January 18, 2004.

14. A. C. Nielsen Annual Survey of Trade Promotion Practices, 2000.

15. Robert J. Alberts and Marianne M. Jennings, "The Ethics of Slotting: Is This Bribery, Facilitation, Marketing or Just Plain Competition?" *Journal of Business Ethics* 20 no. 3(July 1, 1999): 207–15.

16. Federal Trade Commission, *Report on the Federal Trade Commission Workshop on Slotting Allowances and Other Marketing Practices in the Grocery Industry* (Washington DC: U.S. Government Printing Office, 2001).

17. David Balto, "Recent Legal and Regulatory Developments in Slotting Allowances and Category Management," *Journal of Public Policy & Marketing* 21 no. 2 (fall 2002): 289–94.

18. Dale Bugs, "The New Deal," *Sales and Marketing Management* (June 2002): 24–30; and www.grainger.com.

19. Gordon Storholm and Eberhard M. Scheuing, "Ethical Implications of Business Format Franchising," *Journal of Business Ethics* 13 no. 3(March 1994): 181–88.

20. Kathryn Graddy and Diana C. Robertson, "Fairness of Pricing Decisions," *Business Ethics Quarterly* 9 no. 2(April 1999): 225–43.

21. This paragraph and the following two are adapted from Erin Hankes "Franchising Ethics" paper submitted in partial fulfillment of the requirements of a MBA Marketing Ethics class (December 2003).

22. Michael J. McCarthy, "Taking the Value Out of Value-Sized," *Wall Street Journal*, August 14, 2002, D1, D3.

23. Paul Whysall, "Stakeholder Management in Retailing: A British Perspective," *Journal of Business Ethics* 23 (January 1, 2000): 19–28.

24. Joseph P. Guiltinan and Alan C. Sawyer, "Pricing Strategy, Competition, and Consumer Welfare," *Handbook of Marketing and Society*, ed. Paul N. Bloom and Gregory T. Gundlach, 232–62 (Thousand Oaks, CA: Sage, 2001).

25. Edward D. Zinbarg, *Faith, Morals and Money* (New York. Continuum, 2001): 93.

26. Faith Keenan, "The Price Is Really Right," *Business Week*, March 31, 2002, 63–66.

27. Barbara Ley Toffler with Jennifer Reingold, *Final Accounting* (New York, Broadway Books, 2003): 116.

28. Miriam Jordan, "Brazilian Consumer Companies Reduce Quantities in Packages," *Wall Street Journal*, August 27, 2001, A8.

29. Gregory L. White and Karen Lundeguartd, "Sticker Shock: Detroit's Hidden Price Hikes," *Wall Street Journal*, April 10, 2002, D3.

30. Howard Millman, "Customers Tire of Excuses for Rebates That Never Arrive," *New York Times*, April 17, 2003.

31. Michael G. McPhie, "Consumer Product Rebates: The Role of the Rebate—Ethical," Paper submitted in partial fulfillment of the requirements of a MBA Marketing Ethics Class (December 2003): 6.

Chapter Five: Ethics in Advertising and on the Internet

1. http://www.adage.com and Tim Burt, "Global Advertising Boosted by Signs of Recovery in US," *Financial Times*, June 30, 2003, 17.

2. Michael J. Etzel, Bruce J. Walker, and William J. Stanton, *Marketing*, 12th ed. (Burr Ridge, IL: McGraw-Hill/Irwin, 2001): 540.

3. Patrick E. Murphy, "Ethics in Advertising: Review, Analysis and Suggestions," *Journal of Public Policy & Marketing* 17 no. 2(1998): 316–19.

4. The text of this section is adapted from Gene Laczniak, "Advertising Ethics," in *The Blackwell Encyclopedic Dictionary of Business Ethics*, ed. Patricia H. Werhane and R. Edward Freeman, 6–10 (Malden, MA: Blackwell Publishers, 1997).

5. An ethical analysis of market segmentation and targeting in advertising that pays special attention to children is in Agnes Nairn and Pierre Berthon, "Creating the Consumer: The Influence of Advertising on Consumer Market Segments—Evidence and Ethics," *Journal of Business Ethics*, 42 no. 1(January I, 2003): 83–99.

6. Logan, J. D., "Social Evolution and Advertising," *Canadian Magazine* 28 (1907): 333.

7. Richard W. Pollay, "The Distorted Mirror: Reflections on the Unintended Consequences of Advertising," *Journal of Marketing* 50 no. 2(April 1986): 18–36.

8. M. R. Hyman, R. Tansey, and J. W. Clark, "Research on Advertising Ethics:

Past, Present, and Future," *Journal of Advertising* 23 (1994): 5–15.

9. Morris Holbrook, "Mirror, Mirror, on the Wall, What's Unfair in the Reflections on Advertising," *Journal of Marketing* 51 no. 3(July 1987): 95–103; and Geoffrey P. Lantos, "Advertising: Looking Glass or Molder of the Masses?" *Journal of Public Policy & Marketing* 6 (1987): 104–28.

10. John E. Calfee and Debra J. Ringold, "The 70% Majority: Enduring Consumer Beliefs about Advertising," *Journal of Public Policy and Marketing* 13 no. 2(fall 1994): 228–38.

11. Hyman et al., "Research on Advertising Ethics."

12. http://www.bbb.org/advertising/adcode.asp.

13. Ivan L. Preston, *The Tangled Web They Weave: Truth, Falsity, and Advertisers* (Madison: University of Wisconsin Press, 1994).

14. Paul O'Sullivan and Patrick E. Murphy, "Ambush Marketing: The Ethical Issues," *Psychology and Marketing* (July 1998): 349–66.

15. Pontifical Council for Social Communications, *Ethics in Advertising* (Vatican City: Pontifical Council for Social Communication, 1997).

16. Murphy, "Ethics in Advertising."

17. Thomas H. Bivins, "Applying Ethical Theory to Public Relations," *Journal of Business Ethics* 6 no. 3(1987): 195–200.

18. Robert Audi, "The Ethics of Advocacy," *Legal Theory* 2 no. 1(1996): 1–31.

19. www.caru.org.

20. www.the-dma.org/guidelines/ethicalguidelines.shtml.

21. Clifford G. Christians, Kim B. Rotzoll, Mark Fackler, and Kathy B. McKee, *Media Ethics: Cases and Moral Reasoning*, 6th ed. (New York: Longman, 2004).

22. http:www.glreach.com/globstats.

23. Robyn Greenspan, "Wireless Surfers Grow," *Cyber Atlas*, September 6, 2002 (http:cyberatlas.internet.com).

24. "Internet," *Marketing News*, July 8, 2002, 20.

25. Joseph Turow, *Americans and Online Privacy: The System Is Broken* (Philadelphia: Annenberg Public Policy Center, 2003): 3.

26. Yochi J. Dreazen, "Consumers Are in the Dark on Web-Site Privacy," *Wall Street Journal*, June 25, 2003, D2.

27. Eve M. Caudill and Patrick E. Murphy, "Consumer Online Privacy: Legal and Ethical Issues," *Journal of Public Policy & Marketing*, 19 no. 1(Spring 2000): 7–19.

28. Victoria D. Bush, Beverly T. Venable, and Alan J. Bush, "Ethics and the Internet: Practitioners' Perceptions of Societal, Industry, and Company Concerns," *Journal of Business Ethics* 23 no. 3(February I, 2000): 237–48.

29. http://www.vatican.va/roman_curia/ponti...cs_doc20020228_ethics-internet_en.html. Accessed July 5, 2003.

30. Richard F. Beltramini, "Application of the Unfairness Doctrine to Marketing Communications on the Internet," *Journal of Business Ethics* 42 no. 4(February 2, 2003): 393–400.

31. J. J. Boddewyn, *Global Perspectives on Advertising Self-Regulation* (Westport, CT: Quorum Books, 1992); for another view on international advertising self-regulation, see D. Harker and M. Harker, "The Role of Codes of Conduct in the Advertising Self-Regulatory Framework," *Journal of Macromarketing* 20 no. 2(fall 2000): 155–66.

32. www.worldprfesitival.org. Accessed January 22, 2004.

Chapter Six: Personal Selling Ethics

1. The authors are indebted to Ms. L. A. McGilvary Ludwig, former MBA student at Notre Dame, for drafting this scenario.

2. Michael J. Etzel, Bruce J. Walker, and William J. Stanton, *Marketing*, 13th ed. (New York: McGraw-Hill/Irwin, 2004): 511.

3. See, e.g., Jennifer Gilbert, "A Matter of Trust," *Sales and Marketing Management* 155 no. 3(March 2003): 30–35.

4. An extraordinary tale of how mutual greed can injure all parties is in Dean Foust, "Wiped Out," *Business Week*, February 24, 2003, 114–18.

5. David M. Holley, "Information Disclosure in Sales," *Journal of Business Ethics* 17 no. 6(April II, 1998): 631–41.

6. The authors thank Professor Joseph A. Bellizzi of Arizona State University for suggesting the examples in this section.

7. Christopher Stewart, "Desperate Measures," *Sales and Marketing Management* 155 no. 9(September 2003): 32–36.

8. Nancy B. Kurland, "Trust, Accountability, and Sales Agents' Dueling Loyalties," *Business Ethics Quarterly* 6 no. 3(July 1996): 289–310.

9. Archie B. Carroll and Ann K. Buchholtz, *Business & Society: Ethics and Stakeholder Management*, 5th ed. (Marion, OH: Thomson-South-Western Publishing, 2003): 288–89.

10. Ibid., 287–88.

11. For a review of research on selling ethics, see Nicholas McClaren, "Ethics in Personal Selling and Sales Management: A Review of the Literature Focusing on Empirical Findings and Conceptual Foundations," *Journal of Business Ethics* 27 no. 3(October I, 2000): 285–303.

12. Joseph A. Bellizi and Ronald W. Hasty, "Supervising Unethical Sales Force Behavior: How Strong Is the Tendency to Treat Top Sales Performers Leniently?" *Journal of Business Ethics* 43 (April I, 2003): 337–51.

13. Leslie M. Dawson, "Ethical Differences Between Men and Women in the Sales Profession," *Journal of Business Ethics* 16 no. 11(1997), 1150.

14. Julia Lawlor, "Stepping over the Line," *Sales and Marketing Management* (October 1995): 90–101.

15. Robert S. Greenberger and David Bank, "Justices Deal Blows to Telemarketers," *Wall Street Journal*, May 8, 2003, D2.

16. P. Kotler and G. Armstrong, *Principles of Marketing*, 10th ed. (Upper Saddle River, NJ: Prentice Hall, 2004): 556.

17. Erin Strout, "Selling on a Prayer," *Sales and Marketing Management* (November 2002): 38–45.

18. P. Gnazzo and G. Wratney, "Are You Serious about Ethics?" *Across the Board* 40 no. 4(July/August 2003): 46–50.

19. Thomas Garrett, *Business Ethics* (Englewood Cliffs, NJ: Prentice Hall, 1966).

20. Clarke L. Caywood and Gene R. Laczniak, "Ethics and Personal Selling: 'Death of a Salesman' as an Ethical Primer," *Journal of Personal Selling and Sales Management* 6 no. 2(August 1986): 81–88.

Chapter Seven: Implementing and Auditing Ethical Marketing

1. Keith H. Hammonds, "Harry Kraemer's Moment of Truth," *Fast Company*, Issue 64, p. 93, online at http://www.fastcompany.com/online/64/kraemer.html.

2. Allen Questrom, Penney CEO, letter to P. Murphy on March 19, 2001; and see Mary Ellen Oliverio, "The Implementation of a Code of Ethics: The Early Efforts of One Entrepreneur," *Journal of Business Ethics* 8 no. 5(May 1989): 367–74.

3. P. Murphy, "Corporate Ethics Statements: An Update," in *Global Codes of Conduct: An Idea Whose Time Has Come*, ed. O. Williams, 295–304, (Notre Dame, IN: University of Notre Dame Press, 2000).

4. Energy East, *Code of Conduct*, February 2001, 28.

5. Patrick E. Murphy, *Eighty Exemplary Ethics Statements* (Notre Dame, IN: University of Notre Dame Press, 1998).

6. P. E. Murphy, "Survey on Ethics Statements and Training," Working paper, 2004.

7. Ibid.

8. Jon G. Auerbach, "To Get IBM Ad, Sites Must Post Privacy Policies," *Wall Street Journal*, March 31, 1999, B1–B4.

9. Murphy, 2004, *op.cit.*

10. Leonard L. Berry, *Discovering the Soul of Service* (New York: Free Press, 1999).

11. Robert C. Solomon and Kristine R. Hanson, *It's Good Business* (New York: Atheneum, 1985): 171.

12. Al Golin, *Trust or Consequences* (New York: AMACOM, 2004).

13. James Collins, *Good to Great* (New York: Harper Business, 2001).

14. Linda K. Trevino, M. Brown, and L. Pincus-Hartman, "A Qualitative Investigation of Perceived Executive Leadership: Perceptions from Inside and Outside the Executive Suite," *Human Relations* 56 no. 1 (January 2003): 5–37.

15. Boston Scientific, *Integrity in Everything We Do—Code of Conduct,* http://www.bostonscientific.com/common_templates/singleDetailList.jhtml?task=tskVisionValuesMission.jhtml&sectionId=2&relId=1,10, 2.

16. http://www.suez.com/group/english/valeur/telecharger.htm, p. 34.

17. For a discussion on the different types of audits, see John Rosthorn, "Business Ethics Auditing—More than a Stakeholder's Toy," *Journal of Business Ethics* 27 nos. 1–2(September 2000): 9–19.

18. N. Craig Smith, "Marketing Strategies for the Ethics Era," *Sloan Management Review* 36 (summer 1995): 85–97.

19. Alan R. Andreasen, ed. *Ethics in Social Marketing* (Washington, DC: Georgetown University Press, 2001).

20. William L. Wilkie and Elizabeth S. Moore, "Marketing's Contributions to Society," *Journal of Marketing* 63 (Special Issue 1999): 198–218.

21. Richard Lacayo and Amanda Ripley, "Persons of the Year—The Whistleblowers," *Time,* December 30, 2002–January 6, 2003.

22. Luigi Zingales, "How to Stop Corporate Fraud: Pay the Whistleblowers," *South Bend Tribune,* January 22, 2004, A9.

About the Authors

Patrick E. Murphy is the C. R. Smith Co-Director of the Institute for Ethical Business Worldwide and Professor of Marketing in the Mendoza College of Business at the University of Notre Dame. He served as chair of the Department of Marketing for ten years. During 1993–94 he was a Fulbright Scholar at University College Cork in Ireland. Previously, Professor Murphy was a faculty member and Marketing department chair at Marquette University. He specializes in business and marketing ethics. His work on these topics has appeared in leading ethics and marketing journals and his most recent book is *Eighty Exemplary Ethics Statements* (Notre Dame Press, 1998). Murphy was named in 1997 as one of the top researchers in Marketing for sustained contribution to the field. His articles and cases have received awards from the *Journal of Macromarketing* and the European Case Clearing House. Professor Murphy served as editor of the *Journal of Public Policy & Marketing* and is now section editor for marketing at *Business Ethics Quarterly* and on the editorial review boards of five journals. Currently, he is an Invited Fellow of the Ethics Resource Center (Washington, DC) and an Academic Advisor to the Business Roundtable Institute for Corporate Ethics. He holds a BBA from Notre Dame, an MBA from Bradley, and a Ph.D. from Houston.

Gene R. Laczniak is the Wayne and Kathleen Sanders Professor of Marketing at the Straz College of Business Administration at Marquette University. He is a former chair of the Marketing Department there with ten years of service. From 1998 to 2002, Laczniak was the Associate Vice President/Provost for Academic Affairs at the university. He has been a Visiting Professor or Visiting Fellow at the University of Western Australia (Perth) on several occasions. Laczniak's research focuses on the influence of marketing strategy on society especially on questions of ethics. He has published numerous articles and papers and has previously co-authored two books with P. E. Murphy including *Ethical Marketing Decisions* (Allyn and Bacon, 1993). Laczniak was a member of the editorial review board of the *Journal of Marketing* for 15 years and currently serves on four other editorial review boards. His bachelor's degree is from Marquette University and he holds an MBA and Ph.D. from the University of Wisconsin-Madison.

Norman E. Bowie is the Elmer L. Andersen Chair in Corporate Responsibility and a Professor, and former chair, of the Department of Strategic Management in the Carlson School of Management at the University of Minnesota. He is a frequent contributor to scholarly journals in business ethics. His most recent book is *Business Ethics: A Kantian Perspective* and his most recent edited book is *Blackwell Guide to Business Ethics*. His *Management Ethics* is in press. The seventh edition of he co-edited text *Ethical Theory and Business* was published in 2004. He has held a position as Dixons Professor of Business Ethics and Social Responsibility at the London Business School and has been a fellow at Harvard's Program in Ethics and Professions. Professor Bowie is also a member of the Academic Advisors to the Business Roundtable Institute for Corporate Ethics. He holds a bachelors degree from Bates College and a Ph.D. in Philosophy from the University of Rochester.

Thomas A. Klein is a Professor Emeritus of Marketing and Coordinator of the Business Ethics and Social Policy Program at the University of Toledo. He is also a past president of the Northwestern Ohio chapter of the American Marketing Association and is the author of numerous published articles, monographs, research papers, and a book, *Social Costs and Benefits of Business*, published by Prentice Hall in 1977. He is a member of the Editorial Policy Board of the *Journal of Macromarketing*. He has also been a visiting faculty member at the University of Rochester, St. Mary's University of Texas, the University of California, Berkeley, Simon Fraser University in Vancouver, the Netherlands Graduate School of Business, Nijenrode, and the University of Notre Dame. He has been the chairman or trustee of several nonprofits including the YMCA and Arts Commission of Greater Toledo, the Toledo Catholic Diocesan Board of Education, University of Dayton, and currently, Goodwill Industries and Catholic Charities of Northwest Ohio. He holds a B.S. from the University of Dayton, an MBA from the University of Detroit, and a Ph.D. from the Ohio State University.

Name Index

Aaker, David A., 252 (3)
Abela, Andrew, 252 (3)
Abernathy, Kathleen, 251 (2)
Achenbaum, Alvin A., 251 (2)
Adams, Chris, 248 (1)
Ahmen, Zafar, 250 (1)
Alberts, Robert J., 253 (4)
Alford, H. J., 249 (1)
Alsop, R., xxi
Anderson, R. E., 202 (Ex. 6-5)
Andreasen, Alan R., 257 (7)
Aristotle, 31, 32, 33, 34 (Ex. 1-7), 249 (1)
Armstrong, G., 256 (6)
Audi, Robert, 255 (5)
Auerbach, Jon G., 256 (7)
Avila, R., 190 (Ex. 6-2)

Baker, Stephen, 27 (Ex. 1-5)
Ball, Jeffrey, 89 (Ex. 3-3), 251 (3)
Balto, David, 254 (4)
Bank, David, 256 (6)
Bardaracoo, Joseph, 226 (Ex. 7-6)
Barrabes, Carlos, 115
Beard, Alison, 252 (3)
Beekun, Rafik Issa, 39 (Ex. 1-9), 250 (1)
Bellizzi, Joseph A., 256 (6)
Beltramini, Richard F., 255 (5)
Bentham, Jeremy, 249 (1)
Berk, Christina C., 252 (3)
Bernkert, George, 251 (2)
Berry, Leonard, L., 223, 252 (3), 256 (7)
Berthon, Pierre, 254 (5)
Bischoff, Dan, 253 (3)
Bivins, Thomas H., 255 (5)
Blankenship, Al, 50
Blomstrom, R. L., 119 (Ex. 4-2)
Boddewyn, J. J., 255 (5)
Bodhipaska, 250 (1)
Bowen, Michael G., 252 (3)
Bowers, Diane, 251 (2)
Bowie, Norman, 249 (2)
Boylan, Michael, xxi
Brenkert, George, 251 (2)
Brown, K., xxi
Brown, M., 256 (7)
Buchholtz, Ann K., 248 (1), 256 (6)
Bugs, Dale, 254 (4)
Burke, James, 9
Burt, Tim, 254 (5)
Burton, Thomas M., 253 (4)

Bush, Alan J., 202 (Ex. 6-5), 255 (5)
Bush, Victoria D., 255 (5)

Calfee, John E., 255 (5)
Campanella, Peter, 22
Carey, John, 251 (3)
Carman, James M., 248 (1)
Carroll, Archie B., 248 (1), 256 (6)
Carter, Craig R., 253 (4)
Carter, Meg, 108 (Ex. 3-7)
Cassidy, Hilary, 252 (3)
Caudill, Eve M., 174, 251 (2)
Caywood, Clarke L., 256 (6)
Chappell, Tom and Kate, 101
Christians, Clifford G., 250 (2), 255 (5)
Christiansan, Kirk, 108
Cicero, 18
Clark, J. W., 254 (5)
Cleland, K., 252 (3)
Cohen, L., xxi
Collins, James, 256 (7)
Converse, Jane, 226 (Ex. 7-6)
Cooper-Martin, E., 75 (Ex. 2-8)
Costa, Tom Dalla, 36 (Ex. 1-8)
Cross, Frank B., 252 (3)

Daft, Douglas, 114
Davidson, Kirk, 251 (3)
Davis, K., 119 (Ex. 4-2)
Dawson, Leslie M., 256
DePree, Max, 226 (Ex. 7-6)
DesJardins, Joseph, 85 (Ex. 3-1), 249 (1)
DeSpain, James, 226 (Ex. 7-6)
Dewhirst, Timothy, 252 (3)
Dillion, William R., 250 (2)
Dobbins, Steve, 122
Dominguez, Luis V., 248 (1)
Donaldson, Thomas, 29, 31, 249 (1)
Dreazen, Yochi J., 255 (5)
Drumwright, Minette, 165 (Ex. 5-2)
Dunfee, Thomas, 29, 249 (1)

Earnest, Leslie, 251 (2)
Edmondson, G., xxi
Etzel, Michael J., 16, 254 (5), 255 (6)

Fackler, Mark, 251 (2), 255 (5)
Faircloth, James, 70 (Ex. 2-7)
Fatsis, Stefan, 253 (4)
Ferrell, O. C., 16, 207 (Ex. 6-7)
Findley, G., 16

Moore, Elizabeth S., 73, 187 (Ex. 5-1), 257 (7)
Morey, Roger, 238 (Ex. 7-8)
Morse, Dan, 250 (2)
Mukhtar, Syeda-Masooda, 250 (1)
Murphy, Patrick E., xxi, 16 (Ex. 1-3), 27
    (Ex. 1-5), 34 (Ex. 1-7), 66 (Ex. 2-6), 70
    (Ex. 2-7), 100 (Ex. 3-6), 149 (Ex. 4-9), 165
    (Ex. 5-2), 174 (Ex. 5-4), 197 (Ex. 6-4), 248,
    249 (1), 250, 251 (2), 254, 255 (5), 257 (7)

Nairn, Agnes, 254 (5)
Narvaez, D., 42, 43 (Ex. 1-10), 250 (1)
Nason, Robert W., 248 (1)
Naughton, M. J., 249 (1)
Newman, Matthew, 172 (Ex. 5-3)

O Brien, Steve, 62
O Sullivan, Paul, 253 (5)
Oliverio, Mary Ellen, 256 (7)
Olson, J., 53
Oretskin, Nancy A., 252 (3)
Ossip, Al, 251 (2)
Oswald, Lynda, 117 (Ex. 4-1), 138 (Ex. 4-6),
    251 (3)

Paine, Lynn S., 251 (2)
Paolilla, G. P., 250 (1)
Parloff, Roger, 252 (3)
Pastin, Mark, 224 (Ex. 7-5)
Pava, Moses, 249 (1)
Perez-Katz, Ana M., 252 (3)
Pichler, Joseph, 235 (Ex. 7-7)
Pincus-Hartman, L., 256 (7)
Plank, Richard E., 253 (4)
Pollay, Richard, 93, 252 (3), 254 (5)
Polonsky, Michael, 101 (Ex. 3-6)
Power, F. Clark, 252 (3)
Preston, Ivan L., 159, 255 (5)

Questrom, Allen, 256 (7)

Rachels, James, 249 (1)
Rados, David, 141 (Ex. 4-7)
Rawls, John, 29, 249 (1)
Reich, Robert, 234
Reingold, Jennifer, 254, 255 (4)
Rest, J., 42, 43 (Ex. 1-10), 250 (1)
Richards, J., 252 (3)
Ringold, Debra J., 255 (5)
Ripley, Amanda, 257 (7)
Rittenberg, Terri L., 70 (Ex. 2-7)
Roberts, Julie S., 124, 253 (4)
Robertson, Diana C., 254 (4)
Rojas, T. H., 252 (3)
Rosa, J. A., 251 (2)
Rosthorn, John, 256 (7)
Rotzoll, Kim B., 251, 255 (5)

Saeed, Mohammad, 250 (2)
Sautter, Elsie Truly, 252 (1)

Savina, Williams, 251 (2)
Sawyer, Alan C., 254 (4)
Scheuing, Eberhard M., 253 (4)
Schneider, Kennith, 52, 58 (Ex. 2-1)
Schweitzer, P., 253 (3)
Schweitzer, R., 253 (3)
Schwepker, C., 191 (Ex. 6-2)
Scwartz, Marvin, 252 (3)
Seabrook, John, 253 (3)
Seeger, Matthew W., 250 (1)
Severson, Gary, 122
Smith, N. Craig, 75 (Ex. 2-8), 236, 257 (7)
Solomon, Robert, 248, 249 (1), 251 (2), 256 (7)
Sottosanti, Vincent, 148 (Ex. 4-8)
Staton, William J., 254 (5), 255 (6)
Stewart, Christopher, 256 (6)
Storholm, Gordon, 253 (4)
Strout, Erin, 189 (Ex. 6-1), 256 (6)

Tamari, Meir, 249 (1)
Tansey, R., 254 (5)
Thomas, J. L., 250 (1)
Tigret, Isaac, 40
Toffler, Barbara Ley, 143, 254 (4)
Toy, D., 53
Traub, Daniel M., 253 (4)
Trevino, Linda K., 256 (7)
Turow, Joseph, 255 (5)

Ulmer, Robert R., 250 (1)

Valentine, Sean, 70 (Ex. 2-7)
Varela, Francisco J., 250 (1)
Veblen, Thorstein, 252 (3)
Venable, Beverly T., 255 (5)
Viswanathan, M., 251 (2)
Vitell, S., 250 (1)
Vogel, David, 249 (1)

Wade, Worth, 70 (Ex. 2-7)
Walker, Bruce J., 254 (4), 255 (6)
Walton, Clarence, 136
Warren, Susan, 251 (2)
Wee, Victor, 250 (1)
Werhane, Patricia H., 249 (1)
White, Christina, 27 (Ex. 1-5)
White, Gregory L., 254 (4)
Whysall, Paul, 254 (4)
Wilkie, William L., 257 (7)
Williams, Frances, 252 (3)
Williams, M., 191 (Ex. 6-2)
Winslett, Brenda J., 252 (3)
Wood, Graham, 253 (4)
Wratney, G., 256 (6)
Wright, L., 53

Yost, Mark, 113 (Ex. 3-8)

Zhivago, K., 252 (3)
Zinbarg, Edward, 254 (4)
Zingales, Luigi, 257 (7)

Subject Index

Utilitarianism, 22
  act, 22
  cost-benefit, 23
  limitations of, 24
  rule, 22

Values statement, 219, 221
Views of marketing ethics, 2
  industrial, 5
  organizational, 3
  personal, 3

societal, 5
  stakeholder, 6
Virtue ethics, 30
  corporate character, 34
  ethic of the mean, 32, 33
  for international marketing, 34
  virtues test, 44

Web of Laws, 172
Wheeler-Lea Amendment, 191
Whistleblowing, 209, 239